Unraveling Abolition

Unraveling Abolition tells the fascinating story of slaves, former slaves, magistrates and legal workers who fought for emancipation, without armed struggle, from 1781 to 1830. By centering the Colombian judicial forum as a crucible of antislavery, Edgardo Pérez Morales reveals how the meanings of slavery, freedom and political belonging were publicly contested. In the absence of freedom of the press or association, the politics of abolition were first formed during litigation. Through the life stories of enslaved litigants and defendants, Pérez Morales illuminates the rise of antislavery culture, and how this tradition of legal tinkering and struggle shaped claims to equal citizenship during the anti-Spanish revolutions of the early 1800s. By questioning foundational constitutions and laws, this book uncovers how legal activists were radically committed to the idea that independence from Spain would be incomplete without emancipation for all slaves. This title is also available as Open Access on Cambridge Core.

Edgardo Pérez Morales is Assistant Professor of History at the University of Southern California. He specializes in Colombia and its connections with the Caribbean and the Atlantic World. He is the author of *No Limits to Their Sway: Cartagena's Privateers and the Masterless Caribbean in the Age of Revolutions*.

T0384814

ANKERWYCKE YEW

STUDIES IN LEGAL HISTORY

See the Studies in Legal History series website at http:// studiesinlegalhistory.org/

STUDIES IN LEGAL HISTORY

EDITORS

Sarah Barringer Gordon, *University of Pennsylvania*
Holly Brewer, *University of Maryland, College Park*
Lisa Ford, *University of New South Wales*
Michael Lobban, *London School of Economics and Political Science*
Reuel Schiller, *University of California, Hastings College of the Law*

Other books in the series:
Edgardo Pérez Morales, *Unraveling Abolition: Legal Culture and Slave Emancipation in Colombia*
Sara M. Butler, *Pain, Penance, and Protest: Peine Forte et Dure in Medieval England*
Michael Lobban, *Imperial Incarceration: Detention without Trial in the Making of British Colonial Africa*
Stefan Jurasinski and Lisi Oliver, *The Laws of Alfred: The Domboc and the Making of Anglo-Saxon Law*
Sascha Auerbach, *Armed with Sword and Scales: Law, Culture, and Local Courtrooms in London, 1860–1913*
Alejandro de La Fuente and Ariela J. Gross, *Becoming Free, Becoming Black: Race, Freedom, and the Law in Cuba, Virginia, and Louisiana*
Elizabeth Papp Kamali, *Felony and the Guilty Mind in Medieval England*
Jessica K. Lowe, *Murder in the Shenandoah: Making Law Sovereign in Revolutionary Virginia*

Michael A. Schoeppner, *Moral Contagion: Black Atlantic Sailors, Citizenship, and Diplomacy in Antebellum America*

Sam Erman, *Almost Citizens: Puerto Rico, the U.S. Constitution, and Empire*

Martha S. Jones, *Birthright Citizens: A History of Race and Rights in Antebellum America*

Julia Moses, *The First Modern Risk: Workplace Accidents and the Origins of European Social States*

Cynthia Nicoletti, *Secession on Trial: The Treason Prosecution of Jefferson Davis*

Edward James Kolla, *Sovereignty, International Law, and the French Revolution*

Assaf Likhovski, *Tax Law and Social Norms in Mandatory Palestine and Israel*

Robert W. Gordon, *Taming the Past: Essays on Law and History and History in Law*

Paul Garfinkel, *Criminal Law in Liberal and Fascist Italy*

Michelle A. McKinley, *Fractional Freedoms: Slavery, Intimacy, and Legal Mobilization in Colonial Lima, 1600–1700*

Karen M. Tani, *States of Dependency: Welfare, Rights, and American Governance, 1935–1972*

Stefan Jurasinski, *The Old English Penitentials and Anglo-Saxon Law*

Felice Batlan, *Women and Justice for the Poor: A History of Legal Aid, 1863–1945*

Sophia Z. Lee, *The Workplace Constitution from the New Deal to the New Right*

Mitra Sharafi, *Law and Identity in Colonial South Asia: Parsi Legal Culture, 1772–1947*

Michael A. Livingston, *The Fascists and the Jews of Italy: Mussolini's Race Laws, 1938–1943*

Unraveling Abolition

Legal Culture and Slave Emancipation in Colombia

EDGARDO PÉREZ MORALES

University of Southern California

CAMBRIDGE
UNIVERSITY PRESS

Shaftesbury Road, Cambridge CB2 8EA, United Kingdom

One Liberty Plaza, 20th Floor, New York, NY 10006, USA

477 Williamstown Road, Port Melbourne, VIC 3207, Australia

314–321, 3rd Floor, Plot 3, Splendor Forum, Jasola District Centre, New Delhi – 110025, India

103 Penang Road, #05–06/07, Visioncrest Commercial, Singapore 238467

Cambridge University Press is part of Cambridge University Press & Assessment, a department of the University of Cambridge.

We share the University's mission to contribute to society through the pursuit of education, learning and research at the highest international levels of excellence.

www.cambridge.org
Information on this title: www.cambridge.org/9781009514415

DOI: 10.1017/9781108917513

First published 2022
First paperback edition 2024

A catalogue record for this publication is available from the British Library

ISBN   978-1-108-83152-9   Hardback
ISBN   978-1-009-51441-5   Paperback

Cambridge University Press & Assessment has no responsibility for the persistence or accuracy of URLs for external or third-party internet websites referred to in this publication and does not guarantee that any content on such websites is, or will remain, accurate or appropriate.

...for perhaps these laws that we are trying to unravel do not exist at all.

Franz Kafka, *The Problem of Our Laws*

Contents

Maps

x

Acknowledgments

This book began as my doctoral dissertation in history at the University of Michigan, co-advised by Rebecca J. Scott and Richard L. Turits. Long after my dissertation defense was over, their insight, guidance, and support remained crucial to this work. Along with Julius S. Scott, Jean M. Hébrard, Susan Juster, and Javier Sanjinés, Rebecca and Richard deserve much credit for the shaping of this book. I extend my warmest thanks to them for their lessons and hope they will forgive any errors or roughness in the final product, which are my own.

Unraveling Abolition was developed in dialogue and collaboration with the help of many dear Colombian colleagues. At Universidad Externado de Colombia (Bogotá), Daniel Gutiérrez Ardila, whose scholarly work has advanced the historiography of revolutionary Colombia by leaps and bounds, deserves special thanks. Over the last decade, Daniel has been generous in sharing both his knowledge and his home with me, providing many of the documents, references, and ideas found in these pages. At Universidad Nacional de Colombia (Medellín), Roberto Luis Jaramillo remains an exceptional mentor and friend – his recognized authority on matters of Colombian history and legal culture, ranging from the intricacies of Spanish medieval legacies to the choppy waters of genealogy and the secrets of our fractured geography, has been invaluable. Also at La Nacional, Orián Jiménez Meneses and Juan David Montoya Guzmán have been constant allies, helping me track down documents, test ideas, and consider the deep colonial roots of revolutionary and republican polities. Finally, it was Oscar Almario García who first pointed me in the direction of the Colombian Pacific and the old lands of Popayán, providing early and crucial insight for this project. At Universidad de Antioquia (Medellín), Juan Sebastián Gómez González has extended a cordial welcome every time I visit. His nudge in the right direction has helped me not only to make meaningful connections in my work, but also to widen my scope to consider histories and fictions from far and wide. At Western Michigan University (Kalamazoo), I am grateful to Ángela Pérez Villa whose work continues to pose exciting questions that are always reminding me why we must strive to bridge historiographies. For well over a decade now, Armando Martínez Garnica, at Universidad Industrial de Santander (Bucaramanga), has been gracious in sharing his understanding of Colombian history, and has opened both his house and his archives to me a number of times; the depth of his knowledge is only rivaled by the extent of his generosity.

In Colombia, Cuba, Ecuador, France, Spain, Germany, and the United States, I would like to thank Paulina Alberto, Ernesto Bassi, Guillermo Bustos, Sueann Caulfield, María Eugenia Chaves Maldonado, Adriana Chira, Luis Miguel Córdoba Ochoa, Marcela Echeverri, Ada Ferrer, Sybille Fischer, Rebecca Goetz, Max Hering Torres, Jesse Hoffnung-Garskof, Marial Iglesias Utset, Peter Linebaugh, Peter Mancall, Graham Nessler, Francisco Ortega, Nathan Perl-Rosenthal, Jean-Frédérique Schaub, Sinclair Thomson, Isidro Vanegas, Barbara Weinstein, and Michael Zeuske. Special thanks also to Juliana Álvarez Olivares and Antoine Vilotte in Paris. In New England, New York, the Great Lakes, and Cascadia, further thanks must go to Ben Cronin, Valentine Edgar, Ryan Gordon, Naomi Kirk-Lawlor, Michael Leese, Kate Rosenblatt, Anthony Ross, Eric Schewe, David Schlitt, Shelley Selim, Amy Warhaft, and Sarah Zarrow; and in Alta California, to Richard Antaramian, Jason Glenn, Josh Goldstein, Wolf Gruner, Paul Lerner, Maya Maskarinec, Ketaki Pant, as well as to the Ellita Place crew: Stephanie Candelaria, Zoa López, Alex Nuño and all the rest.

I am grateful for the patient and meticulous work of Cambridge University Press and the Studies in Legal History series, especially that of Holly Brewer, Cecelia Cancellaro, Sarah Barringer Gordon, and the editorial staff. I would also like to thank Matthew Mirow and a second anonymous reviewer for their evaluations and helpful feedback.

Finally, a heartfelt thanks and much love to both my families in Antioquia and Michigan, especially to Carly who has remained patient and supportive throughout this unwieldy project, and has done the most to help me unlock the secrets of writing in English.

Abbreviations

AAI	Archivo Anexo I, in AGN
ACC	Archivo Central del Cauca (Popayán, Colombia)
ACCR	Archivo de la Casa de la Convención de Rionegro (Rionegro-Antioquia, Colombia)
ACH	Academia Colombiana de Historia, in AGN
ACHSC	*Anuario Colombiano de Historia Social y de la Cultura*
AGI	Archivo General de Indias (Seville, Spain)
AGN	Archivo General de la Nación (Bogotá, Colombia)
AGS	Archivo General de Simancas (Simancas, Spain)
AHA	Archivo Histórico de Antioquia (Medellín, Colombia)
AHC	Archivo Histórico de Cali (Cali, Colombia)
AHCI	Archivo Histórico de Cartagena de Indias (Cartagena de Indias, Colombia)
ANE	Archivo Nacional del Ecuador (Quito, Ecuador)
BLAA	Biblioteca Luis Ángel Arango (Bogotá, Colombia)
C	Colonia, in AGN
CGE	Centro Geográfico del Ejército (Madrid, Spain)
DA	*Diccionario de Autoridades* 1st ed. 1726-1739. Madrid: Real Academia Española, Gredos, 2002, 3 vols.
DHPC	*Documentos para la historia de la Provincia de Cartagena de Indias, hoy Estado Soberano de Bolívar en la Unión Colombiana*, Manuel Ezequiel Corrales, ed. Bogotá: Imprenta de Medardo Rivas, 1883, 2 vols.
DRLJ	Joaquín Escriche, *Diccionario razonado de legislación y jurisprudencia*. Paris: Garnier Hermanos, 1869.
FHL	Family History Library (Salt Lake City, Utah-USA)

HRC	José Manuel Restrepo, *Historia de la revolución de la república de Colombia en la América meridional* 1st ed., Paris, 1827, 2nd ed., Besançon, 1858. Medellín: Universidad de Antioquia, 2009, 2 vols.
JC	Juicios Criminales, in AGN
NEA	Negros y Esclavos de Antioquia, in AGN
NEB	Negros y Esclavos de Bolívar, in AGN
NEC	Negros y Esclavos del Cauca, in AGN
RCD	*Rebelión comunera de 1781. Documentos*, Juan Friede, ed. Bogotá: Instituto Colombiano de Cultura, 1981, 2 vols.
TLC	Sebastián de Cobarruvias Orozco, *Tesoro de la lengua Castellana, o Española*. Madrid: Luis Sánchez, impresor del Rey N. S., 1611.

This title is part of the Cambridge University Press *Flip it Open* Open Access Books program and has been "flipped" from a traditional book to an Open Access book through the program.

Flip it Open sells books through regular channels, treating them at the outset in the same way as any other book; they are part of our library collections for Cambridge Core, and sell as hardbacks and ebooks. The one crucial difference is that we make an upfront commitment that when each of these books meets a set revenue threshold we make them available to everyone Open Access via Cambridge Core.

This paperback edition has been released as part of our Open Access commitment and we would like to use this as an opportunity to thank the libraries and other buyers who have helped us flip this and the other titles in the program to Open Access.

To see the full list of libraries that we know have contributed to *Flip it Open*, as well as the other titles in the program please visit www.cambridge.org/fio-acknowledgements

Prologue: Antislavery, Abolition, and the Judicial Forum

"It is criminal selfishness to seek liberty and independence from Spain for ourselves, if we wish not to grant it to our slaves." With these stern words, the lawyer Félix José de Restrepo addressed his colleagues, the delegates to the first General Congress of the Republic of Colombia, in 1821. As the delegates worked out the new republic's constitution and foundational laws, Restrepo invited them to consider the problem of slavery: were slaves, like other humans, "children of Adam" and thus eligible for equal rights? Were "whites" entitled to dominate "blacks"? Was any government that upheld slavery a "criminal" government by definition? Should independence from Spain automatically lead to liberty for slaves? As the South American independence movement reached its climax, Restrepo forcefully developed clear-cut questions.[1] But would they find the clear and forceful answers hoped for by many slaves and some free people?

In 1821 Restrepo defended freedom over slavery on behalf of humanity, religion, and the decorum of the nascent country. He introduced a manumission bill, ostensibly aimed at ending coerced labor. It is indispensable to "annihilate slavery," he insisted. In Restrepo's view, the General Congress represented the ideal opportunity to restore enslaved individuals to their human "dignity" while giving neighboring countries an example of "justice." Ending slavery, moreover, would dignify the revolution against Spain, guaranteeing future economic and political stability for this new republic. Restrepo asserted that it remained a contradiction to pray to God for deliverance from foreign tyrants while keeping thousands of people in captivity. Providence, he predicted, would throw Colombia back into the hands of Spain "if we refuse to exercise mercy with our brothers."[2]

Yet in the end the interests and prejudices of the masters prevailed over such grave considerations. Restrepo posed clear questions but, along with most other delegates to the 1821 Congress, the answers he offered were ambiguous. Restrepo's proposed legislation called for a protracted end to slavery, rather than an immediate release of all those held as slaves. Approved on July 19, Restrepo's bill became Colombia's law "On the manumission of slaves." It declared international slave trading illegal, stipulated that slavery would no longer be transmitted from mother to child, and called for the gradual emancipation of deserving individual slaves, compensating their masters with public funds.[3] Some change now seemed possible, but the right to own others remained intact. People continued to be bought and sold like property.

Although bondage remained legal, Restrepo asserted that "the freedom of the womb" constituted the "radical remedy for slavery." By declaring all new-born children of enslaved women free, Restrepo told delegates, the "political cancer" of slavery would be terminated.[4] As it turned out, however, this approach would prove unable to end slavery. Over the next decades, committed slaveholders systematically undermined the mechanisms for slave emancipation stipulated by law in 1821. It would take a new generation, a new legislative act, and a civil war to finally end slavery in 1852.[5] Still, in 1821 Restrepo and his colleagues celebrated their efforts as the "abolition of slavery," and presented Colombia as a country that was simultaneously committed to ending slave trading, slavery, and the tyranny of Spain. Furthermore, they described themselves as "slaves" of Spain, a mistress that had cruelly subjugated her New World vassals.[6] Although the metaphor served to support the case for immediately ending political dependence from Spain, ending actual slavery in the new country seemed less urgent.

Most of the 100,000 slaves in the Republic of Colombia (which comprised today's Ecuador, Colombia, Panama, and Venezuela) never obtained emancipation. Of the nearly 50,000 slaves who lived within the borders of current-day Colombia in the early 1820s, around 19,000 (roughly 39 percent) achieved emancipation thanks to the law of 1821. The rest, some 29,000 slaves (roughly 60 percent), never became free. Most of them died enslaved, while others escaped or gained only informal freedom. An indeterminate number (at least several hundred, but possibly thousands) were shipped abroad, often sold alongside their ostensibly freeborn children. Even the children of slaves who stayed in Colombia struggled to effectively gain emancipation at the age of eighteen, as stipulated by the manumission law.[7] Colombia officially praised its citizens who manumitted slaves, thereby formally supporting the idea of a future world without slavery. Its efforts to speed the coming of that era, however, were lukewarm.[8]

A truly radical approach to ending slavery altogether was available as a distinct possibility in 1821. According to a few delegates, immediately ending slavery was feasible and the General Congress would be remiss not to do so. One radical legislator (a printer by trade) vehemently voiced this opinion. He specifically asked for his words to be written down in the proceedings: "there can be no property on men...the right to liberty of any individual is absolutely inalienable."[9] Calling for actually abolishing slavery, this radical delegate opposed the gradual emancipation approach and insisted that "simultaneous and universal" freedom should be granted to slaves. He even proposed that "slaves be manumitted without the need for compensation for those self-titled lords of their freedom." The very words slave and master appeared to him detestable and fictitious.[10] Restrepo and many of his colleagues who strongly criticized the Atlantic slave system supported a politics of *antislavery*. But only a few delegates supported *abolition* as the logical consequence of this critique. This minority defended the idea that the General Congress must immediately end slavery in Colombia.[11] Many slaves agreed that slavery should end at once.

While not all slaves had the inclination or ability to seek individual emancipation or the end of slavery, *Unraveling Abolition* studies how and why some slaves – actively and at great personal risk – proposed that abolition was both politically imperative and feasible. When the Spanish viceroyalty of the New Kingdom of Granada broke up into independent provincial states (1810–1816), some slaves quickly questioned whether slavery could coexist with these burgeoning free societies. In this emerging struggle for independence, they were the first to express a radical commitment to the principle that "emancipation" from Spain should also mean the immediate, unconditional end of domestic slavery. As early as 1811, enslaved individuals reportedly argued that if their masters were now emancipated from Spanish enslavement, entitled to the "rights of men they had been born with," then the slaves should also be set free.[12] Some slaves thus stood out as vanguard abolitionists. They appraised the possibility and significance of the final end of bondage in light of current political transformations, criticizing slaveholders who demanded freedom from Spain (their supposed mistress) but meant to keep their own slaves in bondage.

Restrepo personally knew slaves who had examined whether it was imperative to end slavery alongside cutting ties with the Spanish monarchy. In the State of Antioquia, one of the provincial states that pre-dated the founding of Colombia, the republican Constitution of 1812 denounced Spain as a mistress keeping Spanish Americans in a condition of slavery. A group of about 200 slaves petitioned the authorities to clarify whether it was "true" that the new political charter had brought an end to "slavery" and "chains." Among the petitioners were Gregorio, Antonio, and Joaquín, Restrepo's own slaves. If the language of liberty and equality in the Constitution accurately represented the intentions of the revolutionary authorities, the petitioners insinuated, then all the slaves in this new republic should be set free.[13]

Under pressure, Restrepo and the Antioquia legislature passed a free womb, gradual manumission law in 1814, later used as the model for Colombia's 1821 antislavery law.[14] But for many slaves, this gradual approach to their own emancipation seemed tepid. Through their dynamic grapevine, slaves whispered that Antioquia's manumission law had ended slavery altogether. Slave leaders gathered to discuss ways to find the law's abolitionist potential. They were even willing to pay taxes to help end slavery immediately.[15] In these discussions and plans, slaves resorted to a rich tradition of legal tinkering. They dissected republican antislavery with the same tools they used in discerning the Spanish laws and local practices of slavery and freedom. Under the Spanish king, slaves had sometimes sought legal redress from the masters, struggled to make claims before magistrates, and offered their own opinions as witnesses or accused parties during trials and litigation. Both the slaves' as well as Restrepo's antislavery politics had evolved in these legal instances.[16]

Unraveling Abolition considers the politics of antislavery and the politics of revolution together, identifying and explaining their overlapping legal origins, leitmotivs, ambivalences, and tensions. The following chapters probe slaves' legal undertakings, seeking to understand how the enslaved themselves envisioned slave emancipation during the transition from the late New Kingdom of Granada to early Colombia. Enslaved people interested in obtaining freedom only rarely turned to violence against the masters.[17] Some imagined a peaceful, complete end of slavery, aspiring to become law-abiding, God-fearing free parishioners, first as vassals of the king and, later, as citizens of the early republics. Authorities only rarely took these aspirations seriously, however. But by carefully looking into the slaves' legal encounters with masters and magistrates, it becomes possible to analyze litigation and the law as crucibles of antislavery. This is the messy story of a vanguard politics playing out over fraught legal exchanges that often took place in jail and under torture.

To tell this tangled tale, therefore, this book turns to the judicial forum as its privileged site of observation. It understands litigation, claims-making, and even criminal trials as instances of cultural exchange in which people – enslaved and free alike – proposed, debated, and co-constructed ideas about slavery, freedom, justice, and political belonging. In all manner of judicial encounters, people appropriated, re-shaped, and even coined legal concepts through mutual understanding, misunderstanding, and influence, neither entirely "from above" nor purely "from below."[18] Lawyers and magistrates, such as Restrepo, first considered the legal dimensions of slavery during litigation initiated by slaves, former slaves, and their allies. Those jurists would go on to write the first constitutions in the Spanish-speaking world and further develop the idea that antislavery principles were the fundamental tenets of representative, republican government.[19] Enslaved legal activists, in turn, would critically scrutinize revolutionary constitutions and antislavery laws.

Following the thread of slaves' painfully articulated preoccupations and opinions is a powerful way to chart new social and cultural geographies in the history of slave emancipation. Vibrant strands of antislavery and abolitionism intersected in the judicial forum. In Spanish-speaking, Catholic South America, debates over slavery and freedom (discussions over the privileges and obligations of masters and

slaves, the legitimacy of captivity itself, and the legal and social implications of authority and power) did not occur in the spaces more
commonly associated with antislavery activism and abolitionist agitation. Before 1810, no independent newspapers existed in the New
Kingdom of Granada, no abolitionist societies, and no churches that
would accommodate or catalyze antislavery debate. Instead, debates
over slavery and emancipation unfolded in the judicial forum – the
sometimes oral, but most often handwritten transactions through
which people typically sought "justice" and "mercy."

The judicial forum operated through a series of face-to-face encounters and, more often, through less direct communications via paper
exchanges. It unfolded in several spaces, at different moments, rather
than exclusively within the confines of a government building. We
ought not to imagine litigation and other legal encounters as confrontation in a courtroom. The judicial forum came into being when
individuals appealed to magistrates (knocking on their doors or
approaching them in the street), when judges tried people (for criminal
and civil accusations), and through the ensuing conversations and
extensive document exchanges. Judges, lawyers, scribes, and witnesses
exchanged memorials, depositions, petitions, opinions, decisions, and
sentences. These documents captured people's thoughts on a myriad of
political issues. Complaining against abusive masters, claiming the
"right" to seek a more benevolent owner, suing for freedom, and
speaking over unwelcome interrogations, enslaved individuals and
families provided judicial agents with information on their lives, their
expectations, and their ideas. Influencing one another, participants
(both literate and illiterate) left handwritten records that reward careful attention.[20] Those documents are the empirical foundation for this
study, alongside official and private correspondence, administrative
and notarial records, periodicals, treatises, legal codes, constitutions,
and laws.

Although most people never participated directly in their creation,
judicial documents kept in Colombian archives and libraries hum with
the voices of humble litigants, such as poor tenants, widows, Indians,
and slaves. The extant sources reveal that litigants often showed
tremendous insight into their own situations, even expressing radical
notions that challenged the existing social and political order. Some
denounced the tyranny and injustice of their social superiors. A few

slaves predicted that God, the king of Spain or an African monarch would right the wrong of slavery. Others even aired their aspirations to equality before the law and access to property as concrete ways to make their freedom meaningful.[21] Pedro Antonio Ibargüen, a former slave briefly represented by Restrepo, thus claimed in 1793 that both masters and ex-slaves, as "equal vassals of His Majesty," should be afforded equal opportunities to possess land and resources. In 1827, Ibargüen would denounce powerful slaveholders as an arrogant set of fallen "aristocrats," rejoicing that "equality is inscribed in the destiny of Colombia."[22]

The judicial forum was inextricably linked to people's everyday, communal life. Spanish legal culture thoroughly permeated society, with property, labor, family, jurisdictional, and even religious issues understood in light of the law and often settled through litigation. Most people would not have recognized a distinction between private and public affairs, between lay life and legal life. This was a world with no political parties and only limited elections (up to 1811 there were no provincial assemblies and only a few elected local magistrates, who were voted into office by local elites). Consequently, the judicial forum often became the political arena *par excellence*, the place where people stirred up conflict and forged amity. Unsurprisingly, what happened during litigation easily spilled outside the magistrates' bureaus. People from all walks of life eagerly learned about the developments and outcomes of civil, criminal, and ecclesiastical proceedings.[23] Shaped by Spanish legal theories and practices, finally, the judicial forum remained active long after independence.

Yet close attention to the judicial forum lays bare shifts in the understanding of the hierarchical legal order of the Spanish monarchy, revealing the place of slaves and antislavery politics in the criticism and undoing of *ancien régime* societies. In this way, the judicial forum opens up compelling avenues to unravel republican abolition, allowing us to discover its ambiguities as well as some of its pre-revolutionary roots, including shifting habits and ideas from the old regime that would have a significant bearing on the revolutionary era.[24] Colombian legislators presented their 1821 "abolition" plan as con-substantial to the new legal order, but the impetus to think about slavery as an illegitimate relationship of power, and the earliest voices to end it altogether, first emerged in the Spanish era. Across the 1700s, elite families and corporations defended their interests and allegedly natural social positions, but critical patricians and non-elite people like slaves increasingly turned to litigation to challenge the "perks of birthright, privilege, and custom."[25] Over litigation, jurists and litigants raised and re-imagined, subtly and explicitly, fundamental legal questions: was emancipating individual slaves and favoring freedom over slavery in the best interest of the polity? Should lawgivers and magistrates aim to foster happiness on earth, including the happiness of those in bondage? Should judges presume equality before the law?

As litigants, their legal aides, and even college students and law professors sought to untangle the very logic of the inegalitarian, corporatist order of society under Spanish rule, competing and overlapping legal visions of the law and slavery emerged. Some emphasized a more traditional perception of the magistrates as agents of the king's "grace" who dispensed "justice" on a case-by-case basis. Others pushed for a more innovative understanding of "rights" and the law as independent from the person of the magistrate (or the king), emanating from "nature" and thus self-evident and universally valid. Still others took eclectic approaches, combining seemingly contradictory legal doctrines.[26] Some voiced patently unorthodox propositions. As early as 1777, two judicial forum practitioners advocated for a new understanding of the slaves' "nature" and standing, questioning whether their legal status was founded on the law of war. They implied that slaves should not be treated as domestic enemies. In 1791, the lawyer Restrepo and the former slave Ibargüen expressed the idea that lawgiving was a matter of "State" rather than a privilege of the sovereign alone. Well-crafted legislation, they claimed, should afford equal protection to all subjects, even promoting the wellbeing of ex-slaves.[27]

For many formally trained lawyers and other magistrates, confidence in legal reform was founded on confidence on what they called "modern philosophy." By modern philosophy they meant critical, practical, and experimental learning in all fields, in contrast with the scholastic following of church-approved "authorities" and the concentration on theology and canon law. Often, modern philosophy enthusiasts brought to bear on litigation conceptual tools and political positions originally developed in college classrooms, boarding houses, and in *tertulias* – salon-like meetings for socializing and learning.

We must note, however, that the modern philosophical corpus went beyond the French *philosophes*, privileging instead seventeenth-century natural law theorists such as Samuel von Pufendorf and contemporary publicists such as the Neapolitan author Gaetano Filangieri.[28] Most of these sources, including some by Spanish-speaking glossators and writers, contained critical thoughts on slavery. José Marcos Gutiérrez and Antonio de Villavicencio, for example, contributed crucial antislavery turns of phrase and concepts.[29]

After 1810, modern philosophy enthusiasts with revolutionary inclinations adopted Filangieri as a most relevant source on law and antislavery.[30] In *La scienza della legislazione* (1780–1791), Filangieri studiously developed a doctrine of modern lawgiving as the means to reform the unequal, antiquated world of European monarchies and their overseas possessions. Even more forcefully than other publicists of the time, he presented the Atlantic slave system as the most egregious example of a decadent old order that had bred illegitimate institutions.[31] Some slaves, Restrepo, and many of his revolutionary colleagues, expressed similar propositions. Slavery was a tyrannical manifestation of the Spanish regime. If the old New Kingdom of Granada was to become a new, independent polity, its legislators had to end slavery as a matter of principle.[32]

And yet the Colombian framers allowed slavery to coexist with antislavery in the nascent legal order, clinging to long-held stereotypes to support their ambiguous choice. Some of his colleagues, Restrepo reported, believed that "blacks" lived "dominated by all manner of vice: they are lazy, liars, thieves." Others asserted that the slaves lacked "enlightenment" and had to be properly educated before freedom. Otherwise, they would cause "evils" to society and destroy themselves. "This is exactly the reasoning of the Spaniards in regards to Independence," answered Restrepo, meaning that Spain likewise treated overseas vassals like people unfit to govern themselves.[33] Still, he argued that suddenly granting freedom to slaves would be "precipitous." "Social liberty" came in degrees. To fully enjoy it, enslaved individuals needed to be induced to a "certain disposition" – even after ridiculing Spain for demanding a similar preparation from those who sought emancipation from the metropole, Restrepo never clarified why the slaves needed a change of disposition and how they might achieve it.[34]

For generations, most masters and magistrates had conceived of slaves as men and women who constantly conspired to turn the world upside down, allegedly seeking to become free by criminally laying waste to cities and fields with sword and fire. Slaves were allegedly sinful by nature, and even their free descendants were labeled children of sin. Even a "virtuous action" by a slave, Restrepo recognized, could pass in the master's view for a "grave crime." Still, he reiterated that people in bondage posed an existential threat to the body politic. Comparing slavery with "electric fire," Restrepo reasoned that it had to be "slowly" ended to avoid "the effects of a violent explosion."[35] Save the physics metaphor, there was nothing new to these ideas. Occupying the lowest rung of the social pyramid, enslaved people were typically described as untrustworthy.[36]

Paradoxically, by virtue of their baptism slaves and freed people belonged in the spiritual community of the Church of Rome, the single religion under both the Spanish Catholic monarchy and the early independent polities. Slaves and former slaves thus had a basic moral personhood and the potential for legal personhood and communal belonging. Some acted on this potential by engaging in litigation and joining professional guilds and spiritual brotherhoods. After all, most enslaved workers in the late New Kingdom of Granada and early Colombia were born on the land, spoke Spanish, and practiced popular Catholicism. They descended from West Africans unwillingly brought across the Atlantic generations earlier.[37]

Many slaves had long trusted that an end to their captivity was in sight, that a new species of social contract was possible. With particular energy over the period 1781–1821, some insisted that kings and queens – including "black" and "African" monarchs – had set out to free the slaves or to ameliorate the conditions of servitude. Some tried to organize collective legal challenges to their enslavement, seeking to shift their status not only to free denizens but to enfranchised members of society. They even suggested that the stigma of their enslaved past should not prevent their political incorporation. Still, most masters and magistrates continued to insist that slaves acted solely out of their wicked determination to destroy the world around them.

Even across these transformative decades, it proved impossible to dislodge entrenched prejudice and vested interests. Some people continued to believe the old order might be as immovable as clergymen and magistrates had long asserted – especially following the 1781 Comunero Revolution. This event had raised serious alarms, making viceregal officials consider the possibility that vassals would seek to separate this Kingdom from the Spanish monarchy. Officials painted the 1781 upheaval as a radical attempt to undo hierarchy by usurping the king's authority. Priests reminded people that monarchical rule was God-given, therefore unchangeable. They emphasized that the same sacred bonds of authority and obedience binding together the king and his vassals also bound together masters and slaves, husbands and wives, the metropole and its overseas territories.[38] These tensions around patriarchal, corporate, and Spanish authority would shape the ambiguous slave emancipation that followed. Our journey thus begins not in the most visited landmarks of the French and Haitian Revolutions (1789, 1791) or Napoleon's occupation of Spain (1808), but in the year 1781.

I

Raynal in the New Kingdom?

The Comunero Revolution in 1781 was the most serious uprising against Spanish authorities in the New Kingdom of Granada prior to the crisis that ended with independence from Spain (1810–1821). In the populous east of the viceroyalty, around 20,000 people in arms took over several districts and came close to marching on the viceregal capital, Santa Fe (present-day Bogotá). The protesters revolted against recent fiscal and political measures. Common men and women opposed new taxes and restrictions on tobacco and alcohol production and sale. Even some elite *criollos* (vassals of Spanish stock, born in the New World) carefully mobilized against their replacement in administrative posts with *peninsulares* (people born in Spain). Indian communities protested a continuing assault on their landholdings. Fearing for their lives, high officials made some concessions, though they later recanted and ordered the execution of the leaders. Besides the protest near the capital, smaller groups of people revolted in other districts, even deposing and killing local magistrates.[1]

Although the new policies seemed terribly burdensome, it was the abrasive way they were introduced that most deeply concerned many of the protesters. Traditionally, taxes and policies were implemented after consultation with locals, who had the privilege to petition the king and negotiate over the scope of change. Some bureaucrats warned that a different, unilateral approach might meet with stiff resistance, but Madrid paid little attention, since ministers were by then engaged in efforts to transform government by compromise into absolute rule. They planned to extract as much revenue as possible from Spain's overseas domains, utilizing those lands as true "colonies" – a concept they borrowed from the vocabulary of French and English policymakers.[2]

Many of the protesters in 1781 relied on Castilian political concepts and practices. Accustomed to petitioning the authorities for redress, orally and especially via written memorials known as *representaciones*, many free vassals now felt affronted by officers who refused to listen.[3] The protesters called themselves *comuneros*, thus signaling that they spoke for the communities or "the people." Even though the label had a latent subversive implication, the comuneros emphasized that they complained not about the king but rather about his ministers, in this case an envoy with special powers and his associates. The comuneros' rallying cry in 1781, which they did not invent but borrowed from earlier generations of protesters, captured this alleged simultaneous hatred of the ministers and love for the monarch: "Long live the King, death to bad government!" the protesters shouted.[4]

Yet many people, especially viceregal officials and the clergy, believed that rising up against ministers constituted a crime against the king and a terrible blow to the sacred hierarchical order of society. Bureaucrats in the upper echelons of administration believed the protesters had undermined sovereignty itself, committing a crime of *lesa majestad*. Over the following years and decades, officials would continue to insist that vassals in the viceroyalty had lost their "innocence," their sense of unflinching respect toward the monarch and his ministers. In Santa Fe, subsequent archbishops, viceroys, and judges in the *Real Audiencia* (the high justice and administrative tribunal) maintained that the entire body politic remained vulnerable. They reasoned that no one could question the authority of the ministers without questioning the legitimacy of the king. The idea that the natural order of society could come apart to be replaced with a new, unnatural order became a major concern among the viceroyalty's top administrators following the Comunero Revolution – an important yet rarely noted consequence of 1781.[5]

Slaves and former slaves participated in several movements during the Comunero Revolution, often taking crucial actions for the overall development of the situation.[6] In 1781 and beyond, many slaveholders and officials feared that slaves, defying hierarchy and authority, would rise up and emancipate themselves by force, further breaking society's organic order. What the slaves' actual goals might have been, however, can be gleaned from extant handwritten evidence at the provincial and local levels. The documents come from several districts across the western half of the viceroyalty, where the majority of slaves were concentrated. Written by bureaucrats who described the unrest as the fruit of criminal conspiracy and a mechanistic reaction to foreign events, this evidence demands careful, critical reading.

Authorities' preoccupation about failing loyalties thus preceded the French Revolution and the Haitian Revolution (1789–1804), the events we more commonly associate with challenges to the monarchical form of government and slavery. After 1789, officials would accuse discontent vassals of flirting with French revolutionary ideas and agents, allegedly spreading a set of doctrines that would cause slaves to violently shake off the yoke of servitude. But even before the 1793 decapitation of the French king and the 1794 abolition of slavery throughout the French Empire, authorities in the New Kingdom (as the viceroyalty was called) had begun to articulate the notion that ungodly, anti-monarchical, and egalitarian ideas had contaminated this territory from abroad. In 1781, a slave overseer claimed that ongoing political protest in Peru and Upper Peru would generate slave unrest in the viceroyalty. By June 1789, an officious friar asserted that books by European "libertine philosophers" had stirred up the souls of leaders of the 1781 insurrection. In 1794, even Santa Fe patricians stood accused of conspiracy to end the current form of government and establish French-inspired "equality" and "liberty."

The French abbot Guillaume Thomas François Raynal stood out among the foreign authors listed as alleged sources of revolutionary influence. His works, Spanish officials warned, defied religion and subordination. Alarmingly, Raynal questioned the legitimacy of Spain's conquest and possession of its overseas territories. He even forecast that the slaves in the Americas would liberate themselves and kill their masters.[7] But Raynal's influence in the New Kingdom seems exaggerated, epitomizing the problematic perception of increasing political tensions at home as the direct consequence of foreign designs to destroy the Spanish monarchy. In fact, slaves autonomously discussed or advanced the cause of their own freedom. Raynal's work occupied no special place in the imagination of criollo patricians interested in political theory and modern philosophy. Members of the New Kingdom's intelligentsia were familiar with Raynal, but the towering figures of their political and legal formation were seventeenth-century thinkers such as Samuel von Pufendorf and Hugo Grotius, and eighteenth-century publicists like Gaetano Filangieri.[8]

After 1781, many clergymen and officials told people that any challenge to specific authority figures constituted a broader challenge to the entire political order. Seeking to separate slaves from the authority of their masters, whether individually or collectively, could be easily construed as challenging the system of monarchical government and its corporate, hierarchal nature. By the same token, projects to separate the New Kingdom from the Spanish monarchy also challenged deeply ingrained notions and habits of hierarchy and authority. Anxieties about slaves and their aspirations for emancipation were thus part of a larger set of preoccupations that became visible as early as the year of the Comunero Revolution.

The Year 1781

At the time of the Comunero Revolution, around 800,000 people lived within the borders of today's Colombia. Roughly 52,000 of them were held in slavery. Even though most of the population (around 55 percent) lived in the eastern half of the viceroyalty, most slaves lived west of the Magdalena River. Just over 35,000 (around 68 percent of the total enslaved population) lived on a vast, variegated territory stretching from the southern governorate of Popayán to the northern province of Cartagena. The west also encompassed the provinces of Antioquia and Chocó (with Chocó, in effect, more accurately described as a satellite of Popayán). While many slaves worked in towns and cities, and many more herded cattle and toiled the fields, most of them spent their lives working in gold mines. Therefore they concentrated on the west, a land cursed with robust mineral deposits, many of them exploited since well before the Spanish conquest.[9] (See Map 1)

The economy of the viceroyalty relied on slavery to carry out this gold mining. Even though they only represented close to 7 percent of the total population, slaves were responsible for this crucial sector of the economy: they extracted gold dust and gold nuggets from rivers,

MAP 1 The lands of Cartagena, Antioquia, and Popayán in the New Kingdom of Granada. Map by Gerry Krieg.

small streams, and slopes. Some of the resulting bullion became ingots and coins in the Royal Mints of Popayán and Santa Fe. And all of it, regardless of shape or form, served as cash in local, provincial and, most importantly, overseas transactions. Between 1784 and 1793, total exports amounted to just over 21 million *pesos*, of which 19.2 million was gold. Gold would continue to be the most salient export long after independence. And because pre-industrial mining techniques would only begin to improve slowly after 1825, slaves remained the decisive, most expensive investment in the mining business. The idea that riches, including royal revenues, depended on enslaved labor became deeply rooted in the imagination of many slaveholders and bureaucrats. The well-being of the polity, many argued, rested on the continued subordination of slaves.[10]

In 1781, as officials introduced new taxes and tried to tighten Spain's political control over the viceroyalty, popular protests took place in the western, gold-producing districts of Antioquia and Popayán. During judicial interrogations, anxious magistrates forced some protesters and alleged conspirators to speak their minds in front of clerks who wrote down their words. Slaves and former slaves who took part in the events thus expressed their grievances and aspirations. Most magistrates, however, distorted or misunderstood their testimonies, insisting that the discontent had been motivated by outside influence, caused by the spread of foreign revolutionary senti- ments. Magistrates also claimed that protesters were not motivated by political aspirations but criminal intentions. Antioquia's governor asserted that malicious slaves planned to end their bondage by means of wholesale slaughter and destruction.[11] Yet the sources reveal that many slaves sought to turn 1781 into an opportunity to realize their long-held hopes of deliverance from slavery while remaining faithful to the king and living in peace with their neighbors. Despite the distortions, magistrates and their scribes left records that provide glimpses of the legal imagination of the enslaved.[12]

Even the situation unfolding at the epicenter of the comunero move- ment should not be understood as a direct trigger of what transpired in Antioquia. To be sure, news of the massive movement in the northeast of the New Kingdom reached slaves and free folk in this province. Fleeting reports from the province of Mariquita, Antioquia's neighbor to the east, even suggested that a comunero leader had offered freedom to a group of slaves in exchange for their joining his forces.[13] But slaves made their political choices keeping in mind their own predica- ments and based on local information. In Antioquia, some slaves took advantage of the 1781 crisis to voice their aspirations for freedom, but these aspirations pre-dated the comunero movement.

Although obtaining freedom was rare, Antioquia slaves witnessed a few manumissions every year, usually paid for by slaves themselves, and occasionally heard of some masters freeing their captives.

By 1781, slaves who belonged to well-off masters seem to have been particularly hopeful about impending freedom. They were closely watched, poorly fed and clothed, and apparently more harshly treated than slaves owned by less powerful masters. Over the previous fifteen years, people had paid attention to one case of collective emancipation. A rich widow, Javiera Londoño, had manumitted 122 of her slaves, leaving instructions for the emancipation of another thirty-two after her death. Not surprisingly, Londoño's heirs pitched a fierce legal battle to thwart those manumissions, alleging that the widow had lost her mind – an old trick employed to block similar liberations.[14]

A few well-off masters who owned dozens of slaves kept some of their captive workers in Antioquia's San Nicolás plateau, where people had mined for gold since the late 1600s (see Map 2). Some of the Londoño slaves lived in the area, where they worked the gold mines alongside people of color and poor criollos. These free folks were known as *mazamorreros*, gold prospectors who ran small operations, rarely owned mine titles or land, and did not have much cash to spare. Some mazamorreros owned a few slaves. Through the time-tested panning technique, and with little government intervention, they extracted the prized gold out of rivers and creeks.[15]

In 1781, however, the enterprise of gold mining in San Nicolás suddenly stood threatened by new fiscal measures. In June, mazamorreros publicly aired their resentment at a new tax on their earnings. They also expressed their opposition to newly established country stores, where they were required to purchase duly taxed supplies from royal agents.[16] When the free miners rose up against these measures in the hamlet of Guarne (see Map 2), slaves found themselves in the midst of political upheaval. And with provincial governor Cayetano Buelta Lorenzana and other officials now pressing for more revenue, some slaves seem to have reasoned that they might be able to accelerate collective emancipation in exchange for offering to pay taxes – in contrast with long-standing patterns of tax evasion. Some slaves aspired to become reliable free vassals of the king, joining the ranks of the humblest mazamorreros. The situation proved delicate from the beginning, but some slaves found time to discuss what the crisis might mean for their own aspirations.

The Londoño manumissions and the ensuing legal challenge had become a *cause célèbre* throughout the province, stimulating

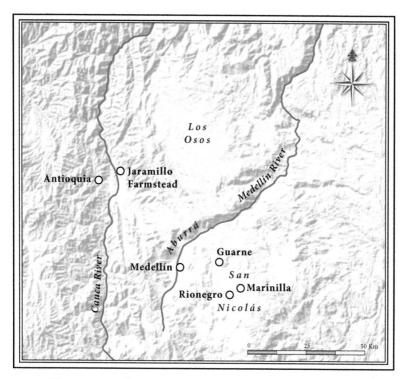

MAP 2 The province of Antioquia. Map by Gerry Krieg.

aspirations of collective legal emancipations. This may have been especially true among the slaves of the powerful priest Sancho Londoño Piedrahíta. His aunt, the rich widow Javiera, had appointed him to provide her manumitted slaves with legal advice, for she anticipated other relatives would not let the manumissions stand without a fight. With about 230 slaves to his name, the priest was the largest slaveholder in Antioquia. His aunt's decision had placed him in a paradoxical position: here was a master defending dozens of people seeking to shake off the yoke of slavery while trying to keep his own slaves under subordination. In the eventful year of 1781, the priest seems to have reached his wits' end. He accused slaves of conspiracy to rise up, but he also claimed that slaves had a plan to demand the publication of a royal decree granting them freedom – a fast-spreading rumor among other groups of slaves.[17] Meanwhile, the governor also alleged that slaves throughout the province were planning to rise up on

January 1, 1782. According to governor Buelta Lorenzana, the slaves believed officials had concealed a very important document from them, a decree by the king setting them free.[18]

Buelta Lorenzana quickly moved to uncover what he described as an alliance among slaves from different districts within the province, including San Nicolás, the Aburrá valley, and the city of Antioquia – the provincial capital (see Map 2). It was a despicable enterprise, he told other magistrates in a letter, put together by wicked slaves who planned to "kill their masters" and "all the whites," "proclaim freedom," and make themselves "owners of everything." These were quite stereotypical accusations, based on thin and dubious evidence. The governor himself mentioned that, at first, he had only had the slightest clues that such a slave conspiracy even existed. Yet he looked for evidence and, finally, "a fuerza de azote," by the force of the whip, he got a slave to confess and to name names.[19]

Under torture, the witness mentioned the slaves of La Mosca, a mining enclave near Guarne, where the troubles had taken place in June and where the Londoño family had some of their slaves. There, a local magistrate soon obtained confessions that a young man who worked as a muleteer had told slaves in the area to join forces because "the whites" were keeping an important secret from them. José Ignacio, a slave captain and a witness in the case, specifically believed the secret to be a royal decree granting freedom to the slaves. But even under pressure, the witnesses mentioned no plans to kill, destroy, or upend social order. After all, their aspirations for freedom through a royal decree, or from testamentary manumission, pre-supposed that they would challenge the bonds of subordination only through legal means.[20]

Slaves in the Spanish Indies had a vague legal personhood, but they could file claims against their masters, and even sue for emancipation. Allowed to enjoy legal counsel, slaves on occasion found sympathetic magistrates to plead their cases. When they stood accused of crimes, slaves had advocates appointed by the judges. Held to be "wretched" and "unfortunate" humans, they could aspire to protection by the king and his ministers. In practice, however, legal avenues to redress and emancipation remained difficult to traverse. Typically, such avenues would not easily open unless some pressure was exerted – but slaves exerted pressure in calculated rather than spasmodic fashion.[21]

What fearful masters and bureaucrats saw as an uprising conspiracy may have been the result of a careful dialogue among some slaves on how to capitalize on political unrest in 1781. Slave leaders appeared to be mostly interested in pressing for manumissions legally granted by masters or the king but illegitimately withheld by inheritors and magistrates. In the criminal inquest into the supposed conspiracy, the leading slave Pelayo provided revealing details. He told of a conversation with fellow slaves and their idea that a group of "fifty blacks" could present a *cabildo* (municipal council) with a written petition for collective freedom. Some slaves believed that they should organize as a group and travel to the provincial capital to plead their case before authorities. Slaves who talked about the rumored royal decree in their favor, moreover, believed the document called for freed people to pay taxes "like Indians," suggesting that slaves could become free vassals with clearly defined privileges and duties, fully enjoying the king's protection rather than his commiseration alone.[22] For some slaves, obtaining freedom meant something close to transitioning into mazamorreros, rural denizens fulfilling the duties and enjoying the privileges of the free folk with whom they lived in close proximity and to whom they were related in some cases.

The idea that a group of enslaved people could modify their status by making claims before municipal magistrates resonated with the actual legal roles of cabildos. As both administrative and judiciary bodies, cabildos functioned as the highest local tribunals, corporations responsible for exercising distributive justice on behalf of the monarch.[23] The would-be petitioners were not entirely misguided in their hopes that perhaps cabildo magistrates would finally bring to light that emancipatory decree from the king. Some slaves imagined that a plan existed to do just this on January 1, 1782, the day the governor anticipated the slaves would rise up to become the new masters.[24] The first day of each year had an important political meaning for municipal business. Patricians in the Spanish world set New Year's Day aside to meet and elect new cabildo members, the magistrates who would rule their urban centers and rural jurisdictions for the following twelve months.

So maybe there was a plan to kill the patricians as they met to choose new aldermen, as Buelta Lorenzana imagined. But Pelayo himself asserted that they would only resort to arms as a last resource.

Moreover, the organized slaves anticipated seeking refuge far away from towns, not to destroy them; they planned to make a living away from the masters and to pay taxes to the king ("like Indians" and mazamorreros) if possible. With rare insight, the slaves' advocate argued that if there had been any plan at all it had probably been to plead before the magistrates on a politically auspicious day.[25] This legal counselor's voice proved to be a lone cry in the desert, however.

The Antioquia case thus suggests a rich, painstakingly and hopeful legal imagination among the enslaved. Pushed to the lowest of social stations and living under the constant threat of violence, while collectively accounting for only a marginal proportion of the population, slaves had to think long and hard before taking arms to speed their freedom. Rather than violent action, many saw individual or collective manumission as the best way to achieve freedom without risking life and limb, even though emancipation remained rare. In Medellín, a day's travel east of the provincial capital (see Map 2), scribes recorded an annual average of twenty-three slave sales but only formalized three or four manumission acts per year.[26] Captivity seemed to have no end. Although the misrepresentation of slaves' intentions was relentless, some slaves still appear to have trusted that the king would take pity and grant them freedom, thereby bringing about the end of coerced work and offering protection by the magistrates in exchange for loyalty and tribute.

This emerging picture of legal thought and action by slaves relies on a critical approach to the surviving documentation. Accounts of slaves' deeds and words as criminal conspiracy typically appear in unsympathetic reports and proceedings. Instead of taking such accounts at face value, we must pay careful attention to the polyphony and subtleties of the judicial forum. In the back and forth between accusers and the accused, some expressions were written down that reveal a vibrant convergence of hope and legal awareness among the enslaved, suggesting the existence of communal efforts to effect change. In the governorate of Popayán, even though the surviving evidence is somewhat thin, we can also see how masters typically painted slaves' mutual help efforts and discrete expressions of discontent as near-apocalyptic threats to the monarchy.[27]

In Popayán's districts of Tumaco and Barbacoas (see Map 3), popular protests turned particularly tense, with slaves and other

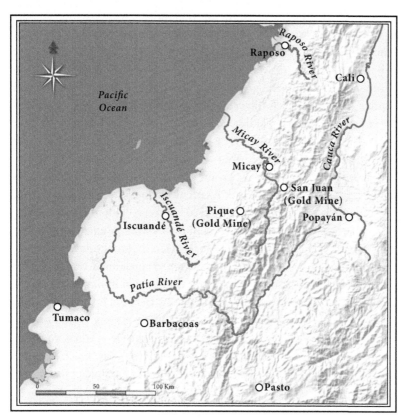

MAP 3 The governorate of Popayán. Map by Gerry Krieg.

commoners rejecting recent measures affecting tobacco and *aguardiente* (a popular alcoholic beverage distilled from sugar cane). In the Pacific port town of Tumaco, a crowd deposed the lieutenant governor in November 1781, replacing him with Vicente de la Cruz, a former slave. He assumed control of the town for the following ten months but was later arrested and sentenced to forced labor.[28] In April 1782, people in the mining town of Barbacoas also took to the streets, demanding to roll back tobacco sale restrictions. The cabildo had to yield. The aldermen, however, sent alarming reports to the viceroy, claiming that the local "nobles" were on the brink of destruction at the hands of criminal "plebs." Moreover, they suggested that the threat extended to the entire monarchy. Should they become the victims of "insurrection," cabildo members insisted, the king would lose the revenue from gold extraction. Local notables worried that coerced workers might escape their control, preventing slaveholders from sending bullion to Popayán's Royal Mint.[29]

Barbacoas' masters seem to have interpreted the events of 1781 as another symptom of the growing collaboration between free folk and captive workers, which they claimed would lead to the end of slavery. De la Cruz's leadership had been especially alarming precisely because he and his followers could not be easily distinguished as either slave or free.[30] Most humble families in the district in fact straddled slavery and freedom. Not only did some slaves abscond permanently or temporarily, but some obtained formal emancipation and then tried to help their captive relatives out of slavery. Hoping to purchase freedom for themselves or their relations, slaves panned for gold on their free days (on Saturdays, and even secretly on Sundays and other Catholic holidays) while free folk poached unclaimed or unguarded streams. The masters claimed that self-emancipation happened alarmingly frequently, and that the acquisition of freedom by any individual slave set a bad example for the rest. Slaveholders saw collaboration between slave and free as collusion to undermine slavery and gold production. During the comunero crisis, the Barbacoas cabildo ordered emancipated slaves to settle down in hamlets instead of illegally prospecting for gold.[31]

Despite the obvious anxieties about slaves' efforts for self-emancipation and the fiscal motivations of the unrest, officials and slaveholders claimed that news about uprisings elsewhere caused the local riots. As early as March 18, 1781, Marcos Cortés, from an infamous clan of masters and slave drivers, predicted that any opposition to the new taxes in Barbacoas would ultimately lead to a slave uprising. It would be "natural," Cortés anticipated, for people in bondage to "shake off the yoke of servitude...devouring the lives of every white man." But Cortés also explained that news about the uprising in the northeast of the viceroyalty would lead to unrest. The movement, he even claimed, would be partially caused by the troubles in Peru and Upper Peru, where thousands had joined powerful anti-colonial uprisings in 1780.[32]

Even though the situation stabilized quickly after 1782, the planned fiscal and political overhaul of the viceroyalty had been disrupted and a sense of political calamity settled among some. High authorities in

Santa Fe typically thought that the year 1781 had revealed a deep-seated contempt for the current political order in the New Kingdom, a polity they continued to see as being on the brink of upheaval over the following two decades. The dubious moral and spiritual fiber of vassals, Spanish administrators believed, fueled the viceroyalty's unstable political climate. Although quick to blame foreign ideas and agents for political tensions at home, many bureaucrats also believed that wicked locals simply abhorred the peace and virtue of life under the Spanish monarch and the Catholic church. Officials typically painted aspirations for change as challenges against the sacred order of society. The comuneros, people were told, had challenged the holy bonds of vassalage binding together king, ministers, and subjects.[33]

Throughout the districts where the 1781 uprisings had been most serious, missionaries preached that the movement had not merely been a protest against taxation but a most egregious crime against the sovereign, the monarchy, and the church. The officious Capuchin friar Joaquín de Finestrad wrote a treatise re-visiting the basic political grammar of the New Kingdom and of the monarchy as a whole – a grammar allegedly defied by the comuneros. The New Kingdom, he reminded his audience, was constituted as a corporatist, inegalitarian, and mystical society. This conception of society rested on three doctrines. First, the sacred organization of the body politic in the form of a monarchy. Rising up against the king's ministers was "the most horrendous sacrilege," for the monarch's temporal authority emanated from God. Second, the organic constitution of society in the likeness of a human body. The political body had different members, each with specific functions. As the head of the body, the king was the most important member. While the ministers' function was to govern on behalf of the king, the vassals' role was to "venerate and blindly obey his royal commands." Finally, this "political and Christian order" was eternal: it should not be challenged or altered in any way, for doing so risked the breakup of civility, peace, and virtue. "Without the subordination of the limbs to the head, neither the natural body can survive nor the political [body] preserve itself."[34] The entire system was underpinned by the principle of authority: slaves had to obey masters for the same reasons that all vassals obeyed the king and all students their teachers. In the turbulent 1790s, following the outbreak of revolution in France and its Caribbean

colonies, many would reiterate that these principles and doctrines were
under threat from dangerous French agents, godless French ideas, and
unruly, easily impressionable slaves.

The French Scare

Some Spanish administrators specifically saw foreign political principles, which they believed had entered the viceroyalty via French
books, as a cause of the 1781 troubles. The idea that political contagion had affected the viceroyalty thus predated the outbreak of
revolution in France. Before learning about the events at the Bastille,
Finestrad already asserted that works by French thinkers had inspired
the leading comuneros. He referred to those thinkers as the "new
philosopher" or the "libertine philosopher" – French publicists
allegedly characterized by their envy of Spain's glories and their
impious character. In Finestrad's view, those "philosophers," who
dangerously wrote with "little respect" against the church and the
principle of authority, had gained secret sympathizers in the New
Kingdom. Among these thinkers, Finestrad listed the famous Raynal.[35]

Raynal epitomized the dreaded French philosopher, co-writing a
French-language critical history of European colonization in the East
and West Indies that first appeared in 1770 and remained popular
in the 1780s. Some people in the viceroyalty illegally owned this
prohibited work, which specifically touched on the New Kingdom of
Granada, openly discussing the notion that the territories so cruelly
conquered and poorly managed by the Spaniards had the potential to
become independent.[36] Following the increasingly radical French
Revolution in the early 1790s, the notion that French ideas and events
had direct consequences on the political fate of the viceroyalty became
even more entrenched. Authorities, however, looked at events in
France in light of the Comunero Revolution.

Because viceregal officials continued to interpret the comunero protest as a crime against the sovereign, in the 1790s they emphasized the
French Revolution as a most execrable example of exactly this kind of
crime. Following the decapitation of the French monarch (a cousin of
the Spanish king) and the outbreak of war between Spain and France
in 1793, animosity against people from France and its overseas territories increased dramatically. The year 1793 also saw the liberation of

the slaves in the restive French colony of Saint-Domingue, with increasing participation of freed people in the conflict as soldiers and privateers. The French government declared the abolition of slavery throughout its territories early the following year. Wary about a revolutionary reprise in the New Kingdom, Spanish officials and masters of slaves became suspicious not only of newly arrived French speakers but even of longtime French and other foreign residents.[37]

In January 1793, on orders from Madrid, the viceroy expelled foreigners from the viceroyalty, except those who would swear allegiance to the king of Spain. About a dozen French people resided in Santa Fe at this time, some of them married to Spanish subjects. The group included Juan Francisco de Rieux. A medical doctor from Montpellier, Rieux had traveled to Saint-Domingue in a scientific expedition in the 1780s. He later traveled to Cartagena de Indias, where he worked in the military hospital before moving to Santa Fe in 1792 (see Map 1). As the owner of a rural estate with ninety slaves, Rieux might not have been interested in promoting revolution, but with his brother still living in Saint-Domingue and he himself traveling regularly between the inland provinces and coastal Cartagena, Rieux received letters, heard news of the events unfolding in the French world, and talked to his relatives and friends about it all.[38]

Spanish authorities maintained that people like Rieux would transmit French ideas of "liberty," "equality," and "disobedience" to Spanish subjects. In Santa Fe, Audiencia judges and other viceregal officials asserted that those notions had spread among notables and college students. The main suspects were members of tertulias, gatherings of men and women of considerable social standing interested in reciprocal learning, the discussion of current events, and what they called modern philosophy. Participants shared printed and handwritten materials, reading aloud and discussing foreign books, gazettes, and correspondence. The French doctor Rieux assiduously participated in Antonio Nariño's tertulia.[39] With the largest personal book collection in the Kingdom (boasting an impressive 1,617 volumes in 1794), Nariño emerged as a leading intellectual and was accused of harboring revolutionary inclinations.[40]

Authorities knew that foreign books were read and circulated among the local intelligentsia, including, though not limited to, French texts. Nariño owned books by Voltaire, Montesquieu, and Raynal.

These authors criticized and mocked the Catholic church, European monarchies, and colonialism with writings that were included in the Inquisition's list of prohibited books. Almost all "French books" were considered "suspicious" at the time.[41] To counteract the potential effect of this literature, Santa Fe's only gazette, the officially sanctioned *Papel periódico de la ciudad de Santafé de Bogotá* (in circulation 1791–1796), denounced what its editor, a fervent monarchist, termed the "political anarchy of France." Defending the natural, wise, and perfect character of monarchies, the editor praised this form of government as the only political system capable of bringing happiness to humankind.[42]

Such a strong defense of monarchies made sense in reference to events in France as well as in the viceroyalty. Defending kings and condemning regicides worked as warnings against a potential revolution in the New Kingdom, where loyalty to the monarchy, high officials believed, remained vulnerable since the year 1781. Indeed, the *Papel periódico*'s coverage of events in France argued that a pathway toward revolution existed, and that the New Kingdom had already taken steps down this very path. The French Revolution, the editor explained in a series of issues, had taken place within a specific chain of events. One chapter in that process, the Flour Wars, appears in the *Papel periódico* as a first "attempt" to throw France into revolutionary turmoil. In the spring of 1775, rioters throughout the French Kingdom demanded a solution to the high price of flour and impending generalized hunger, but in spite of the radical character of the movement, authorities pardoned most of the participants. According to the *Papel periódico*, this misguided policy of compassion toward the "perverse leaders" had allowed the revolutionary spirit to stay alive. The reference to the Flour Wars as an antecedent of the French Revolution resonated among readers of the gazette as a warning that the spirit of the Comunero Revolution still haunted the viceroyalty.[43]

The message that connections and parallels existed between revolution abroad and the political situation at home was directed at intellectually curious patricians. The editor and his sponsoring officials knew that tertulia habitués read the *Papel periódico*. The coverage of the French Revolution thus identified written works by French thinkers as causes of ungodly social disorder, warning readers against foreign "philosophers." Metropolitan and viceregal authorities believed that these authors, especially Raynal, embodied a root cause of revolution: disobedience to the principle of authority. They obsessively denounced Raynal, even though his work was infrequently cited among tertulia participants and other readers.[44] Announcing Raynal's death, the editor of the *Papel periódico* labeled his work "arrogant and boastful," ironically lamenting this great loss for humankind.[45]

Following the 1793 radicalization of the French Revolution, fresh assertions that French egalitarian doctrines directly threatened spiritual and temporal order appeared in the *Papel periódico*. To establish the "system of equality" promoted by French thinkers, the editor insisted, would be absurd. Any and all political transformations were to be prevented. Change, he warned, would amount to sacrilege: just "thinking about the reform of a political establishment" would be an "impious project, tyrannical, and inhuman." For political change could not be achieved without the destruction of "the most sacred objects of Religion, the most sacred bonds of Society, the most useful interests of common good."[46] To transform society in any way would be to interfere with God's plan for his people. And to transform it by undermining the mystical bonds of vassalage seemed particularly terrible.

The importance of faith and subordination to hierarchical rule in this society can hardly be overstated, as duly explained by the friar Finestrad. If the majesty of the king emanated from God, crimes against the monarch constituted offenses against religion.[47] Even the very thought of changing the social order, particularly by promoting the idea of "equality," threatened the bonds binding together naturally unequal groups and corporations, all enmeshed in the single spiritual community of the baptized. "We are all vassals of the one same king and members of Jesus Christ," Finestrad wrote. Everybody, he insisted, must fulfill the duties specific to their social stations.[48]

A notion of tremendous negative connotations, equality presupposed an alteration of the reigning political and spiritual order. Finestrad and the *Papel periódico* thus defended hierarchy and inequality, insisting on the proper subordination of the lower to the upper social echelons: the vassals to the king; the viceroyalty to the mother country; the provinces to Santa Fe; the hamlets to the cities; the faithful to the clergy; every nun to her abbess; plebeians to patricians; the slaves to the masters. We must keep in mind that, under

Spanish rule, no common rights applied equally to all individuals.[49] Alarmed authorities claimed that the comuneros first, and now Revolutionary France and the former slaves of Saint-Domingue were bent on turning this status quo on its head, making everybody "equal."

The Rights of Man and Citizen?

The remarks on the French Flour Wars and the "system of equality" published by the *Papel periódico* appeared in a moment rife with political tensions. Before dawn on August 19, 1794, someone attached pasquinades to the front walls of several buildings in Santa Fe. These pamphlets, which threatened the lives of the viceroy and viceregal officials, mentioned, both specifically and obliquely, not only the 1781 comunero movement but also an ongoing plan to establish the "liberty...enjoyed by the French." The pasquinades also suggested that, due to the government's bad policies, "our Sovereign" would "lose the Indies." The anonymous writings thus linked the events of 1781 with the current situation, forecasting the possibility of radical political transformations in the very near future. The writings even announced that Santa Fe "will be finished" in a conflagration.[50]

Despite the seriousness of the pasquinades, the idea that a full-blown French-inspired movement to upend society was afoot only fully crystallized two weeks later. When someone denounced Nariño for secretly translating and printing the French Declaration of the Rights of Man and Citizen (originally drafted in 1789), the viceroy and Audiencia judges hastened to assert a connection between the translation and the pasquinades. Nariño, they reasoned, had participated in a conspiracy to upend the Kingdom and adopt the French form of government.[51] Nariño was arrested, sent to the infamous dungeons of Cartagena, and later shipped to Spain. The viceroy and judges further thought that the Frenchman Rieux, also detained and sent to Spain, had undermined Nariño's respect for authority and loyalty to the monarchy. Officials displayed, once again, the idea of revolutionary contagion from abroad.[52]

But we must not lose sight of the home circumstances behind the judges' repressive approach. To begin with, tertulia goers and other patricians in Santa Fe had lived under close watch from authorities well before 1794. As part of the same measures opposed by the comuneros, authorities had eroded Santa Fe elites' influence on the viceregal administration by excluding criollos from high office, appointing people born in Spain instead. Nariño himself was a member of the Álvarez clan, a local family whose impressive grip on the viceregal court bureaucracy had been dissolved by 1780. Born in 1765, he was old enough to remember the affront.[53] Patricians in similar situations had collaborated with the comuneros, whose leaders demanded that "the nationals of this America" be preferred for office. After 1781, the struggle over royal posts would facilitate a more clear-cut articulation of differences between criollos and peninsulares, even though elites from both sides of the Atlantic were intricately linked by blood, marriage, patronage, and customs.[54]

Nariño's 1794 arrest and the imprisonment of many others, including young students, caused outrage among many criollos. They resented yet another blow to their ranks, one executed with a harshness unfitting to their high social station. The Santa Fe cabildo (controlled by criollos) requested to take part in the investigation on the pasquinades and the translation. The judges and viceroy, however, argued that the matter was outside of the cabildo's jurisdiction. Members of the cabildo were thus unable to help the detainees. In a report to Madrid, the viceroy suggested that Santa Fe's cabildo had to be re-shaped, forcing Americans to share municipal posts with Europeans. Rieux would later claim that the 1794 conspiracy never existed, that it was all false accusations brought forward by people seeking to garner favor at court by manipulating existing tensions.[55]

Increasing tensions in the late 1700s led some observers to believe that a separation between the New World viceroyalty and the Spanish monarchy was possible.[56] Even in the absence of organized movements for independence or clearly articulated plans for a republic, open calls for the rejection of the monarchical form of government and separation from Spain – as opposed to the traditional "long live the king, death to bad government" – began to spring up. An anonymous handwritten letter to the viceroy in Santa Fe, for instance, announced the coming of independence, stating that "the great men" currently imprisoned would soon get out of jail, for the "spirit of the hatred of Monarchism" now possessed "all the souls of those who are not traitors to the Fatherland."[57] Presumed "seditious" papers also appeared in the city of Quito on October 21 and November 21, 1794, and March 21, 1795. One of the documents explicitly called for armed struggle against the "tyrant King." Considering the French 1793 regicide of a Bourbon sovereign, the expression raised serious concerns among authorities. The doctrine of tyrannicide, developed by Spanish theologians in the 1500s, was now removed from the curriculum in the Kingdom's educational institutions.[58]

The doomsday scenario anticipated by pasquinades, accusations, and judicial proceedings failed to materialize. The viceroy ordered all provincial governors to keep him informed of any disturbances of "public tranquility"[59]; however, things remained relatively calm. Moreover, authorities never fully substantiated the accusations against the alleged 1794 conspirators. The judges found no copies of Nariño's translation of the Rights of Man and Citizen. In Madrid, Rieux was cleared of any wrongdoing and even received authorization to return to Santa Fe.[60] After escaping from prison in Spain and fleeing to France, Nariño allegedly slipped back into the viceroyalty. According to the Count of Torre Velarde, an Audiencia judge in Santa Fe, Nariño came back to spark a general uprising and to establish a "republic."[61]

Torre Velarde and other officials rejected the French doctrines of equality and republic. They continued to believe that social bonds could break, including the bonds between slaves and masters. Their fears only grew after Spain's rapprochement with the French Republic in 1797. For despite all the rhetoric and heightened apprehension about foreigners, authorities had no choice but to occasionally welcome people from the French world – including liberated slaves from the French islands. Much to the chagrin of viceregal, provincial, and local authorities, Spain alternately rejected and welcomed French royalists and French republicans, depending on shifting international alliances and wartime developments in Europe and the Caribbean.[62] Though officials hated the abstract "libertine" French "philosopher," they could not easily keep people from France and French territories at bay.

Most people who came to the New Kingdom from French colonies like Saint-Domingue and Guadeloupe were liberated slaves. In these French territories, some masters had been killed, many plantations and some cities burnt, and slavery abolished. Ex-slaves from those places thus embodied an explicit case of the dissolution of the traditional chains of subordination. Their presence in places where slavery still existed, authorities believed, could fuel hopes of freedom among local slaves. Some even reasoned that the former slaves could help others still in chains in the killing of their masters, thus turning the world upside down. But those coming to South American shores may not have been all that much interested in promoting revolution. They were mostly people down on their luck or traveling for work: prisoners of war, privateersmen, soldiers, stranded sailors, re-enslaved people, refugees, and assistants to French agents.[63]

In the eyes of bureaucrats, however, all people from the French Caribbean were potential agents of revolution, regardless of the complexities of their particular circumstances. In February 1803, a ship from Guadeloupe arrived near Chimare, on the north coast of the Guajira Peninsula (see Map 1). The ship brought over 200 refugees, mostly people of color described as "French blacks." They apparently sought refuge among the Guajiro people, who inhabited the area. The viceroy was alarmed by the news: so many people of African descent from an island where slaves had been emancipated and allowed to work as soldiers and sailors, he believed, could set a terrible example for local slaves. From the viceroy's perspective, the refugees constituted "a class of people infected with the ideas of liberty, equality and others that have been so pernicious and have caused many ravages and horrors on the unhappy French Islands." Fearful that they might make their way into the inland provinces, the viceroy requested they be thrown in jail, sent to public works, or interrogated and deported to their place of origin.[64]

These people had left their homes unwillingly and had likewise not chosen their place of destination, and though the provincial governor was able to arrest some of these refugees, he did not deport them to Guadeloupe. The official believed that the French had orders to throw those people "alive into the sea." With the conflicts in Saint-Domingue and Guadeloupe now turned into a war over French colonial presence and against the re-establishment of slavery, drowning had become yet another weapon in the bitter fighting.[65] Aware of this drama, a Spanish bureaucrat would occasionally take pity on refugees of color, setting aside fears that they might be dangerous revolutionaries. Usually, however, slaves and former slaves were subjected to odious and repressive treatment.

* * *

Following the 1781 Comunero Revolution, masters of slaves and Spanish authorities in the New Kingdom developed the idea that a terrible infection had taken root in the body politic of the viceroyalty. This disease, which they claimed had been introduced from abroad via vectors of revolution such as books by "libertine" philosophers and conspiracies led by foreign agents and local traitors, allegedly ate away at the foundations of the monarchy: faith, authority, and hierarchy. The suspects included increasingly dissatisfied criollos such as Nariño, suspicious tertulia goers such as Rieux, and slaves and former slaves seeking redress. According to the authorities, it was Raynal's godless doctrines that had contaminated their spirits. After all, Raynal's book had prophesied that the slaves would rise up to avenge the New World. Finestrad even claimed that his work partially accounted for the comunero movement, an idea that gained further adherents after the execution of the French monarch.

After 1793, people from the troubled French Caribbean, most of them traveling in search of work or safe heaven, also came to be judged as vectors of revolution. Most had been recently liberated from slavery, and odious labels bestowed upon them such as "negros franceses," and even "negros franceses esclavos revolucionarios" were not neutral references to place of origin, African ancestry, or linguistic backgrounds. Such monikers were meant to represent a heterogeneous group of people as an infectious collective, contaminated by a political disease that might be transmitted to local, presumably impressionable, slaves.[66] Most officials thus tended to gloss over the complexities of the situation in which those held as slaves found themselves. Enslaved families and individuals in the New Kingdom neither mechanically replicated foreign examples of revolution nor idly stood by as increasing political uncertainty offered new chances to further their aspirations.

Throughout the Americas, a "culture of expectation" already existed among many slaves, keeping alive hopes that redress, individual freedom, and even general emancipation would materialize, giving respite to those in bondage.[67] Some took steps to advance the realization of those hopes, pressing masters and inheritors to deliver on their promises of manumission, requesting clarification from authorities about the rumor that the king had ended bondage, and attempting to file petitions with local magistrates to further clarify these issues. What Antioquia officials denounced as a cabal for the destruction of the social order was actually an early manifestation of the cross-district collaborations among slaves seeking to enter the judicial forum on a more tolerable basis to make claims about their status.

Slaves' culture of expectation was neither predicated on boundless violence against "white," free people, nor guided by news from abroad. As we shall now explore in more detail, slaves' hopes were underpinned by their own leitmotifs: they were bound up in local conditions, and they often crystallized in plans for legal endeavors – a fact that authorities at the time usually brushed aside and that present-day historians also tend to bypass. In spite of efforts by officials and masters to simplify slaves' efforts as criminal conspiracy and their ideas as mere byproducts of French agitation, some of these complexities are still discernible in the judicial sources.

2

Landscapes of Slavery, Rumors of Freedom

Long before the Comunero Revolution and the electric 1790s, many free people in the New Kingdom of Granada believed slaves lived in a near-constant state of conspiracy to destroy the masters, kill "all the whites," and upend the social order. For generations, masters and other observers resorted to the trope of slaves trying to take over cities and shatter the reigning order. Although the plots could rarely be confirmed, many officials reiterated that slaves, as a matter of course, sought to turn the world upside down. It was thus better to kill the suspects than for free folk to wait to be murdered or turned into serfs, many believed. Over the centuries, hundreds of slaves perished in the recurring crazes.[1] The physical and social destruction of cities by slaves, however, almost never happened. Rebellious slaves typically left urban centers, avoiding direct confrontation with authorities and masters.[2]

Blanket characterizations of slaves as criminal conspirators gained more currency toward the turn of the nineteenth century. Already evident during the Comunero Revolution, stock accusations became salient in the wake of the French and Haitian Revolutions. Age-old fears of slave uprising decidedly shaped masters' understanding of the potential home effects of social upheaval abroad. As we zoom in to study the three most relevant slave societies in the viceroyalty (the jurisdictions of Cartagena, Antioquia, and Popayán) during the turbulent change of the century, we shall see how prejudiced, stereotyped perceptions of slave action were present across the board. People in power reproduced formulaic ideas about slaves allegedly seeking emancipation through violent means and, by extension, the destruction of all that was sacred and natural.

These simplifications rested on the ways in which people in corporate societies essentialized others. Legal inequality allowed ample room for individuals to believe that innate, natural traits characterized different groups of people. The idea that vice and virtue accrued according to people's social station, religious confession, political background, and genealogy was widely accepted. Many Spanish-speakers took it as fact that Jews were duplicitous, Indians drunk, the French godless, and slaves deceitful and treacherous.[3] They took rumor of slave conspiracy seriously. As the old Spanish saying went, one would be wise "not to discard altogether rumors spread by the common people."[4] This led to judicial scrutiny, biased interrogation, and torture to corroborate the presumptions.[5]

Moreover, people mobilized these convictions to fit their own purposes and advance their interests. The challenge for the historian is to probe the ways in which specific New Kingdom officials and slaveholders interpreted and used the specter of slave insurrection to further their own political agendas and special interests. This approach will allow us to sketch a more accurate portrait of slaves' culture of expectation, the necessary counterpoint to the stereotypes propagated by unsympathetic commentators. This culture of expectation encompassed the actual notions about the end of slavery shared by many slaves, as well as their actual tactics to improve their working conditions or accelerate the coming of emancipation. Both dimensions had an undeniable legal tinge that was already apparent in the sources regarding the year 1781. Evidence of the legal imagination of the enslaved appears even more clearly within the interstices of sources from the 1790s and early 1800s.

Clues from those records show that many slaves envisioned their deliverance from captivity as a peaceful process. Many enslaved communities told hopeful tales of liberation and legally recognized emancipation, and the rumor that a merciful monarch had decreed collective freedom reappeared periodically.[6] For some slaves, the hope continued to be based on manumission promises by masters; others thought that God would somehow end slavery and punish the masters;

and many hoped that they could become full members of the body politic (paying taxes, obeying magistrates and priests, even living in their own towns) after emancipation.

Typically, slaves made their points during unwelcome criminal interrogations, and these judicial forum encounters were fraught with dangerous possibilities. Unequal access to the judicial sphere, however, did not stop slaves from monitoring the circumstances around them to find the right moment to advance their aspirations. During the crisis of 1781, for instance, Antioquia slaves from across various districts planned to appeal to the monarch's mercy by collectively petitioning before local and provincial officials – a legal tactic used widely by free vassals but typically outside the reach of the enslaved.[7] Slaveholders and magistrates, however, worked hard to stymie these requests, accusing petitioners of criminal conspiracy. Such accusations took on even more alarmist tones after 1791, when slave action was alleged to be modeled after the example of slave unrest in the Caribbean. Let us then peel back those accusations starting in the province of Cartagena, where some officials touted the idea that slaves would emulate or collaborate with their counterparts from the French islands.

Cartagena and the Specter of "French Blacks"

Located on the Caribbean coast, the province of Cartagena extended across the northern plains of Colombia, hugged by the Caribbean Sea to the west, bound by the Magdalena River to the east and north. The region had a relatively dense network of roads and waterways, and the provincial territory was large and directly connected with the Atlantic. The Magdalena, in turn, facilitated access to the rugged interior. Most merchandise and travelers bound for the mountain provinces passed through this territory, traveling by boat before continuing the overland route up the steep slopes of the Andes. Aside from commerce with Spain, trade and smuggling with British Jamaica and Dutch enclaves off the coast of Venezuela was prevalent. The province had a total population of around 120,000 people, including around 10,000 slaves.[8]

Only a small proportion of Cartagena slaves worked in gold mines. Most worked on rural estates, growing sugar, cacao, cotton, and herding cattle. A small number worked for merchants and smugglers.

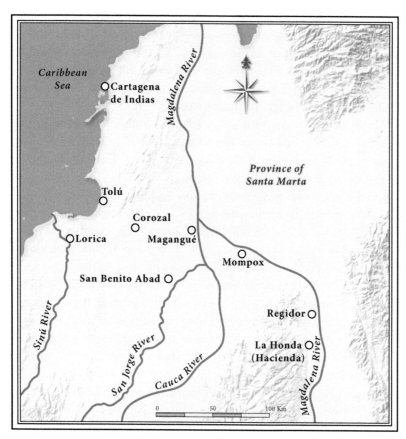

MAP 4 The province of Cartagena. Map by Gerry Krieg.

Around 2,000 lived in the provincial capital, the city of Cartagena de Indias, but some lived in smaller urban centers (see Map 4). In the provincial capital, many slaves were hired out. Others, however, served in the palatial homes of patrician families who were proud to live in the most important port town of the viceroyalty and the second most important city after Santa Fe. A crucial military and commercial hub – in effect the front gate to Spanish South America – the walled city of Cartagena resembled Havana in Cuba or Cádiz in Spain.[9]

The province had remained particularly calm during the Comunero Revolution, but the 1790s here, as elsewhere in the Caribbean, would be characteristically troublesome. In 1793, Cartagena was rattled by news of arson and accounts of a potential slave conspiracy in the rural hinterland, where the majority of slaves lived and worked. The events unfolded in Mompox, the second most important urban settlement in the province (see Map 4). In January, a series of seven individual conflagrations consumed over 400 houses in this prosperous freshwater port on the Magdalena. Although the matter was never clearly understood, slaves were the main suspects.[10]

Mompox was home to a group of rich families who lived in fine townhouses with their slaves and retainers, and whose patriarchs held sway over the local corporations and royal posts. This upper echelon of the local patriciate had large rural estates, where slaves and peons worked year-round. Some even exploited a few gold mines and other mineral deposits. With the town built on a strategic point on the Magdalena, the richest slaveholders had important commercial interests too. The docks, warehouses, and merchants' homes were stages for a thriving exchange and transshipment of merchandise.[11]

Although fires were by no means rare in this preindustrial town with its numerous thatched houses, in 1793 the flames seemed unstoppable and were oddly similar. Structures were engulfed by flames on January 5th, 6th, 11th, 14th, 15th, 17th, and 29th, and several of the fires began between two and three in the afternoon. Before long it was insinuated that slaves might be involved.[12] The notion that slaves might set towns ablaze was not difficult for free people to imagine; indeed, slaveholders and bureaucrats in the Americas were quick to accuse slaves of arson. Some slaves did occasionally use fire as a weapon against the masters, but false accusations seem to have been more frequent than actual instances of arson. The resentful, arsonist slave motif, moreover, is one that features regularly in narratives about slave conspiracy from ancient Rome to seventeenth-century Barbados and beyond.[13]

While slaves might not have been involved in stoking this crisis, some hazarded the chance of turning it into an opportunity to broadcast their hope that slavery might be disrupted, if not by men, then by spiritual forces. Such was the case with Juan Santiago Fontalvo, who was accused of arson by his mistress, the rich widow Mariana Damiana González. Fontalvo made subtle but legible statements about the iniquities in Mompox, where slaves were mistreated, poorly fed, and barely clothed, and his words had connotations of divine judgment, seemingly referencing the Bible. The widow González claimed that Fontalvo had predicted the conflagration of the 15th, causing her to rush to pack garments and valuables in preparation for what he called a "great fire." The widow asserted that he had foretold the fire from "the looks of the sun."[14] Fontalvo later said, his mistress claimed, that "two legions of Demons" had caused the inferno. During interrogation, Fontalvo corroborated his mention of mystical descriptions and made them more explicit: people should leave town, he advised the magistrates, for God had vented "the arm of his justice."[15] "Mine arms shall judge the people," reads the book of the prophet Isaiah (51:5).

The expectation that divine judgment was potentially imminent functioned as a statement on the sins of the people of Mompox. Among the enslaved, such expectation may have implied the meting out of punishment for their masters. This aspect of Fontalvo's message made patricians uncomfortable. They did not care to be seen as the subject of a coming reckoning, and when Pablo Álvarez (the *fiscal* or prosecutor) prepared his accusation against Fontalvo, he seems to have intentionally dropped any suggestions of prophecy and judgment.[16]

Instead of focusing on the content of Fontalvo's message (divine judgment, and by extension the sins of Mompox), Álvarez focused on the form (the act of prophecy). In order to undermine Fontalvo's message, the prosecutor sought to paint him as a sinner. Prophecy, Álvarez wrote, could only happen in two ways: by actual knowledge of things about to take place or by the "Gift of revelation." As a sinful man (during his depositions he had been led to confess to illicit sexual liaisons and nearly pushed to admit theft), Fontalvo could not be admitted the privilege of revelation, argued Álvarez. It followed that he had to be "adivino" or "agorero:" a diviner, a practitioner of the "vain art of divination" through omens that were often associated with readings of the sun.[17] Álvarez believed that Fontalvo had relied on "diabolical art" for his divination and even recommended that the prisoner be tortured to extract a full confession. This was admitted because Fontalvo was "vile," a man of "servile condition," and thus presumed to be guilty and allowed to be tortured (patricians were legally protected from torture).[18] Silencing this would-be prophet prevented a potential identification of Mompox as the collective subject of divine judgment. Although the fires continued after Fontalvo's arrest, his imprisonment dragged on for another two and a half years.

He languished in jail, isolated from anyone who might pay heed to his message.

However, there were some who believed that clashing elite families were responsible for the crisis. The lieutenant governor, the top local magistrate, intimated that the "conspiracy" was a byproduct of a feud among patricians.[19] Circumstantial evidence suggests that there may indeed have been other local tensions at play. While the González clan repeatedly distanced themselves from Fontalvo (who, as their slave, was seen as a member of their household and an extension of their will), a member of their rival clan, the Mier family, came to his aid.[20] In 1795, someone from this family advocated on behalf of the jailed slave, marking the only time anyone of influence interceded on his behalf. Although the *procurador*, who had a legal responsibility to defend slaves, managed to avoid defending Fontalvo, it took the open intervention of a member of the Mier family to finally bring Fontalvo's case to a head, ending in a final sentence of three years forced labor.[21]

While no mention of any potential connections with events abroad was made during the Mompox fires, fears of contagion from the French Caribbean emerged around this time. Cartagena slaveholders were acutely aware of the epochal events unfolding in places like Saint-Domingue and Guadeloupe. News from the French islands made it to Cartagena shores in a matter of days. Sailing from Cartagena, it took about five days to get to southern Saint-Domingue. By contrast, it could take more than a month to travel to Santa Fe, which was located inland at 8,612 feet above sea level. Masters and officials understood the unusual character of the events in Saint-Domingue: as far as anyone could tell, it was the only large-scale slave insurrection in recent memory; nonetheless, accounts from the neighboring islands seemed merely to confirm prejudices about slaves' criminal impulses.[22]

In their interpretation of slave uprisings on the French islands, Cartagena's officials relied heavily on ready-made notions. The Spanish secretary of state ordered administrators to avoid getting involved in Saint-Domingue's struggles. He exhorted officials to lend a helping hand to those who could be affected by *malhechores* (bandits), pirates, and *negros* from the French colony, who, he suggested, no doubt intended to "destroy" white people.[23] This vocabulary served to validate stereotypes about those held in slavery as well as about people who came from the French world. The sum of two great fears, *negros franceses* was shorthand for the combined apprehension about criminal slaves and godless French-speakers.

In April 1799, a "French black" conspiracy was allegedly uncovered in the provincial capital. Framed by stock accusations and the idea of foreign influence, governor Anastasio Cejudo's reports on the events reflect how entrenched these stereotypes were. He reported that a group of slaves from the French Caribbean, in cahoots with local slaves, planned to murder him, take over the walls and fortresses, kill the "whites," and loot the city. The biased imagery did not stop there. Cejudo reported that he had foiled the plot at the very last minute, the night before it was all supposed to happen. Indeed, last minute, quasi-providential foiling of criminal plots is yet another motif that features across many instances of conspiracy accusations against slaves.[24]

The label "French blacks" used by Cejudo seems clear-cut, but this expression did not neatly map onto clearly identifiable people. Cejudo never mentioned any of these "French blacks" by name. Rather than recalling specific individuals, Cejudo used the expression to evoke a set of concerns that had become commonplace by 1799. The foreigners, he claimed, had struck an alliance with local militiamen of color, bringing people together across the lines of slavery and freedom to separate Cartagena from the Spanish government. The plan was not just to emancipate the enslaved but also to bring political liberty to other commoners. In the governor's parlance, the suspects carried the "detestable maxims of liberty and disobedience."[25] The conspirators thus allegedly challenged both the authority of masters over slaves as well as the power of the king over the viceroyalty.

Such loaded terms, however, potentially mask the local dynamics behind this alleged discovery of a devastating plot. Cejudo was keen to underscore that he remained in full control of a jurisdiction that had come within hours of full-blown revolution. However, his grasp on the government had been tenuous ever since taking office as governor in 1796. Cejudo's promotion came after twenty years of work as a local military officer; thus, he took charge of the post with plenty of enemies and found himself entangled in further power struggles.[26] Cejudo's position turned even more delicate when he proved unable to discharge one of the most crucial obligations of the post: keeping the city well-supplied and its soldiers fed. War with Great Britain interrupted flour supplies in 1796, and Cartagena's maize fields were damaged by floods in 1798.[27] With corn jobbers storing much of the remaining grain, Cartagenans began to feel the pinch. Even the Queen's Infantry Regiment, its numbers already dwindling due to tropical disease, seemed at risk, and Cejudo fretted over the dangerous prospect of hungry soldiers. A subsistence crisis in a time of war loomed at the horizon for the troubled governor. Threatened on multiple fronts, Cejudo overstated his role in keeping at bay a much-touted threat from foreign agents, perhaps in an attempt to rally his opponents behind him.[28]

Like the magistrates dealing with the Mompox fires earlier that decade, Cejudo carefully selected what he wished to highlight and to silence when he talked and wrote about the challenges he faced during his governorship. For instance, his surviving reports fail to mention a serious episode of slave action unfolding in alarming synchrony with the alleged near destruction of the provincial capital. Considering that this episode took place in La Honda, an important rural estate south of Mompox (see Map 4), Cejudo must have been aware of it. Pressed by masters seeking to regain control of La Honda, the magistrates in Mompox opened criminal proceedings. The surviving depositions and letters are abundant, allowing us to catch a glimpse of the many ways in which slave tactics and goals defied the stereotypes.

Formulaic depictions of arsonist slaves can be counterpointed with the actual steps taken by slaves on the La Honda sugarcane hacienda. With just over 100 slaves, this was one of the biggest such estates in the Kingdom. In mid-April 1799, the slaves declared themselves free and expelled their overseer. The tactics and legal strategy employed by these captive workers hoping to achieve emancipation emerged clearly during the early stages of the movement.[29] Aware that their master had promised them manumission (effective after his death), La Honda leaders insisted that they had patiently waited for his passing, all the while diligently doing their jobs. When the day finally arrived, they took their own freedom by expelling the late master's proxy, but the use of force stopped there. They stayed put in the estate, arguing that their master's promise (in fact formalized in his last will) rendered their course of action legal. Furthermore, they hoped authorities would now recognize this hacienda as a formally incorporated settlement of free people. They would defend themselves if attacked, slave leaders insisted, but they would much rather live peacefully.[30]

The people of La Honda's aspiration to form a settlement of free vassals living in peace was underpinned by their understanding of the Spanish hierarchical municipal regime. In conversations later retold before Mompox magistrates, the slaves Antonio, Ascención, Valerio, and Vicente revealed that they hoped to continue to live on the former estate but under the authority of a priest and a magistrate, paying tithes and taxes. They thus voiced their desire to live *en policía*: settled around a church and abiding by the laws of "both majesties" – God and the king. The La Honda people clearly understood that successfully achieving freedom and peace did not depend on manumission alone; they also had to form a corporation adhering to the land within the Spanish political order.[31] Their aspirations to transition into free vassals, though articulated with different legal references, resembles the aspirations of some Antioquia slaves who, back in 1781, imagined themselves paying taxes "like Indians" or mazamorreros. By May 1803, however, the master's inheritors had retaken the hacienda, causing death, flight, and the final disintegration of the La Honda community. In the end the former slaves had to fight – and their emerging town was destroyed as a result – but they did not choose violence to speed their freedom.[32]

Most slaves usually waited for specific windows of opportunity (a political crisis, the death of a master, the replacement of an overseer) to take steps toward making their lives more tolerable or achieving emancipation. Some patiently saved money to purchase their own freedom or to pay for the emancipation of their loved ones.[33] Many slaves even nurtured the hope that a powerful person would come to deliver them from slavery. Rumor spread from time to time that a distant king had ordered the masters to set all people in bondage free. Such anticipations of freedom were not uncommon on the Caribbean islands, and, as we have already seen, they also existed in the Andean province of Antioquia, but these rumors must also be carefully examined.

Antioquia and the Rumor of "Candanga"

Cartagena's neighbor to the south, Antioquia was an Andean province bound by the Chocó to the West and the Magdalena River to the East. The Magdalena provided navigable access to Cartagena and the world beyond, but this river marked the outermost confines of the province. Antioquia's epicenter, the neighboring valleys of Cauca and Aburrá and the adjacent plateaus of San Nicolás and Los Osos, struggled to efficiently communicate with the Magdalena. It took two or three weeks to descend to the river. Small, tightly packed, and tucked away, Antioquia's provincial heartland is best described as landlocked (see Map 2). However, Antioquia had gold, and this important and easily portable commodity linked its economy to wider trade networks. Out of a total population of close to 80,000 people at the turn of the nineteenth century, around 10,000 were slaves, and most of these slaves worked for gold mines.[34]

Panning for gold in the cool highlands of San Nicolás and Los Osos during the rainy season, many slaves also toiled the fields or tended cattle in the warm valley of Aburrá and the hot Cauca River valley, especially over the dry months. They thus moved up and down through the four areas where both population and resources concentrated, all located within one or two days of travel from each other. Most slaves lived in small groups, but they easily communicated with others across jurisdictions. (In Cartagena, by contrast, slaves faced more travel restrictions and longer distances.) Some Antioquia slaves also split their time between the countryside and the two main urban centers: the city of Antioquia (the provincial capital), and the crossroads town of Medellín. These urban enclaves resembled modest Spanish towns in Andalucía and Extremadura.[35]

Masters and magistrates in Antioquia worried that slaves would organize an uprising, and that revolutionary contagion from France might help catalyze revolt. This preoccupation was further stoked by their knowledge that slaves from different districts regularly exchanged opinions about their potential emancipation. The exchanged messages included familiar narratives, model fables that people drew on when emancipation seemed possible, rather than tactical signals to accelerate freedom through violent means or by replicating events from abroad.[36] One prevailing fable was that the monarch had decreed emancipation, but the masters and magistrates kept the freedom decree secret.[37] Times of political uncertainty seemed to lend more ubiquity to such ideas. As we have already seen, in the year 1781 the provincial governor insisted that captives from three different districts (San Nicolás, Aburrá, and the provincial capital) were in cahoots and planning a wholesale destruction which would be followed by making themselves "owners of everything."[38]

One might be tempted to see the expectations of royal clemency that surfaced again in Antioquia during the turbulent turn of the century (in 1798 and 1806) as yet another mischaracterization of slaves' ideas by anxious masters. However, the legal tinge of one model fable relayed by word of mouth suggests that these ideas and forms of communication underpinned the slaves' culture of expectation. Most of the freedom tales told and retold by slaves circulated as rumor. Though the message traveled through whispers, it consistently communicated a core idea: freedom was coming, perhaps for all slaves, and in a shift of status not only legitimate but sanctioned by sacred and royal majesties.[39] To grasp the texture of this culture, however, we must read our sources with an eye for potential political manipulations and the ever-present specters of homegrown unrest and foreign influence.

Let us begin in 1794, when the rich peninsular merchant Juan Pablo Pérez de Rublas, a cabildo member and interim governor in the provincial capital, informed the viceroy that individuals with revolutionary, egalitarian sentiments were wreaking havoc on the social order. Aware of the pasquinades affair in Santa Fe, Pérez de Rublas assumed that, in all likelihood, the "pernicious maxims of the French" had reached Antioquia.[40] A reader of the *Papel periódico de la ciudad de Santafé de Bogotá*, the merchant drew on the anti-French sentiments prevalent at the viceregal court, but he was careful in choosing who to accuse as the agent of impending trouble in Antioquia.[41]

A successful merchant, Pérez de Rublas accused the taxman Francisco José Visadías of being the malevolent egalitarian threatening the established hierarchy. Already engaged in a legal battle against Visadías over issues of taxation and the creation of a new Royal Mint in Medellín, Pérez de Rublas had strong reasons to undermine this royal treasury official. Along with a business partner, Pérez de Rublas controlled 40 percent of legal trade in Antioquia's capital. He was a man of consequence, taking advantage of his interim governorship to further merchants' goals. Visadías firmly opposed him.[42] The merchant reported that Visadías was a depraved, irreligious womanizer who was bent on inciting plebeians to revolt and on stoking a fire that would "embrace and consume this unhappy city and the entire province."[43] Pérez de Rublas could not substantiate his accusations, but he insisted that Visadías had suspiciously friendly relationships with plebeians in the capital city's jurisdiction, where less than 2000 people could claim Spanish status.[44]

Pérez de Rublas asserted that Visadías promoted revolutionary collaboration among slave and free alike, highlighting Visadías' "unnatural" association with slaves and people of enslaved ancestry. Pérez de Rublas also mentioned that Visadías treated "mulato" families – who straddled slavery and freedom – as though they were of noble stock. He even suggested that this cabal had already tried to turn the world upside down during the Comunero Revolution. Visadías' public pronouncements in favor of "liberty," he claimed, had stimulated slave conspiracy in 1781. Pérez de Rublas now recalled that, as a cabildo member, he himself had helped stop a slave uprising in that fateful year. Encouraged by Visadías and hoping to "see themselves freed from captivity," Pérez de Rublas told the viceroy that slaves now seemed ready to strike again.[45]

If the patrician Visadías broke conventions by interacting with his social inferiors, he was not the only one and his activities were much less dangerous than suggested. Pérez de Rublas and other merchants regularly associated with people known or rumored to have enslaved ancestry, some of whom gained wealth and political prestige. Most of these people remained in their social stations throughout their entire lives, but service to the king, economic achievement, and ascendancy could sometimes officially clean a "stained" genealogy, raising an individual's *calidad*. Most usually, a few people improved their social position patiently and silently as they expanded their businesses and respectability. After 1795, some people would translate such good fortunes into firmer political belonging, entering the group of Spaniards (criollos) by obtaining *gracias al sacar*. A paid-for royal grace, this document granted the status of "white" regardless of the beneficiary's genealogy. Changes in calidad, whether officially recognized or not, rarely happened free from tension and uncertainty.[46]

This struggle between treasury officials and merchants, and their anxieties about slaves and free people of color, unfolded against the backdrop of a gold boom in Antioquia. With population growth and the exploitation of new deposits, the provincial economy was already expanding by 1781. From 1780 to 1799, Antioquia mined some

236,000 pesos worth of gold: four times what it had mined between 1750 and 1779. Prospecting, rather than large-scale gold mining or agriculture, allowed some people in Antioquia to better their lot by accumulating some riches. With a predominantly rugged terrain, the cultivation and export of a cash crop had no chances of success. By producing valuable and portable gold, however, miners had better fortunes, especially those who could afford to buy a few slaves.[47]

Commerce increased and some humble people benefited from this expansion, but the social structure remained strong. Although trade was difficult, merchants began to introduce more manufactures and other goods from Santa Fe, Cartagena (via Mompox), and Quito (via Popayán). Petty traders expanded their own operations too. In a telling detail, two Antioquia brothers of enslaved ancestry who participated in this boom ranked among the very first people ever to obtain gracias al sacar in Madrid.[48] But improvement of one's calidad remained rare. Not unexpectedly, in the end nothing came of Visadías' alleged social leveling plans. Still, anxieties about restive commoners and social climbers did not go away. And neither did the rumors of freedom, which slaves revived again in 1798.

As people prepared for the end-of-year festivities in December 1798, news spread in Medellín that slaves believed freedom was about to materialize. Cabildo magistrate José Joaquín Gómez Londoño reported that the slaves were determined to "violently" shake off the yoke of servitude. Nevertheless, his source indicated that slaves expected emancipation through legal means. Gómez Londoño himself wrote that slaves believed a "high order" granting them freedom existed, albeit currently withheld by magistrates. Relying on information provided by a spy, Gómez Londoño also reported that slaves believed the cabildo would soon enforce "general freedom." With the coming cabildo meeting of January 1, expectations may have been unusually high in December. The rumor of the emancipatory decree gained traction. Partly coinciding with hopes reported back in 1781, the spy reported that slaves expected an official announcement of their freedom on New Year's Eve.[49]

As had happened seventeen years earlier, other clues indicate that the slaves may have been preparing for legal action rather than insurrection. Gómez Londoño reported that some slaves expected to be allowed to buy their freedom at the price of one gold peso, hoping to live in their own, separate town under their own elected magistrates. Like the slaves of La Honda near Mompox, some slaves in Medellín hoped to become free vassals living *en policía.* Slaves of the Restrepo clan, a family of influence in Medellín, seem to have talked seriously about the prospects of legal, general emancipation. A slaveholding patrician reported that the slaves José Manuel and Pablo, belonging to two of the Restrepos, had stated that, should freedom be withheld after the end of the year, they would travel to request their liberty from the king himself. Another master testified that Javier de Restrepo's slave was raising funds to litigate for collective freedom.[50]

Some slaves also expected Providence rather than human action to speed their freedom. The slave Miguel, owned by José María de Restrepo, denied any knowledge that slaves were about to rise up, conceding nonetheless that "God was to punish all the whites for holding them as slaves." Even more explicitly than the slave Montalvo in Mompox, this man expected divine justice, not insurrection, to come to right the wrong of slavery.[51] José Ignacio, another skeptical slave, believed that freedom would come from God, not from men.[52] Though at first glance somewhat restrained, the suggestion that the masters were about to face divine reckoning was a radical one. It turned the murky issue of slavery and freedom into a clear-cut matter of good versus evil.

Gómez Londoño, however, obfuscated the complexities of slave testimony by intentionally distorting his information about the slaves' ideas and plans. Víctor Salcedo, the provincial governor, did not fully trust Gómez Londoño. Because the latter was a native of Antioquia, the governor presumed his reports might be motivated by intricate entanglements of friendship and hatred. The governor did think that slaves may in fact be on the verge of insurrection, yet he also mentioned that Gómez Londoño was known for his bad temper and litigious inclinations. Hoping to gain a better grasp of the situation, the governor sent his lieutenant Antonio de Viana to Medellín. Viana arrived on December 31. Gómez Londoño then admitted he had no evidence to prove that the slaves were planning an insurrection.[53] New Year's Day, 1799 arrived and nothing happened.

Nevertheless, further evidence on coordination across several districts suggests vigorous organizing for collective legal action among the enslaved in Antioquia. Viana gathered information indicating that slaves in Medellín held communication and coordinated with slaves in San Nicolás – the epicenter of the 1781 events.[54] Back during the comunero movement, slaves from different jurisdictions had been in communication about how best to make claims before local and provincial magistrates. Some slave leaders probably tried to enter the judicial forum via written or oral petitions, seeking to express their hope to legally end their captivity. But masters and magistrates stifled their voices, preventing slaves from exercising the privilege to petition for redress, which free folk had regularly exercised for generations.[55]

The barriers preventing slave leaders from making claims through written petitions stimulated the oral nature of their culture of expectation as well as the spiritual, though somewhat unconventional tenor of its contents. Although Gómez Londoño's reports painted slaves' plans as a full-fledged insurrection, he also left behind some non-stereotyped evidence on the contents of their conversations: he wrote that the slaves had "baptized their revolution, or designs, with the name of La Candanga." The word Candanga was prevalent among slaves in the Medellín district.[56] Unrestrained by the formalities that would have shaped their vision on a written legal document, people in captivity freely used this word as part of their sustained conversations on emancipation. One of its potential meanings points in the direction of monarchs of African origin and Christian virtue as deliverers of freedom.[57]

Among the enslaved in Medellín, the use of the name Candanga was probably connected with the fable of an African queen, perhaps the mythical Candice of Ethiopia (Candaces or Kandake in Spanish), who had come to enact emancipation.[58] Known as the "Queen of Ethiopia," the biblical figure of Queen Candice (Acts 8:27) was recognized as a member of the "illustrious" cadre of black people who had allegedly belonged in the Catholic church.[59] Inducted into the rudiments of the Christian history of salvation, slaves may have referred to this queen by the name of Candanga. While the 1798 records do not offer much detail, the liberating queen shows up again in later documents.

The name Candanga resurfaced in Medellín a few years later, and this time the symbolic connection with an emancipatory black queen is more tangible in the evidence. In March 1806, rumor spread among slaves in Medellín that a royal decree for their liberation existed but the local postal administrator kept it secret.[60] Believed to be in alliance with slaves in Los Osos, the slaves of Medellín were again accused of planning insurrection.[61] One of the witnesses in the criminal inquiry declared that he had heard from a woman that a "black Queen" had arrived in Antioquia to grant all the slaves their freedom. The Queen was hiding away, the woman had added, and "she heard mass every day from a priest at her hide-out." This queen, presumably African, like Queen Candice, also seemed to be perceived as a pious Catholic monarch.[62] Benevolent like her Spanish counterpart, this justice-delivering sovereign was also a virtuous Christian.

Slaves' dialogues on where their freedom might come from, how best to speed the hour of their deliverance from slavery, and what type of legal status they might enjoy afterwards elicited accusations that they were out to undo the entire social order. Entangled in local struggles and relying on prejudices about unfree people and people of color, the accusers ignored or misrepresented these vibrant dialogues. Throughout the lands of Popayán, similar dialogues and accusations also took place. With a master class that had more to lose, Popayán's political and economic order was starkly predicated on continuing enslavement. Those at the top in this order staunchly defended it as everlasting. Nonetheless, we can catch glimpses of the slaves' culture of expectation, including something of their repertoire of familiar narratives anticipating change.

Popayán and the "Black Queen" in the Americas

The governorate of Popayán had the largest jurisdiction in the New Kingdom, spreading across most of today's southwestern Colombia. With its blurry southeastern limits lost in the Amazon jungle and bound by the Pacific Ocean to the west and the Andes central cordillera in the northeast, Popayán bordered with Antioquia to the north. Two mountain passes allowed communication with Santa Fe and Cartagena, via the Magdalena River valley. Popayán also communicated with Quito, its neighbor to the south, and had ties with Lima. Traveling was a long and costly enterprise in this variegated landscape, but people and merchandise entered or passed through the governorate. The population concentrated on large and fertile Andean valleys, where haciendas produced agricultural goods for urban centers and the rich gold mines of the Pacific piedmont and lowlands. Formed by several constituting provinces, which together contained about 140,000 people, this kingdom within the Kingdom had about 30,000 slaves. Working on the sweltering Pacific gold districts, many slaves lived far away from their owners, who usually lived in the capital city, Popayán.[63] (see Map 3)

At the provincial capital, an elite class of high patricians enjoyed substantial wealth and influence. They controlled the cabildo, held sway over the Pacific mining districts, owned large haciendas, inhabited solid townhouses, and donned garments prohibitively expensive for most people. Spanish *hidalgos* with seigneurial aspirations, Popayán's masters stood at the top of a robust and violent slave society.[64] Here, the famed Prussian naturalist Alexander von Humboldt complained after a visit, lazy young men lived "frightened by the slightest discomfort," "surrounded and served by slaves," "afraid of the sun's rays."[65]

Around 10,000 slaves worked the metal-rich deposits of the Pacific region. Subdivided into five districts (Barbacoas, Tumaco, Micay, Iscuandé, and Raposo), the area was overwhelmingly covered by rainforest (see Map 3). Hamlets and trails barely made a scratch on the land. Grouped in large work gangs, often in the hundreds, these slaves lived much farther away from significant urban centers than their counterparts in Antioquia and Cartagena. The trip to the capital could take up to three weeks over the wet seasons. Trails were difficult even in the dry months, with porters instead of mules bringing in crucial supplies. Other goods entered by sea and river from Panama, Guayaquil, and Callao. The mining slaves rarely saw their absentee masters, urban dwellers who also spent much time on their near-by rural estates.[66]

As in Antioquia and Cartagena, in Popayán the political troubles of the 1780s and 1790s were bound up with pre-existing issues, especially the tensions between absentee masters and their far-flung slave gangs. Some Popayán families usually found it hard to keep slaves under control. Masters lived in a slow-motion back and forth with enslaved communities, who increased their autonomy by taking advantage of the distance and time mediating between the gold diggings and the capital city. The situation turned even more tense after the year 1781. Some insisted that outside political developments could spark a slave uprising against the king and the masters. However, slaves did not turn into unwitting agents of foreign powers, and never really exercised the type of wholesale violence predicted by officials and struggling masters.

Take the case of the San Juan mine, one of the many gold mining enclaves on the Pacific slopes of the Andes. Originally owned by José Tenorio (as *alférez real* of Popayán's cabildo, he held the most prominent of municipal posts), San Juan was in the district of Micay (see Map 3). As early as June 1782, just months after the Tumaco uprising and well before the death of Tenorio, San Juan slaves were reported to be in a state of disobedience. Like the slaves of La Honda, the captive workers here challenged their master while staying put, holding on to their clearings in the forest, their thatched houses, and their canoes. When the owner died in 1787, San Juan passed into the sphere of influence of Jerónimo Francisco de Torres, a peninsular and the patriarch of the Torres y Tenorio family.[67]

Who exactly owned San Juan and its self-assertive slaves remained bitterly disputed in probate proceedings. This dispute among putative masters opened a new space for slaves to make work and life decisions by themselves. For the Torres y Tenorio family, it became increasingly difficult to keep authority over the slaves while defending their claim to property in the tribunals at Popayán. Because gold was their most important source of income and the mining site was remote, the would-be-masters had to tread lightly. They negotiated with the people of San Juan in order to elicit a modicum of obedience.[68] A temporary working arrangement seems to have been reached by 1794, when the patriarch himself visited San Juan.

But there was always the fear that slaves might be moved to strike against their masters under influence from outside forces and circumstances. While at San Juan, Jerónimo Francisco received a letter from his son, Camilo Torres. The missive came from Santa Fe, where Camilo was a highly respected lawyer and professor of civil law. Officials there had sought to implicate him in the pasquinades affair. Even before Camilo's letter reached his father, slaves had already received news of the tensions at the viceregal capital. Reassuring his father, Camilo asserted that viceregal authorities had blown the recent episodes out of proportion. The slaves, meanwhile, only saw further proof of discord among masters.[69] Moreover, they were also aware of tensions between Spain and the British monarchy. Because of their relative proximity to the coast, places like San Juan received not only unofficial information but also official military instructions from authorities, as well as news of Anglo-Spanish maritime skirmishes in nearby waters.[70]

Rather than dealing with foreign influence and sudden uprisings, however, Popayán slaveholders had to contend with long drawn out and carefully calculated challenges from their slaves. Anxiety about the people of San Juan is evident in the family correspondence, which reveals how difficult it was for absentee owners to govern their slaves. Members of the Torres y Tenorio family may have found it hard to keep slaves at San Juan under control and mining for gold, but this does not mean that slaves refused to work altogether: they exercised different degrees of autonomy rather than fully severing the ties of subordination. Still, Camilo complained that he had never known San Juan to yield any profits, not even in the time of his late grandfather. The slaves, he suggested, were to blame, for "they are even capable of letting their owners starve to death."[71] Shortly thereafter, the same "starving" master presented his betrothed with pearl earrings, a pearl necklace, a diamond ring, a gold belt buckle, and an emerald ring.[72]

As litigation over the mine dragged on, slaves in San Juan more easily challenged or disobeyed commands from people whose positions as legitimate masters remained contested. The masters of today could face a judicial setback and be replaced by a new patrician family tomorrow. Trying to legitimize his possession while keeping the slaves under close watch, Camilo's father seems to have spent most of the time at San Juan at the turn of the century.[73] Camilo's brother, Gerónimo Torres, took charge of family affairs after the passing of their father (around 1804).

The paper trail thins out at this point, and the best source available on what happened at San Juan in the following years is a letter by Gerónimo, penned in 1820. We must take the letter's content with a grain of salt, as these are not only the words of a typically unsympathetic and prejudiced master, but also years removed from the events, not to mention shaped by the upheaval of the wars of Independence, which took a heavy toll on the slaveholding patricians of Popayán and their sense of identity and purpose. Despite its harshness, Gerónimo's letter provides evidence for the culture of expectation of the San Juan slaves. At some point around the year 1800, this community came to believe that the emancipation of all slaves in the mine was possible, and they built their hopes on something even greater than increasing autonomy from the masters.

The letter in question indicates that the people of San Juan believed a redeeming queen of African ancestry had come to their rescue. Gerónimo recalled that during the time of Governor Miguel Tacón, most likely in 1810, the slaves of San Juan seriously challenged their masters on two occasions. First, they refused to work for Gerónimo's brother, Manuel, with the governor punishing the leaders of this action.[74] On a second occasion, the governor had to intervene again, when the captives began to claim that "a black Queen had come to the Americas bringing freedom for the slaves." Also coinciding with a fable that we have encountered before, the people of San Juan claimed that the masters were trying to hide this important development from them.[75]

Gerónimo reported that slaves took further, non-violent steps, holding nightly meetings to discuss how they would attain the freedom to which they now felt entitled by the grace of a monarch. Apparently, the plan was to draw up and send to Popayán a legal petition on behalf of the whole slave gang. But they found it difficult to make any claims through a written document, and the masters relied on the threat of military repression to regain some obedience. In the governorate of Popayán, slaveholders and their proxies worked hard to prevent enslaved communities from making their voices heard through legal means.[76]

Gerónimo, like most other masters, disregarded the slaves' conviction that their freedom would happen with the blessing of a monarch, whether a black Queen or the Spanish king. Instead of recognizing his family's failure to keep their affairs in working order, and the slaves' growing ability to decide when and how to obey commands from masters and overseers, Gerónimo asserted that slaves were naturally prone to disobedience and inclined to hate their superiors. Admitting that the slaves had engaged in continuous attempts to "shake off obedience," Gerónimo believed that this was caused by the slaves' own "innate and irreconcilable hatred" toward their masters, rather than by the burdens of captivity. But then again, he had been raised to believe that "severity and rigor" were the only ways to "govern the blacks."[77] The experience of San Juan and his ingrained convictions about slaves would shape his later political career.

* * *

Collective organizing and dialogues pertaining to their status increased among enslaved communities after 1781, leading to accusations that they were conspiring to turn the world upside down. Relying on ingrained stereotypes about slaves' criminal inclinations, over the three decades before 1810 masters and bureaucrats levied serious charges against people in captivity. It is not unusual to find reports that those held in slavery were interested in defying not just their enslavement but the entire social order of the monarchy, and that they were in cahoots with foreign agents or somehow influenced from abroad. With the memory of the Comunero Revolution still fresh and considering revolutionary events in France and the French Caribbean, typical accusations took on more alarming dimensions after 1793.

A critical examination of the sources, however, reveals that instead of wholesale destruction and sudden revolt many slaves were more interested in thoughtfully figuring out steady avenues toward various forms of freedom: individual, familial, and even for all in bondage throughout entire jurisdictions, mainly at the municipal level. Some even hoped they could become free vassals living in their own towns, abiding by the laws of God and the monarch. Many slaves longed to be peacefully free – even if it meant living under the eyes of a man of the cloth, and under the vigilance of a man of the baton for good measure. Although slaves could in theory aspire to legal aid, it remained extremely difficult for them to effectuate change, or even voice their opinions, by appealing to the justice tribunals and through avenues of their own choosing. Still, some kept on trying, hoping that a better world would one day materialize.

In legal interrogations and over extra-judicial conversations later retold in intricate judicial exchanges, some slaves revealed how they imagined the end of slavery. The evidence indicates that they envisioned a legal and political shift, largely devoid of images of violence and underpinned instead by a repertoire of familiar narratives circulated through rumor. The fables included the notion that justice, in the form of collective emancipation, would be delivered by a monarch. While a distant king or queen was seen as gracious and pious enough to grant emancipation to the slaves, the rumors asserted that masters and officers withheld freedom, partially coinciding with the old claim that the monarch was good but his or her ministers were bad. Slaves' culture of expectation, however, operated on the careful consideration of many local variables. A master's death, quarrels among slaveholders, and protracted probate proceedings could be used as windows of opportunity to press for autonomy and even individual or collective emancipation. While slaves consciously articulated their hope that a life without slavery was possible and reachable through legal means, masters and officials rarely failed to insist that such a change would only come about through unchecked violence from slaves.

Yet from time to time, some individuals expressed less stereotyped ideas. A few even made insightful claims about the legal dimensions and power dynamics at play in the relationship binding masters and slaves together. Relatively free from censorship, the judicial forum served as a space where some lawyers and litigants critically scrutinized certain aspects of the current social order. Some expressed their dislike of slavery and their aspirations for legislative change, relying on an eclectic and somewhat unorthodox application of legal doctrines.

3

Popayán: Prudent Legislation

As early as 1791, the lawyer Félix José de Restrepo showed particular judicial diligence on behalf of individual slaves suing for their freedom. He strongly adhered to the principle that freedom suits should be resolved in *favor libertatis* – in favor of the slaves' petition of liberty. In 1804, Restrepo asserted that slaves deserved judicial compassion, reiterating that magistrates should promote freedom over slavery. Instead of blindly siding with the masters, Restrepo argued, judges should presume that those claimed as slaves were free. Masters, in turn, had to firmly prove their claims to property over fellow human beings.[1] During litigation, Restrepo defied the widespread notion that slaves' words and intentions were not to be trusted, and that they should keep to their natural social station.

Radically expanding on the principle that individual magistrates should favor freedom, Restrepo further asserted that the government ought to facilitate slave emancipation. Allowing slaves ample room to achieve manumission by legal means was the trademark of any "sweet, prudent, and moderate legislation."[2] Restrepo aired these opinions in Popayán, of all places, where the livelihood of most people of his standing hinged on the enterprise of slavery. Moreover, he expressed these legislation opinions in a society in which the king alone could decide on the scope and nature of the laws. In the judicial forum, Restrepo was subtly stepping into a realm reserved for the sovereign and his closest ministers.

Doctrines and practices of modern philosophy and the unorthodox idea of legal equality underpinned Restrepo's propositions. An unusual college education facilitated his critical approach to old doctrines, as did his admiration for Gaetano Filangieri, whose recent work had proposed a new philosophy of legislation. For Filangieri, legal reform was the avenue to an egalitarian and just world, a world in which slavery had no place. As a college professor, Restrepo taught his pupils that long-standing intellectual authorities and convictions must be challenged; and as a lawyer, he proposed innovative interpretations of slavery and freedom, stating that it was proper to promote not only slave emancipation but also equal protection by the law.[3] His assertions were at odds with the widespread convictions that any challenge to authority, hierarchy, and slavery undermined the sacred social order.

By engaging in individual litigation, people of color undermined prevalent prejudice and stimulated legal thought. Judicial quests by slaves seeking freedom and former slaves pressing for new rights shaped Restrepo's legal outlook. Throughout his stints as appointed legal adviser, litigants pushed Restrepo to ponder captivity, inherited privilege, and whether magistrates should favor humble petitioners over rich families. In effect, these litigants tested whether the lawyer's evolving convictions would have any real effect for those with the least legal standing. The former slave Pedro Antonio Ibargüen is a case in point. Ibargüen received Restrepo's advice during the early stages of a lawsuit against a well-connected Popayán clan. Ibargüen went on to defend equality before the law with tenacity, asserting that all vassals of the king, rich and poor alike, deserved the same protection from the magistrates.[4]

Quietly at first, Restrepo, Ibargüen and many others argued that it was the obligation of the "State" to change the legal order, fostering happiness and justice on earth, even for slaves and their free descendants. As they took on their social betters through judicial confrontation, some humble litigants criticized the political grammar of the viceroyalty. More discreetly, in tertulias and over correspondence – robust but little-known spaces of political dialogue – even criticism by patricians must have been increasingly sharp. Secretly, after 1793 some people even questioned the authority of Spain to rule over the New Kingdom.[5]

The Spanish monarchy's authority over the viceroyalty became the subject of more open and urgent discussion following Napoleon Bonaparte's invasion of Spain in 1808. These European events were unprecedented, as were the answers that came from across the Atlantic, resulting in an acute political crisis that shattered the viceroyalty in 1810. Provinces, cities, towns, and even hamlets pulled away from the authority of Santa Fe and refused to obey officials from the occupied metropole. These emerging revolutions opened the door to a more radical questioning of slavery and of the hierarchical links binding up the body politic. Opinions previously exchanged in the judicial forum were projected onto the political crisis. Some patricians quickly came forward with fully formed criticisms of the Kingdom's "pact" with Spain and, using their preferred metaphor to discuss the links with the metropole, they reasoned that the yoke of Spanish "slavery" had to be fully dissolved.[6] Jurists, litigants and many others pondered fundamental questions of state, government, and the law in light of the new crisis.

Enslaved communities also discussed and communicated their own opinions about the place of slavery and emancipation in the growing political wrangle. Across the governorate of Popayán, many of the enslaved discussed what the changing situation and their masters' political choices could potentially mean for those who hoped to be free. In the Pacific mining districts, the San Juan mine slaves took advantage of the crisis, refusing to obey their masters altogether. Some slaves interrogated metaphoric understandings of slavery by calling attention to their actual status in captivity. Their freedom, they asserted, was a necessary extension of the freedom demanded by the masters who were now claiming to be enslaved by Spain. In the governorate's capital, meanwhile, Restrepo had begun to discuss a formal plan for the "abolition" of slavery through legislation. He openly sought to extend the logic of *favor libertatis* to all slaves, though only through a gradual approach.[7]

Restrepo reasoned that prudent lawgivers and magistrates, under a new form of government, were obligated to transform society by ending slavery. But even for this forward-looking early antislavery legislator, it proved hard to let go of the old prejudices. In the end, the plan was to reform slavery while postponing its actual end, thus preventing the alleged chaos that would be caused by liberated slaves.

In short, Restrepo and other thinkers with antislavery inclinations still believed that slaves would seek to turn the world upside down at the first opportunity. This ambivalence in approach often came from those in uncertain social positions: individuals with an increasingly revolutionary outlook but with strong ties with the old order.

Friend and Foe

Although he is usually commemorated as the liberator of slaves, Félix José de Restrepo was nonetheless deeply entangled with Popayán's slave economy. Starting with the sale of his slave José Antonio in January 1789 and traceable in surviving notarial records up to 1801, his involvement in the city of Popayán's slave market, the largest of its kind in the New Kingdom, is not insignificant.[8] In Popayán that year 161 slaves were exchanged; the figure had reached 264 the year before; and in 1801, 113 slave sales would be recorded. Restrepo himself bought at least twelve slaves, but he also bought human beings on behalf of other masters, most likely charging a fee for his services.[9] Before 1810, Restrepo seems to have granted manumission only once (to his slave Leonarda), and this only after receiving 250 pesos in payment.[10] From the vantage point of most captives, Restrepo must have hardly seemed a friend of freedom.

Nevertheless, Restrepo's rank among slaveholders was unexceptional; overall, he was a patrician of modest means. Compare, for instance, the 300 pesos he spent to purchase twenty-year-old Dionisio in 1793 with the 35,100 pesos invested by a Barbacoas master on a group of 135 slaves that same year.[11] Restrepo owned no haciendas or gold mines, and his deal to purchase a house on credit fell through. In 1807, Restrepo, his wife, their five children, and their three household slaves lived under the roof of his brother-in-law.[12]

Restrepo also took part in the enterprises of slavery in a more oblique way. He helped his in-laws, the Sarasti brothers, obtain public posts in the Pacific mining districts, profiting a little from taxes and bribes collected from the wealth created by slaves. Restrepo's in-laws had followed in the footsteps of their father, the lieutenant governor of Barbacoas back in the 1760s. Francisco Sarasti, as *oficial real*, oversaw tax collection from the owners of gold mines in Barbacoas. In 1790, Restrepo provided Francisco with 500 pesos to cover the fees required to take up the post. It is likely that Francisco used his office income to pay Restrepo back with some interest.[13] José Joaquín Sarasti, the lieutenant governor of Iscuandé, requested 100 pesos from Restrepo in 1792. He used the money to pay for the post of *alcabalas* administrator for the districts of Iscuandé and Micay, and he was now in charge of collecting sales taxes.[14] That same year, yet a third brother-in-law, Agustín Sarasti, became alcabalas administrator for the district of Raposo. Agustín obtained Restrepo's formal backing as guarantor.[15]

However, this family's entanglement with the gold economy depended more on political influence than on slaveholding. Always much too uncertain, appointments depended on connections. Moreover, the posts did not always guarantee a stable income, let alone an increase in riches. Restrepo continued to participate in these bureaucratic arrangements, but his apparent wish to rise in the ranks of the local magnates failed to materialize. He tried to build his fortune by shipping goods for retail in Antioquia, to no avail. He also tried reselling slaves and jewelry, both in Antioquia and Cartagena, but he did so by proxy, which was rarely the safest way to turn a small investment into a fortune.[16] Bound up with the world of the slaveholders and profiting from slave labor, Restrepo nevertheless did not, or could not, develop a livelihood based mainly on the ownership of other human beings. In the parlance of the time, he was neither a *minero* (master of gold mining slave gangs) nor an *hacendado* (owner of a rural estate). He had to rely on a myriad of enterprises for his income and position; teaching at a local college was his main occupation, but he also practiced the law and held municipal posts.

His legal occupations further contributed to Restrepo's ambivalent social position and linked him with slavery in yet another way. Though he worked as a lawyer for well-off families, he was occasionally appointed to represent poor people before local magistrates. He thus came into conversation with plebeians seeking justice. These included people in bondage or individuals claimed as slaves. A slaveholder advocating on behalf of slaves may sound paradoxical, but we must recall that slaves, on occasion, relied on certain jurists to litigate their cases. On these rare occasions, some slaves may have seen Restrepo as an ally. Initiated by people seeking emancipation for themselves or their loved ones, such cases were often based on conceptual understandings of slavery and freedom.[17]

Restrepo officiously supported some people who managed to bring their struggles for freedom before the justice tribunals. As a relatively small slaveholder, he may have found it somewhat more practicable to point out the inequities of slavery. In 1791, he helped the slave Alejandro de la Rosa, who had recently obtained *papel* from his master, a document that allowed slaves to look for a new potential owner. Papel was granted to slaves who convinced officials that their current master had abused his or her authority, but de la Rosa's master later accused him of running away. There was more to the case, for de la Rosa had also paid the master over 100 pesos toward his freedom. With Restrepo's legal advice, de la Rosa was able to hold his master to their agreement and secure manumission.[18]

Slaves' freedom suits forced Restrepo to grapple with the meanings of freedom and the ambiguities of its legal underpinnings. In 1804 he defended Clara, born to slave parents and now twenty years old. Although her parents had paid for her freedom when she was baptized, their master attempted to claim her as property. Clara provided Restrepo with evidence of the payment. Although this payment mattered, Restrepo argued that Clara was legally free mainly because she had enjoyed freedom most of her life. It made no difference that her parents' master had not consented to the payment in the first place, as they claimed. Following the principle of prescripción, the lawyer recalled, slaves could obtain their freedom by "lapse of time." After going about "undisturbed" for ten years in the country of their masters, or after enjoying freedom for twenty years elsewhere, slaves could turn their informal freedom into legal emancipation. The *Siete Partidas*, a Castilian thirteenth-century legal code and an important Spanish source of jurisprudence, stipulated prescripción. Restrepo knew the code well and cited it in his written opinions. He also knew that existing legal notions suggested that slavery should not necessarily be regarded as an everlasting status.[19]

The idea that slavery was not a natural state or a fixed status but rather an undesirable, temporary condition emanating from an act of force can be detected in the ambiguous legal vocabulary of enslavement and emancipation. The *Siete Partidas* recognized slaves as human beings in a wretched condition, with slavery described as the most "vile" and "contemptible" thing.[20] The formulae used in notarial records to formalize the sales, purchases, and manumissions of slaves also conveyed that slaves were slaves only through the force of the masters. The expressions natural freedom (*libertad natural*), subject to servitude (*sujeta a servidumbre*), freedom from servitude (*libertad de servidumbre*), under the condition of slave (*bajo la condición de esclavo*), rescue (*rescate*), and redemption (*redención*) suggested that slavery existed only when some people forced captivity on others, and that people could slip in and out of a state of slavery over the course of their lifetime.[21]

Restrepo insisted that the balance of justice should always tip in favor of the slaves. Before handing Clara's case to another lawyer (because of a trip out of town), Restrepo stated that in the "cause of freedom" the law did not require particularly solid evidence to support arguments advanced by slaves and their attorneys. The burden of proof lay with the putative masters, who were obliged to substantiate the captivity status of those they claimed as slaves. Judges, Restrepo further suggested, should find avenues to facilitate the restitution of people to their "natural dignity" (*dignidad natural*).[22] Even when born from enslaved mothers, people were not naturally born into slavery but rather subjected to it by others.

His use of the word *dignidad* suggests Restrepo had begun to think critically about slave emancipation, drawing on sources beyond the Castilian legal canon and language. Traditionally, dignidad referred to the honor and standing of people in positions of authority, especially ecclesiastical "dignitaries." In unequal societies, people received deference and respect in proportion to their standing. Meant only to serve and work, slaves thus commanded little to no respect. Natural dignidad, therefore, presupposed a universal standing for all individuals, with all men and women presumably deserving a baseline or modicum of respect. Often seen as naturally deserving of the harshest judicial treatment, slaves now appeared in Restrepo's arguments as common folk who deserved some basic considerations, and even a measure of special treatment, from the magistrates.[23]

First expressed in Popayán, Restrepo's somewhat innovative legal propositions drew on sources and perspectives from his college years in Santa Fe. Born in Antioquia in 1760, he was homeschooled in "first letters," "arithmetic," and Latin "grammar." On arrival in Santa Fe to request admission at the Colegio de San Bartolomé in 1773, Restrepo was found "superabundant" in Latin; he mastered the Latin canon, developing a special love for Virgil and Cicero.[24] But it was his serendipitous arrival in 1773 Santa Fe that laid the foundation of Restrepo's critical thinking. He joined the only cohort of students officially exposed to modern philosophy during the Spanish period. At this time, instructors and students were encouraged to privilege experimentation, direct observation, and debate over obedience to traditionally accepted authorities and texts. This modern philosophy approach (as opposed to syllogistic and scholastic education) was rolled back in 1779, but Restrepo became *bachiller* in 1776 and *licenciado* in 1778. Alongside many of his cohorts, he believed that modern scholarly knowledge and practical intellectual endeavors should lead to prosperity, happiness, and justice on earth.[25]

Restrepo was appointed professor of philosophy at Popayán's Colegio Seminario de San Francisco de Asís in 1782. He settled, married into a local family, and soon garnered admiration and respect for his pedagogical efforts. Happily for Restrepo, some Popayán elders, including the bishop, supported modern philosophy. At the public opening of the new school cycle in 1791, Restrepo defended the study of mathematics, geometry, geography, and botany. Such practices did not oppose revelation, nor did they endanger salvation, he insisted, rather it was scholasticism that should be rejected, and "reason, not authority, shall have the right to settle our disputes." This critical and utilitarian approach, he told his audience, would lead to a "fountain of happiness."[26]

Modern philosophy encouraged a more general questioning of hierarchy and tradition. Challenging scholastics and inherited wisdom stimulated a critical attitude toward social and political matters. This attitude caused trouble for young pupils involved in the 1794 Santa Fe pasquinades affair. Some, like Camilo Torres, had begun their careers with Restrepo in Popayán. They complied with the scholastic approach but in secret they mocked those teachings, criticized the rollback of educational reform, and continued to steep themselves in modern philosophy through tertulias and private classes.[27] Led by a local notable, Mariano Lemos Hurtado, a vibrant tertulia formed around 1800 in the city of Popayán. Restrepo was a prominent member of this circle.[28] Looking for tools to dissect their society, this intelligentsia re-read the Latin classics, discussed contemporary publicists (such as the Neapolitan Filangieri and others who wrote on *derecho público*), and debated seventeenth-century political theory.

Indeed, in his writings about the "natural dignity" of slaves, Restrepo may have been drawing on the seventeenth-century thinker Samuel von Pufendorf, who wrote extensively about human dignity and human equality. Widely read by lawyers trained during Restrepo's college years and vehemently condemned by the Capuchin friar Finestrad, Pufendorf himself drew on the Roman statesman Cicero and his notion of *dignitas*. With this word, Cicero was indicating the worthiness of men holding civic office – a meaning that would have been familiar to an eighteenth-century Spanish speaker – but he was also highlighting the standing of humankind, who, unlike animals, exercised their reason and learning. Even Roman patricians, Cicero wrote, had to be just to their slaves. Pufendorf, in turn, argued that slaves should not be treated like animals or objects.[29]

In Restrepo's estimation, theoretical knowledge of this link between freedom from slavery and human dignity would ideally lead to legislative action. Like Filangieri (who rejected slavery as a crime supported by illegitimate laws), Restrepo thought of legal reform as the necessary avenue to a better society. In 1804, he wrote that facilitating freedom was part of a "sweet, prudent, and moderate legislation."[30] Though obliquely suggested, this idea of a prudent legislator making laws to benefit the slaves and thus uphold their human dignity had grave implications. Restrepo's turn of phrase seemed to question the king's own prudence – his virtue and ability to distinguish between good and evil. A thorny thought indeed, for it was the sovereign alone who had the prerogative to legislate and was considered "supreme judge."[31]

His ideas on human dignity and the law, moreover, reveal Restrepo's unorthodox conviction that the Spanish government had a duty to offer equal protection to all vassals. Restrepo first endorsed legal equality while representing the former slave Pedro Antonio Ibargüen, who would later further elaborate on equal protection under the law. For Restrepo and Ibargüen, equality was more than an abstract principle, it was a matter of politics, and therefore it was achievable through litigation and legislation. Ibargüen was also entangled in the slaveholding economy of Popayán. Though his social position was no less ambiguous than Restrepo's, his ideas had a radical bent that elicited pushback.

The King's Slave

Ibargüen was probably born in the Chocó, in the northernmost Pacific mining districts (see Map 1). Achieving freedom in this land of back breaking work and cruel overseers was no easy task. In the Chocó, Humboldt wrote, "slaves are treated like beasts."[32] But Ibargüen obtained his emancipation, and then moved south in the 1780s. He started out as a gold prospector in the district of Iscuandé, and by the late 1790s, he had accumulated some money, bought slaves of his own, and hired some free workers to pan for gold. Ibargüen's success eventually allowed for luxuries, including Spanish and French garments, some china, glasses, a rosary, and a reliquary.[33]

The relative success of this former slave gained him some enemies. In 1791, two years after setting up a mine on a stream named Pique (see Map 3), the Castro and Grueso families, two slave-owning clans from Popayán with interests in the area, challenged Ibargüen's activities. According to Ibargüen, the Grueso family ordered their slaves to destroy his house. In what would be the first of a long series of travels and judicial undertakings to gain legal redress and defend his claim to status as a free vassal, Ibargüen left for Popayán. There, after most attorneys in town refused to represent him, he asked authorities to appoint a legal adviser for his case. Thus, Ibargüen and Restrepo crossed paths for the first time in April 1791.[34]

With Restrepo's help, Ibargüen presented a petition before the authorities. Although such petitions often appear to be authored by the petitioner alone, they emerged from a dialogue between legal advisers and claimants. In a detail that reveals his careful participation in the drafting of the petition, Ibargüen signed the document by his own hand. Restrepo also signed the document, which demanded compensation for damages and lost income; moreover, they requested formal legal possession of Ibargüen's Pique mine. Most significantly, the language of the petition transcended the specifics of the case, arguing that it was the government's duty to provide all vassals with the same protection.[35]

Restrepo and Ibargüen's proposition of equality defied the notion that property and usufruct were allotted according to rank, and that they were corporate privileges and prerogatives rather than rights.

Restrepo and Ibargüen argued that the "privileges" of some caused prejudice for others. Specifically, they questioned the restrictive nature of the rank of minero (gold mine owner). Drawing a distinction between minero (a person formally authorized to mine) and a *real de minas* (a royally authorized mining enclave), the duo argued that access to the latter should not be an "exclusive privilege" of a few. Since the land belonged to the king, restricting its fruits to specific families or corporations would be detrimental to "all other vassals," who were "equally entitled to the protection of the government." Equal enjoyment of the sovereign's grace and the protection of his minsters, moreover, was the foundation of what the petition called the "security of the State." Therefore, a specific threat to Ibargüen in the form of the Grueso family's aim to monopolize the Pique gold sources also exemplified a general menace to an imagined political order – a polity in which authorities had the duty to protect all vassals equally as a matter of State.[36]

Both Restrepo and Ibargüen knew perfectly well that justice was distributed on an unequal basis, with the verdicts of the tribunals usually pivoting on familial and corporate privileges and influence. Indeed, another lawyer, citing his connection with the Gruesos, had denied his services to Ibargüen, and in fact Restrepo also recused himself from the case, in deference to his in-laws who were also allies of the Gruesos. Although Ibargüen eventually found magistrates to advise him and managed to obtain favorable rulings, Manuel José Grueso prevented Ibargüen from returning to his mining activities. José Joaquín Sarasti, the lieutenant governor of Iscuandé and Restrepo's brother-in-law, actively supported Grueso.[37] In December 1792, Ibargüen filed a new petition. He denounced Grueso for bribing Sarasti, also claiming that the powerful Arroyo family had advised Sarasti not to favor him, for it was not appropriate "for a black to have his own way."[38]

Besides his pointed criticizing of privilege and monopoly, Ibargüen also attacked the elite families' prejudice against former slaves and commoners. His case, Ibargüen insisted, was an instance of the ongoing struggle between rich and poor, highlighting how patricians disobeyed the magistrates and acted against the king's wishes. In the mining districts, the rich disobeyed the governor's orders and constantly "punished" the poor, even though humble people behaved as "faithful vassals." The poor, who always abided by royal decrees and never claimed the immunities demanded by "gentlemen," thus also deserved the protection of the magistrates.[39] Early and consistently, Ibargüen cast his cause as a transcendental legal issue over authority and privilege, intersecting with and radicalizing the intellectual preoccupations of jurists like Restrepo.

The former slave's legal propositions also shared some features with the legal imagination of slave communities in Antioquia and Cartagena. Ibargüen saw former slaves' incorporation into the Spanish municipal regime as the ideal avenue to equal protection by the law. Like slaves in La Honda or Antioquia, who aspired to form sub-municipal societies living *en policía* after emancipation, Ibargüen also believed that former slaves deserved political belonging: the privilege to hold landed property, thus settling down and living in or near towns ruled by spiritual and temporal authorities. Ibargüen argued that monopoly of the land by the "gentlemen" clearly prevented these rightful aspirations. Even the slaves of powerful gentlemen wrongly called themselves "landowners," while he, an exemplary vassal and a "slave" of the king of Castile, was denied access to his property in Pique. Ibargüen also announced that, if necessary, he would "make a pilgrimage" to Madrid to seek justice before the king.[40]

Although he never did cross the Atlantic, from 1793 to 1810 Ibargüen traveled throughout the Pacific mining districts, made several trips to Popayán, appealed before the Real Audiencia in Quito, and roamed the region looking for Governor Diego Antonio Nieto to make his appeal in person. Despite these efforts, Ibargüen was never able to recover the value of his lost property or to regain access to Pique.[41] But he never held back from appealing to the magistrates and speaking his mind in the judicial forum, broadcasting his political ideas through intense litigation. Unlike most slaves and groups of slaves seeking emancipation or protection from the authorities, Ibargüen was already free, and he was literate. He owned several notebooks, pious texts, and a pair of spectacles, none of which had been obtained through inheritance.[42]

Throughout his endeavors to regain the property he had bought and earned, Ibargüen revisited the theme of inherited privilege again and again. While many powerful individuals accumulated land for no reason other than to keep it for their children, Ibargüen declared poignantly, "I ask for land for my own subsistence." While mineros and hacendados were afforded the protection of the tribunals, a poor person with no connections or established riches received no protection at all. Ibargüen argued forcefully against this injustice. Since rich and poor alike were "equal vassals of His Majesty,"[43] a lack of riches and hereditary privileges should not prevent access to the grace of justice from the king. In short, fidelity to the sovereign should equalize vassals before authorities. Ibargüen's propositions and aspirations caused a stir, and he was imprisoned in 1797. He wrote a new petition. He opened the document with the words "Pedro Antonio Ibargüen, Etíope libre."[44]

The words "free Ethiopian" reveal much about Ibargüen's views on the political standing of former slaves and show that he understood he was fighting to be treated as a free vassal. Masters often treated ex-slaves harshly, and free folk usually referred to them as *negros libertinos*. Tellingly, Patricio Grueso de Agreda threatened Ibargüen with 200 lashes, thus treating him as a slave, and ordered him to keep silent, since, as a "negro," Ibargüen should endure any aggravation and "not speak in his presence or the presence of gentlemen."[45] "Negro" was often used as a synonym for slave. Ethiopian, however, conveyed not just African enslaved ancestry but the dignity of a Christian background. Many so-called Ethiopians, including Queen Candice (or Candanga) and Saint Benedict of Palermo (a freed slave), formed illustrious characters in the histories of salvation and the church.[46] Although not a resident with privileges and obligations in a formally constituted Spanish municipality, Ibargüen nonetheless claimed status as a vassal, one whose ancestry revealed a faithful Christian genealogy rather than the stigma of slavery alone.

Unsurprisingly, his enemies resorted to old canards about slaves and former slaves to silence and subdue him. Early in 1798, the slaveholder José Ignacio de Castro assured authorities in Popayán that "freed people" lived in a state of near "mutiny" and sought to overthrow established authorities.[47] Captives in the mining districts made efforts to end slavery for themselves or their kin, and many individuals insisted that this set a bad example and could lead to the breakdown of gold production. Governor Nieto and patricians from Popayán and Barbacoas petitioned royal authorities to forbid slaves from attempting to obtain their freedom legally without consent from their masters.[48] Ibargüen's legal tactics and his relative success after slavery, especially his becoming a master himself, did not fit the stereotype of mutinous commoners. Nevertheless, in the eyes of his enemies he was living proof that former slaves could not be trusted to know their place.

According to his enemies, Ibargüen's influence over other freed people also threatened the natural order of society and the stability of the monarchy. Ibargüen relied on the labor of his slaves, but he also hired former slaves and possibly runways who formed a semi-autonomous community near Pique. In 1798, Agustín Sarasti, Iscuandé's new lieutenant governor, told Nieto that these people, who communicated with slave gangs elsewhere, would spark a "general uprising." Officials asserted that Ibargüen was the "head of the mutiny," and that force alone could stop this mobilization. Referring to Ibargüen and his neighbors as members of a *palenque*, a term for maroon settlements, slaveholders and officials inaccurately regarded this settlement as a community formed entirely by escaped slaves. Local priest José Varona also denounced Ibargüen and the freed people as rebels, and in 1800, José Ignacio de Castro would insist again that this settlement stimulated the mixing of free and enslaved. The situation was also seen as a threat because "enemies" on the Pacific Ocean, presumably the British, could persuade disorderly people to join their cause and attack Spanish forces.[49]

Under such unrelenting attack, Ibargüen ultimately relied on an illegal maneuver, but it was hardly the violent action his opponents anticipated. Beating a tactical retreat, in May 1798 he fled to Quito after learning that Castro had convinced the governor to throw him in jail once again. In Quito, however, Ibargüen reverted to legal tactics, filing a complaint against Sarasti for drunkenness while performing his duties as a magistrate. Ibargüen thus found himself facing Restrepo during litigation. The Popayán patricians rarely shied away from a legal battle, and on behalf of his kinsman and to fend off the accusation of drunkenness, Restrepo accused Ibargüen of defamation the following year.[50] Within a decade, however, these matters would be set aside to face much broader challenges.

The near-destruction of the Spanish Bourbons at the hands of Napoleon Bonaparte and his allies, beginning with the French invasion of the Iberian Peninsula in 1808, would have enormous repercussions in the New Kingdom. When the storm gathered full pace in 1810, the old tensions that typically found expression in the judicial forum would merge with the new conflict, promising to change the very terms and scope of political reflection on the meanings of slavery and freedom. Restrepo and Ibargüen would cross paths again many years later, but in a world changed by revolution and war. By the time Ibargüen resurfaced again, an upheaval so dramatic had taken place that it was no longer appropriate to appeal to monarchs for justice, and some considered ending slavery a goal of State and government.

The Revolution of Popayán

The French occupation of the Iberian Peninsula elicited strong condemnation throughout the Spanish world. Following the Emperor of the French's imprisonment of Spain's Ferdinand VII and the installation of his own brother as the new king, a war of liberation began in Spain. In the New Kingdom, cabildos openly rejected the intruding dynasty.[51] Still, the delicate situation in Spain created uncertainty about the standing and future of the Spanish monarchy. The absence of the sovereign threw into question the legitimacy of the viceroys, *oidores*, and governors – high officials who directly represented the deposed king. Except for events in Quito, where patricians deposed high authorities but were quickly repressed in 1809, a tense calm set in throughout the viceroyalty.

The situation changed dramatically by mid-1810. News arrived that French forces had gained the upper hand in the Spanish conflict, with an improvised and seemingly illegitimate Regency Council now as acting sovereign. Although it was impossible to tell the extent to which the Regency could command respect and bestow authority, governors and high magistrates hastened to swear allegiance to this new governing body. Spanish bureaucrats and military officers feared that locals would take advantage of the Regency's weakness and ambivalent standing to push for increased autonomy or even independence. Many criollos had been eager for reforms, seeking to expand free trade policies, obtain greater access to royal posts, and to update college education. There were families who still resented officials' harsh response to the pasquinades affair, claiming they were treated like "slaves."[52]

Some criollos now actively concluded that the disappearance of the legitimate dynasty in Spain already implied the independence of all overseas territories. Camilo Torres argued that the collapse of the Spanish monarchy had set the people of the New Kingdom free to choose their own form of government. "What should we do," asked Torres in a letter to a relative, "what measures should we take to sustain our independence and liberty?" With the monarchy "dissolved," the "sovereignty" had reverted to the "nation," Torres asserted, and the "nation" was now at liberty to reject rule by distant authorities. Many people agreed. So long as it led to "happiness," a transformation of the form of government was legitimate, and for many, radical political change now seemed feasible and not sinful. If the slaves of Saint-Domingue, upon recovering their liberty, could form an independent country, freely choosing their own political system, Spanish America and all other peoples might surely also enjoy the same "essential and imprescriptible right."[53] Torres's reference to the former slaves of Saint-Domingue, who had defeated the French and obtained independence six years earlier, was especially significant, if clearly ambivalent.

Increasingly vocal about their aspirations for independence, Torres and other patricians characterized Spain as a cruel mistress who had for centuries subjected the New Kingdom's vassals to the most "horrible" form of slavery. Accustomed to treating the people "like vile slaves," the old Spanish "chiefs" are not good enough "to govern free men," reasoned Torres. Newly acquired freedom from Spain thus meant that "the chain has been broken," and the inheritance of a "shameful slavery" erased. The way forward, Torres further asserted, was for the cabildos to form *juntas*, taking on the task of local and provincial government. Later, juntas should install a congress in Santa Fe in order to settle on a new general government and political system – ideally a federal republic like that in the United States.[54] The very nature and form of the entire polity were now under debate, and the growing criticism of the old system was couched in the language of slavery.

A coup against the governor of Cartagena on June 14, 1810, set off an unprecedented wave of events leading to the formation of juntas and the outbreak of civil war. With the Cartagena government and military garrison now in autonomous hands, elites elsewhere gathered the confidence to push ahead with their own plans. In the past, central authorities in Santa Fe had deployed soldiers from Cartagena to quell unrest in the Andean interior, most notably in the year 1781. Without this garrison, the viceroy had lost the most important means of enforcing his authority.[55] Notables in several towns established autonomous juntas, deposing incumbents and taking up the responsibilities reserved for the king's representatives. By the end of July, autonomist leaders in Santa Fe had formed their own junta, deposing the viceroy himself. The old Kingdom broke down into multiple self-governing units, with some thirty juntas established in the most important cities between July 1810 and June 1811. Given these atomized revolutions, the fear that hamlets would break away from cities, wives from husbands, and slaves from masters took on an entire new urgency for many.[56]

Governor Miguel Tacón of Popayán organized a pro-Regency coalition to prevent the formation of a junta in his jurisdiction. The governor's allies included recent transplants from Spain and their children – up and coming patrician families like the Grueso and Castro clans, whom we may recall as Ibargüen's most vehement opponents. Many members of the clergy also supported Tacón, and even the urban "populace" seemed to be on his side, as Tacón had convinced the Franciscans to preach his cause to parishioners. Many women also sided with him, especially those who owned stores where people increasingly congregated to talk politics. These shopkeepers spread word that challenges to the governor would usher in revolution, rape, and sacrilege. This party was referred to as the *taconistas*.[57]

Despite Tacón's assertive countertactics, autonomists and budding revolutionaries in the capital city also sprung into action. The group consisted of habitués of the Lemos tertulia, including Restrepo and middling officials such as his brother-in-law Agustín. The core leaders included members of old patrician families, though some families straddled social divides. The Torres clan, with both sympathizers and opponents of the governor, came from old Popayán stock via their mother, but also belonged to a newer family on their father's side. Lawyers, professors, merchants, and landholders in this group also had the backing of some members of the local militias and high clergy. In agreement with Camilo Torres, who sent letters and printed matter from Santa Fe to his relatives in Popayán, this coalition insisted that a junta had to be formed to face the current political challenges. The group was known as the *juntistas*.[58]

Anti-Regency elites in Cali, an important city to the north (see Map 3), also moved decisively to curtail Tacón and promote their own autonomy within the governorate. By February 1811, Cali convinced five neighboring cities to form a union commanded by a single, provisional junta, a Confederation of "friendly cities." The so-called confederate leaders aimed to depose Tacón and establish a junta in Popayán with authority over the entire governorate. In this conflict, civil war seemed inevitable. Already in late 1810, Tacón had reinforced some key military positions, sending scouts north to spy on the emerging confederation and intercept their communications.[59] In November, moreover, he organized a parade to declare war on Cali and its allies. Tacón openly displayed his forces, but a portion of the troops was not what it seemed. Though properly attired and armed, some of the potential fighters were slaves. The governor brought them for the occasion from the Quilcacé hacienda, the property of one of the convents in the city.[60]

From the use of decoy slave troops Tacón controversially moved toward openly calling for slaves to join his forces on a formal basis, offering emancipation in exchange for military service. Believing his enemies to have superior forces, Tacón and his allies probably hoped that the emancipation offer would lure their opponents' slaves to their camp. But only a few hundred enslaved heeded the call, which nevertheless generated excitement through the slave grapevine. In early 1811, even before the official announcement, news spread that the governor would grant freedom to slaves willing to become his soldiers.[61] Similar proposals would come from other leaders later, but slaves hesitated to believe such promises, instead preferring to take advantage of the situation on their own terms.[62]

The growing political rift and the governor's call to arms further stimulated slaves' expectations and facilitated some action.[63] As early as January, slaves at the San Juan mine openly declared they would no longer serve their masters. Two deserters from Tacón's army visited the mine, bringing word that the governor had decreed freedom for all the slaves. Well before it was confirmed, the deserters not only communicated Tacón's conditional offer but augmented it into an announcement of the immediate end of slavery. San Juan leaders then sent word to Popayán that the mine no longer belonged to anyone from that city.[64] On February 26, Tacón ordered the slaves of San Juan to return to obedience. He had just recently punished slaves who had announced the presence of a liberating "black Queen" and the coming of freedom, but there was little he could do now. Although nominally still enslaved, the people at San Juan comported themselves as free folk, stayed in their homes, allocated land for their garden plots, and continued mining for gold to pay for tools and other goods. Gerónimo Torres would later accuse them of offering shelter to runaway slaves from other mines.[65]

Some slaves did willingly join Tacón's forces, and many others were recruited by force. A private letter suggests that around 300 slaves participated in the battle that finally took place on March 28, 1811, just north of Popayán. Juan Manuel Mosquera was one of them. A slave who worked on a small sugar estate north of the city, Mosquera, along with six other slaves, rushed to Popayán after hearing about Tacón's freedom offer. As an infantry soldier, Mosquera's sole weapon was a spear. On the day of battle, as soon as the cannon roared, he ran into the woods and hid until sunset. He returned to his masters, but later fled a second time to Tacón's camp to fight; pushed to the front lines, most other slaves perished in the clash. Fleeing south with the royal treasury in tow, a defeated Tacón was also followed by about seventy surviving slaves who expected formal emancipation.[66]

Restrepo and the Sarastis also sought to use their slaves as soldiers for the juntistas, but some of them fled and joined the taconistas instead. Slaves who chose to side with the governor were apparently promised emancipation. Restrepo's relatives turned their Pisolé hacienda into an operational center where they kept arms and ammunition and coordinated with confederate leaders. As it became clear that the Sarastis had decided to make slaves into soldiers, some Pisolé slaves fled to the city, where Tacón recruited them. Such was the case of Agustín Sarasti's slave Victoriano and his co-worker José, Restrepo's own slave. Victoriano would later declare that he intended to defend the city and the legitimate governor rather than seek emancipation. He considered Sarasti and Restrepo traitors and fled south with Tacón.[67] Meanwhile, the triumphant anti-Regency coalition of Popayán, now including representatives from Cali and other cities, established a governing junta on June 26.[68]

The overwhelming majority of slaves distrusted Tacón's initial offer and his subsequent recruitment efforts. Tacón eventually retreated east to the Pacific districts, where he controlled Barbacoas and Tumaco. The region offered him access to gold and crucial logistical connections with pro-Regency forces in Quito and Perú.[69] Here he renewed his slave recruitment plans, but only some enlisted. Most enslaved workers, like those in San Juan, stayed in their homes and refused to obey their putative masters or to trust the governor.[70] In spite of early and constant accusations to the contrary, slaves in the Pacific who saw an opportunity for freedom kept to themselves instead of spreading violence and destruction.

Even though civil war did not unleash the long-touted struggle of the slaves against the masters, at the end of the eventful year 1811 Tacón set out to explain his role in the delicate issue of slave recruitment. He saw the emancipation offer as a blemish on his record. Writing to authorities in Spain, he denied he had ever entertained any "alteration of the slaves," blaming his own allies and maintaining that the pro-Regency Popayán cabildo had offered freedom to slaves against his will. To prevent defeat at the hands of approaching Cali confederates, the cabildo indeed authorized slaves to bear arms. Any slave who volunteered with a gun in hand and a horse for the defense of the city would be compensated with freedom "on behalf of the King." Conscious of slaves' expectations of freedom and political belonging, the cabildo further told slaves that they would be treated as vassals of the monarch, the very of treatment Ibargüen and others had demanded previously. The aldermen also decreed that loyal masters would be compensated for the value of slaves emancipated by virtue of military service. Tacón claimed that his allies in the cabildo had insisted he made public these offers to prevent "rebels" from making similar proposals to the slaves.[71] Without explicit consent from the governor, however, it seems unlikely that cabildo magistrates would have taken these extraordinary steps.

Members of a new cabildo set up in Popayán after Tacón's defeat deemed their opponents' earlier promise of manumission illegal and unwise. An offer that so clearly threatened order and the property of masters, the freshly installed magistrates reasoned, would necessarily lead to a general slave uprising. Relying on the usual tropes, they evoked an alarming image of emancipated slaves: 30,000 "beasts hallucinating with liberty" who would destroy all Popayán and Chocó, leaving the remains to Napoleon, whose agents doubtless stood behind the governor's evil designs. Tacón, they asserted, had tried to spark a slave uprising and to keep his authority by sowing chaos. The Popayán victors even invited their antagonist slaveholders to join forces, destroy Tacón for good, and build an autonomous government without losing their slaves.[72]

Slaves who supported Tacón later learned that emancipation in exchange for soldiering would not be easy to achieve, especially following the governor's final defeat. Mosquera, who had fled the battle scene but later rejoined Tacón's forces, eventually realized that his leader had run out of resources to pay him or even provide him with food and shelter. Dismissed by the governor, he found a job at a tobacco farm near Tumaco. Following Tacón's last stand in January 1812, Mosquera presented himself before the "rebel" captain who defeated the governor. Claiming to be a free man, Mosquera figured the new authorities would keep the promises made by the governor and his cabildo allies. Instead, they treated him as a traitor and returned him to bondage in 1813.[73]

With the 1810 breakup of the viceroyalty and the ensuing civil war, the questioning of established authorities and the potential emancipation of slaves took on new forms and significance. Autonomist leaders and pro-independence thinkers described the conflict through the idiom of slavery and emancipation. The metaphor further stimulated slaves' inquisitive minds and their culture of expectation. The indiscreet spoken, handwritten, and printed assertions of their masters "against the chains of slavery," Tacón wrote, emboldened slaves to take a stand for their own freedom.[74] Moreover, some slaves would point out the inconsistency between the rejection of Spanish chains and the simultaneous continuation of their enslavement. Restrepo would also dwell on this tension between liberation from Spain and domestic slavery. If a new government formed, he and others believed, its chief "obligation" must be the liberation of the slaves through antislavery legislation. The political terms for the relationships between slavery, freedom, and the law were undergoing a radical mutation. The possibility of favoring individual freedom, once intimated through the politics of litigation, was fast turning into a principle of potential general application.

"Supreme Obligation"

Restrepo's expanding arguments on why and how to change the fate of slaves through legislation came into focus through his encounter with Antonio de Villavicencio. A Quito-born noble who had grown up in Santa Fe, had connections with Cartagena, and had owned slaves in Caracas, Villavicencio arrived in the New Kingdom from Spain as an envoy of the Regency. His mission was to invite the elites to recognize the Regency's legitimacy in exchange for reforms.[75] Villavicencio, however, developed a more substantial political position. He believed that Spain had to establish a "liberal and just" system, allowing for all New World jurisdictions to achieve "independence" and to govern themselves while keeping "fraternal, friendly, and equitable" relations with the mother country. Best described as a home rule approach, Villavicencio's prescription would thus differ from what he termed the "old colonial system." Vassals in the New Kingdom, he told Popayán's governor, had no intention of going back to business as usual. Even slavery, according to Villavicencio, had to end. Around January 1811, he shared these ideas with Restrepo.[76]

Villavicencio also likened Spain's New World vassals to abject slaves whose "manumission" was at hand, and he conjured up images of innocent sheep long tyrannized by despotic officials behaving as so many wolves.[77] But unlike Torres, Villavicencio explicitly included domestic slaves in his reflections. He drafted a plan for what he called "the absolute abolition of slavery." Villavicencio's absolute abolition, however, was to be completed through a gradual approach, since he belived that immediate abolition would bring social and economic disruptions, and suddenly freed slaves would naturally give themselves to "disorders," "theft," and "emigration" to avoid work. Still, he maintained, slavery "must be abolished." Otherwise, slaves would end their own captivity via "murder, arson, and another thousand atrocities."[78]

Villavicencio's ambiguous plan to gradually end slavery rested on the free womb principle, a logic that was also adopted by Restrepo. Instead of continuing to regard the new-born children of enslaved women as slaves themselves, Villavicencio's plan granted these babies freedom at birth. Thus, he claimed, the enslaved workforce would slowly disappear. Enacting the free womb principle would prevent the general liberation of slaves that many slaves themselves hoped for. Masters would continue to hold on to their human property and the practice of slavery would eventually end by attrition. In the meantime, the slave trade would be prohibited, old and sick slaves would be set free, and young slaves would be permitted to purchase their own freedom at prices proportionate to the time they had spent in chains.[79]

According to this plan, gradualism was the only way to end the "barbarian and impious system of slavery" without causing economic or physical damages to the "current owners of slaves." With the gradual approach, slaveholders would not lose their investments, and the prospect of freedom might even elicit increased productivity from the enslaved workers.[80] The "security and tranquility" of the slave-holding Americas, Villavicencio wrote, depended on the elites' determination to gradually end the slave trade and slavery. The British Parliament as well as some US legislatures, he reminded his readers, knew this well. They had taken steps to gradually end slavery, skillfully avoiding actual abolition.[81]

Villavicencio's plan, drafted back in 1809, was outlined as a legislative bill to be approved by a reformed Spanish government. He had meant this bill to be debated by the Spanish Cortes, which in 1809 were still expected to convene. Like many other liberals in Spain, he saw the formation of a national parliament as the correct avenue to enact reform and save the besieged monarchy. Villavicencio expected the Cortes to take a "just" and "humane" course of action by bringing slavery to a slow and controlled death. As both a "philanthropic" act as well an unavoidable step, Villavicencio believed that an antislavery law would crown the transformation in the system of government and shape the change that was needed to resolve the crisis. A "liberal and regenerating government" would never fulfill its most "supreme obligation," Villavicencio wrote, unless it destroyed "even the very name of slavery."[82] However, his proposed law destroyed slavery in name only.

Restrepo embraced Villavicencio's propositions for an antislavery law, including its gradualist approach and the language of "abolition." Both men believed that the current crisis should lead to a new form of political association, one that was forged and sustained by prudent and forward-looking legislators who followed principles worked out by publicists like Filangieri. Their ideal legislative achievement, moreover, would be the gradual "abolition" of slavery – a legal oxymoron that protected the master class while containing the alleged violent consequences of an unconditional liberation of the slaves. By contrast, many slaves imagined final emancipation as an immediate but peaceful step. Nonetheless, both Restrepo and Villavicencio believed it made no sense to discuss emancipation from Spain while ignoring slaves' cries for emancipation from slavery.[83]

Aiming to reassure the masters while also threatening to end their livelihood in future, and articulated as part and parcel of a broader political emancipation, this nascent anti-slavery thinking recognized its own paradoxical standing. Restrepo, Villavicencio, and Torres used the word *slavery* as a synonym for tyranny and despotism in government. Villavicencio specifically highlighted that the actual enslavement of people was of a piece with the old despotic ways of both Spain and Napoleon, for if people on both sides of the Atlantic spoke of "liberty, independence from the French yoke, and the rights of man," domestic slaves would not tolerate their "inferior" condition for much longer. It would be a horrendous "contradiction" to wish to "still keep in chains" large groups of people whose human dignity made them worthy of "a better fate."[84]

Villavicencio correctly recognized that slaves themselves would quickly identify and meditate on this ambiguity. Two masters who between them owned around 700 slaves confirmed that, following Tacón's 1811 defeat, some slaves in the mining districts "took advantage" of the unexpected situation and refused "servitude to their masters." If the masters were now free from the "slavery" imposed by Spain and had recovered the "rights of men they had been born with," the slaves reportedly reasoned, then those who had suffered enslavement in the gold mines were equally entitled to their freedom. The two masters reported that among the slaves current opinion nevertheless continued to favor government by the king. They believed only the sovereign could offer protection against the "cruelty" of their owners, and they distrusted new promises that they would keep or expand the minimal protections they already had. Moreover, many still hoped to one day enjoy the same "liberty" as other "faithful vassals," who lived peacefully under the "dominion" and "authority" of the king and his ministers.[85]

This apprehension on the part of the slaves is understandable. While new conceptual and practical possibilities were opening for slave and free alike, the political and military situation remained much too uncertain and open-ended. In Popayan's Pacific districts, much like in Antioquia and Cartagena, most people in bondage continued to believe they could expand their autonomy, privileges, and maybe even achieve freedom within the old Spanish legal order. Yet emancipation in exchange for fighting with Tacón, who had claimed to defend this order, proved very hard to achieve. Even for patricians like Restrepo, the war had turned life upside down, leading him to take up arms himself. When self-proclaimed "royalist" forces invaded the city from the south on April 22, 1812, Restrepo and his students collaborated in the defense of the city. From the windows of the building where he worked as a professor, Restrepo and his pupils fired on the enemy.[86] And after Tacón's final defeat, the new government remained vulnerable to attack, with the city becoming a wartime frontier that would change hands several times over the next few years.

Already in 1811 Restrepo had anticipated a need for specie, and a potential emigration. He visited the Royal Mint, where he exchanged two gold ingots for minted coins. In 1812, he visited the Mint several more times, [87] and by the end of February, he had sold seven gold bars, receiving over 2200 *doblones*. Between March and May, Restrepo sold thirty-three ingots. On May 20 alone, a few days after his one-time taste of battle, he sold seventeen. He now had over 10,700 doblones to cover the expenses of potential exile.[88] At the end of August, the new government evacuated Popayán under fresh pressure from enemy forces. Even though juntistas recovered the city on October 9, Restrepo decided to leave the governorate for good. He took to the road and headed for his native Antioquia.

* * *

In the judicial forum, litigants like Ibargüen and his advocate Restrepo critically considered the social links and hierarchies that bound patricians and plebeians, masters and slaves together. Despite being slaveholders, they also defended legal equality. Ibargüen insisted that former slaves should have equal standing as vassals of the king. Restrepo, in turn, believed that the king's magistrates, and maybe even the king himself as legislator, should uphold slaves' natural dignity by facilitating their emancipation. The old Spanish laws and legal formulae described slavery as an unnatural state, a notion Restrepo pushed farther by asserting that slaves should enjoy the basic respect afforded to free folk and even receive special consideration before the justice tribunals. Slavery should therefore be presumed to be no more than unjust captivity, and that freedom and equality were fair and prudent propositions.

The monarchical crisis and the breakup of the viceroyalty gave new meanings and implications to these propositions, whose transformative potential came into sharper view. With slavery adopted as the preferred metaphor to express the nature of the frayed relationship between the viceroyalty and Spain, challenges and criticisms of masters now appeared more clearly as potentially legitimate challenges to the slave-holding order. Like domestic slavery, the alleged enslavement of the New Kingdom by Spain rested on an act of force. The vassals of the viceroyalty had been cruelly enslaved, and they were justified in break-ing free from the tyranny of the old masters. Some slaves argued that they had suffered bondage too long and should now take control of their own destinies. Though few masters were willing to concede this idea, there were many slaves who already expected general freedom as a possible, legitimate transformation.

The link between lawgiving and slave emancipation became more clearly identified with the broader transformation of the polity. Villavicencio, and Restrepo after him, believed that the "abolition" of slavery should be the primary legislative goal of the liberal govern-ments that seemed poised to replace the old colonial system. Villavicencio proposed that slaves were part and parcel of the ongoing conflict, and slavery a manifestation of political tyranny. However, he called for the postponement of actual abolition, leaving the status of current slaves unaltered, and the privileges of the masters untouched. Restrepo likewise adopted this approach. Many slaves realized that such a balancing act was impossible, and they continued to hope for freedom and political belonging under the king. Many took advantage of the crisis to achieve emancipation through military service, or they increased their autonomy by refusing to obey the masters altogether.

Restrepo's prudent antislavery legislation failed to gain any traction in the context of Popayán's convoluted crisis and with the region's staunch slaveholding patriciate. In Antioquia, however, he eventually achieved his aim –though not without pressure from slaves themselves and help from Juan del Corral. A patrician whose convictions about equality and legislative reform seemed as honed as Restrepo's own, Corral was a native of the town of Mompox in the province of Cartagena. Before 1810, some Mompox patricians had begun not just to preach but to practice equality, which they claimed emanated from "natural law." This doctrine would also underpin Colombia's emerging egalitarian, antislavery thinking.

4

Cartagena: Equality and Natural Law

With the second largest concentration of slaves in the New Kingdom, the province of Cartagena also witnessed pre-revolutionary criticisms of slaveholding and a budding egalitarian sensibility. The process was particularly textured in Mompox, where magistrate Melchor Sáenz de Ortíz condemned slavery altogether in 1804. In the judicial forum, on behalf of the slave María Magdalena Soto, he argued that enslaving others was senseless and inhuman. Slavery, he asserted, only existed in "the legal codes."[1] It was an act of force supported by appalling written laws; according to natural law, however, slavery was illegitimate. Understood as the highest source of individual rights, granted by nature and universally valid, natural law became increasingly crucial for slave litigants and their aides in the decades leading up to 1810. Like Sáenz de Ortíz, some expanded the implications of the doctrine – worked out by seventeenth-century thinkers and scrutinized by eighteenth-century publicists – to reject slavery altogether.[2]

The study of natural law in the colleges and law offices of the viceroyalty accelerated in the mid-1770s. All humans, proponents of this doctrine postulated, were predisposed and authorized to strive for their self-preservation, freedom, happiness, and a peaceful coexistence with others. Such predisposition emanated from the universe rather than from history or social convention. Natural law was, therefore, also at the heart of José Félix de Restrepo's notion that slaves deserved a modicum of respect, and that they possessed the same intrinsic and

basic human dignity as free people. Despite prohibition of this doctrine, many scholars persevered in their explorations, sometimes
through litigation, and later through tertulia encounters and other
intellectual exchanges.[3]

Some circles thus maintained that the enslavement of others defied
the natural order of things, and that the government had a responsibility to ameliorate this situation. As early as 1777, Mompox litigants
and slaves heard of an opinion given by Santa Fe magistrates that
slavery contradicted "natural law." Given that natural law theorists
accepted slavery as a legitimate relationship of power, these magistrates developed their position by questioning the theory that slaves
were former prisoners of war whose lives had been spared in exchange
for servitude. In the absence of a Spanish war in Africa, the magistrates
implied, masters' unlimited power over Africans or people of African
descent held as slaves was unjustified.[4] Like Restrepo in Popayán but
about a decade earlier, the highest magistrate in Mompox even
declared that authorities had a political obligation to help slaves.[5]
Such declarations must have been noticed by enslaved litigants and
even by other slaves and their free kin.

The idea that people were naturally and legitimately inclined to seek
a better, more egalitarian world was also tentatively put into practice
by a sector of the Mompox elite. Forward-looking patricians conceived new institutions and ways of doing things that (though still
within the bounds of hierarchal principles) explicitly sought to bring
about a more egalitarian environment. Mompox's new "economic
society," for example, held all members to be equal regardless of their
genealogical, military, or ecclesiastical rank. Two leading members,
Ramón del Corral and Juan Antonio Gutiérrez de Piñeres, offered cash
prices to peasants who excelled in the cultivation of cotton. One of the
richest merchants in town even established a local college that explicitly allowed admission of free people of color.

Young Mompox patricians like Juan del Corral and the brothers
Vicente, Gabriel, and Germán Gutiérrez de Piñeres grew up in this
environment of judicial struggle, legal argumentation, and social
reform. They were also brought up to further Mompox's cause in its
rivalry with non-local officials. The children of newcomers who had
achieved wealth and influence in local politics, they came to believe
that Mompox's full potential could only be realized by lifting the

oversight privileges of elites and bureaucrats in Cartagena and Santa Fe. Ranked as a *villa* in the municipal hierarchy, Mompox remained a second-rate town despite its obvious prosperity. It was their natural right, many locals believed, to seek a better future and to achieve political autonomy.[6]

This rivalry would boil over in the wake of the 1810 crisis, galvanizing the rise of a revolutionary government that embraced the doctrines of natural law and legal equality in its founding documents and political goals. These included a radical constitution that called for reforming slavery and ending the slave trade. Behind this transformation was a coalition of the Piñeres brothers, other members of the Mompox and Cartagena intelligentsias, and leaders of African descent. Reminiscent of Ancient Rome's Gracchi brothers, the Piñeres brethren coordinated the most popular and radical wing of this alliance.[7] An observer scornfully recalled that they had "a strong party with the mob, and all who had nothing to lose."[8] A more sympathetic witness remembered Germán as a known "patriot" with a strong influence "over the whole people who respected and listened to him as an oracle."[9]

Led by this vibrant coalition, Cartagena became the first province in the Kingdom to declare absolute independence from Spain. Quickly afterwards, it granted equality before the law to all citizens. Other rich merchants and high patricians in the provincial capital resented the autonomist aspirations of their Mompox counterparts, however, and disliked the egalitarian hopes of their plebeian allies. An "aristocratic" coalition formed in the city of Cartagena that found support among rural dwellers. As in Popayán, the emerging political groupings would clash in civil war. While egalitarian, antislavery aspirations prevailed only in limited ways, this revolution offered radical answers to the 1810 crisis. Above all, it placed legal equality, slavery, and the stigmas of slavery front and center in the political debate. With its late eighteenth-century social, judicial, and intellectual effervescence, Mompox holds some of the keys to better understand this process.

It Takes a *Villa*

Over the course of the 1700s, Mompox attracted new migrants seeking fortune in a place known for its easy relationship with contraband

and tax evasion. The fresh arrivals, especially those from Spain, often married well and opened new lines of business. A few obtained substantial land grants, establishing large cattle estates and sugar or cacao haciendas. Some of these new proprietors were also involved in gold mining and sold slaves to miners throughout the western section of the viceroyalty. A few used their landholdings and income to obtain nobility titles – a rare achievement in the New Kingdom.[10] Less interested in land or noble status, later arrivals firmly embedded themselves in the local community through different forms of corporate belonging. Take the case of Ramón del Corral, an immigrant from Galicia and Juan del Corral's father. Though he had a difficult start, by 1769 he had become a member of the cabildo. He also obtained the rank of captain of the first fusiliers' company in the "free colored" regiment, thus establishing direct contact with people of enslaved ancestry. By 1806, he had become sergeant major of the urban militias. He also built and operated a pottery and established robust and diverse social connections.[11]

This businessman participated in Mompox's late eighteenth-century economic boom. The town's population grew from around 7,200 people in 1780 to 14,000 at the turn of the new century.[12] Humboldt, who visited in 1801 and met Ramón del Corral, remarked that commerce here was perhaps more robust than in the city of Cartagena. He recalled a "big smuggling" operation with the English colony of Jamaica and the Dutch entrepôt of Curaçao. Mompox investors, he also commented, revitalized the gold mines of northeast Antioquia.[13] Foreign and local fabrics, metal and wooden manufactures, gold, silver, wine, wheat, maize, tobacco, sugar cane products, tallow, hides, cattle, pelts, and even beaver hats passed through town; local merchants had customers and suppliers in the Caribbean, Europe, the Kingdom of Quito, and the viceroyalty of Peru.[14]

Like others before him, Ramón del Corral used his connections and the special protection afforded by military status for illegitimate purposes. His main income came from trade, both legal and illegal. He was accused of hiding behind his military privileges to avoid prosecution by ordinary justice. Allegedly, he bribed officials who would have reported on his illicit activities.[15] Despite the accusations, his business thrived. In 1785, Ramón bought six storefronts and a warehouse for 800 pesos. Three years later, surviving business records show that

Ramón owned and operated several *champanes* – large canoes used on the Magdalena River trade, operated by slaves and free men of color. In this riverine operation, his main associate was Juan Antonio Gutiérrez de Piñeres, a successful newcomer from Seville.[16] Their children, who grew up in the 1770s and 1780s, inherited and further developed the social connections as well as the "patriotic" and egalitarian sensibilities first developed by their parents.

Successful migrants often tried to prove their worth and love of the host community by coming up with or supporting projects to improve local conditions. Some discussed social, moral, and economic innovation in tertulias. Others advocated for the creation of *sociedades económicas de amigos del país* (economic societies of friends of the country, often called patriotic societies). Established for the diffusion and application of modern philosophy on behalf of the "State" and for the "common good," sociedades formed throughout Spain after 1774. Far less common in the Spanish Indies, patricians in the New Kingdom nonetheless became familiar with the idea, read the proceedings of Madrid's Sociedad, and drew inspiration from this European model.[17]

Ramón and his associate Juan Antonio actively participated in the formation of Mompox's Sociedad Económica in 1784 – perhaps the first one of its kind in the New World. Their principal goal was to promote efficient "agriculture and commerce" of cotton. Given Europe's growing demand, they saw cotton as the safest route to bring wealth and happiness to the province's inhabitants.[18] The Sociedad's early activities garnered praise. For some, it seemed "incredible" that this town, only a villa in the municipal ranking, was teaching people of means in the "the entire Kingdom," including its capital Santa Fe, how to spend their time in a wise and productive way.[19]

This association's goals, moreover, included the promotion of a new, relatively critical attitude toward legal inequality, a crucial component of the current political and social order. From the outset, and following Spanish precedent, the Sociedad was established with no special jurisdiction or privileges. At their meetings, the associates would take seats on a first-come, first-serve basis rather than hierarchically. Rejecting hierarchy, even in this limited space, was a significant innovation. People were expected to take their seats in church or spots in processions and other gatherings according to rank (often causing intense litigation over precedence). The Sociedad remained a gathering of people of means, yet members set aside corporate privileges, practicing their budding egalitarian sensibility. This extended, moreover, to other aspects of their endeavor. Members planned to invite farmers, rich and poor alike, to get involved in their cotton utopia. Ramón del Corral and his associate offered land for cultivation to humble peasants, free of charge for one year. Corral offered cash prizes for the largest cotton producers but specified that these had to be common farmers, people "personally devoted to the countryside" as opposed to estate owners or administrators.[20] Though obliquely articulated, an important subtext was that commoners had a role to play in the building of future economic prosperity.

As they envisioned a brighter future for Mompox, some patrician families resented that their young men had to travel far away for advanced studies. Vicente and Germán Gutiérrez de Piñeres, for example, studied in Santa Fe, where they graduated as doctors in canon law in 1790 and 1793 respectively. Those who would not travel to the viceregal court for schooling had to apply themselves to informal schooling at home. Following his early education in Latin, Juan del Corral engaged in a self-teaching program, learning to read French, English, and Italian (he too would follow the doctrines of Filangieri and other Neapolitan authors). The young Corral also taught himself some geography, political economy, agriculture, and military theory – a modern philosophy-inspired curriculum now prohibited in the colleges of the Kingdom.[21]

Daringly, Mompox's most advanced leaders embarked on a project to establish the systematic teaching of modern philosophy in their *villa*. They wanted their offspring to officially learn the kind of practical lessons that Restrepo had helped to keep alive in Popayán despite the prohibitions. To facilitate this project, Pedro Martínez de Pinillos, a migrant from Old Castile with considerable wealth and no children, decidedly championed the cause of a college for Mompox. He set aside an impressive 176,500 pesos to fund the "Colegio y Universidad de San Pedro."[22] Decidedly practical, the three-year school cycle designed for San Pedro aimed at giving students the skills to lead society toward wealth and happiness. According to the 1806 curriculum, professors should spend less time in perfecting their pupil's Latin, altogether dropping syllogism and scholastics, and concentrate instead on advanced mathematics, geometry, physics, chemistry, meteorology, botany, zoology, and even commercial accounting and bookkeeping. The true "philosopher" should be able to discuss and practice basic agriculture, crafts, and trade. The Neapolitan Antonio Genovesi's *Lezioni di commercio* was mandatory reading. The College aspired to support student's travels to Madrid, Paris, and London, and the travelers, according to the plan, would bring back books, scientific instruments, and new lessons to teach.[23]

More strikingly, an egalitarian tinge also characterized the college founders' plans. Pinillos was known for treating with "notable humanity" all "humble people." Even his slaves, a local priest reported, were looked upon by Pinillos with the "warmth of children," an attitude he promoted among his relatives.[24] If the priest exaggerated Pinillos' open-mindedness, the college's "Constitutions" nonetheless reveal that the founder and his associates aspired to look passed the stigmas of slavery. Existing regulations excluded the descendants of slaves from college education, a privilege only granted to criollos and peninsulares able to prove their *limpieza de sangre* and *hidalguía* (purity of blood and gentry, old Christian background). At San Pedro, however, the plan was to offer admission to some "negros" and "esclavos." "We are not to be too scrupulous," the Constitutions stated, "on hidalguías and limipeza."[25] At least on paper, the founders admitted that people of enslaved ancestry also deserved a modicum of respect and opportunity, and a release from the burdens of segregation. The college began operations around 1808, but whether people of color enrolled remains unknown.

Other members of the local elite likewise espoused somewhat egalitarian attitudes. The priest Juan Fernández de Sotomayor, a native of the provincial capital, became parish rector of Mompox in 1803. With impeccable genealogical and academic credentials, he also held the post of adviser to Cartagena's Tribunal of the Inquisition. He believed that common folk had to be catechized in Spanish and patiently brought toward Christian virtue. Ordained only in early 1801, Sotomayor immediately went to work with the Indians of Tubará, north of Cartagena, where he experimented with a less rigid approach to preaching. On Sundays, before the Latin mass that would have been beyond the grasp of most parishioners, he explained doctrine "in a clear and intelligible voice for everybody with no distinction of person." He claimed to have replicated this tactic in Mompox, plainly teaching doctrine to parishioners in Spanish and avoiding segregation of the laity by gender.[26]

These forming egalitarian attitudes among members of Mompox's elite had sharp limitations and ambivalences. The college founders, for example, continued to uphold old stereotypes, believing stock accusations against slaves and former slaves: the Constitutions indicated that, if possible, slaves and freed people should not be hired by the institution. Their service was very "risky," the document stated as a matter of fact, because of their "infidelity" and their "communicable ailments." Still, the Constitutions tangentially criticized slaveholding. People served by slaves, the authors believed, became accustomed to harshly treating not just their human property but other individuals too. The slave trade had caused this failure in character among criollos, and greater evils were to be expected from the curse of slavery. The document mentioned "conspiracies" in the Carolinas, Jamaica, Cartagena, and, above all, the "horrendous catastrophe" of Saint-Domingue as examples of how far slaves were willing to go to break their chains.[27]

Although many forward-looking people continued to obfuscate the emancipation expectations of many slaves, critics of slavery spoke their minds with unusual emphasis in Mompox. They articulated critical perspectives on human bondage, sometimes going beyond the typical arguments occasionally used to legally defend slaves against abuse. Some magistrates built on the particulars of each case to point to the iniquities of Mompox slaveholders and the unacceptable injustice of slavery in general, while others expressed the idea that "nature" could not permit the enslavement of humans under any circumstances. The notion that a natural, equal order trumped the artificial, unequal legal order of society underpinned the antislavery positions emerging in the judicial forum.

Tribunes of the Plebs

Understandings of natural law as a source of individual rights with universal validity converged with the concept of nature as a guiding force. Besides describing slavery as the "vilest and most contemptible thing that can exist among men," for example, the *Siete Partidas* stated that slavery had been instituted "contrary to natural reason."

According to "nature," the medieval code read, no "distinction" exists between free and slave, with all people naturally loving and desiring freedom. Understood as an inherent guiding force steering humanity toward good, nature in the Catholic world traditionally appeared inseparable from the will of God. The idea that bondage (like grave sins) was an offense to nature had crucial religious implications. Further, this was a compelling proposition when the enslaved people under consideration were Christians.[28]

Relegated to an unnatural status, slaves appeared in written laws as people inclined to change their fate by preventing abuse from masters or even reverting to their natural state of freedom. As Christian people living in a wretched condition, slaves in the Spanish monarchy enjoyed, in theory, some protection by the law and the magistrates. The *Partidas* called for masters not to "kill or wound" slaves, and slaves in turn could "complain to the judge" if their masters treated them with excessive cruelty. Magistrates were encouraged to pay attention to these cases. They could even remove cruelly treated slaves from the authority of their owners and sell them to a different master. Spanish lawgivers restated these and similar commands over the centuries. Rarely, however, did jurists go out of their way to denounce cruel masters or to emancipate slaves.[29] Unnatural in theory, slavery was in practice seen and perpetuated as a normal situation.

Slaves themselves had to initiate legal action against cruel masters or file petitions for their own freedom, though they seldom found opportunity to do so. Although people could bring complaints before local authorities orally (who sometimes solved issues over spoken, legally binding exchanges), the preferred and most common form of jump-starting legal proceedings remained a written petition.[30] Very few slaves were literate, however. Some literate slaves used their skills to advance their individual causes.[31] Collective petitions, as we have seen in the cases of Antioquia and Popayán, were almost impossible to file. Slaves who could not write and had no access to ink and paper sometimes hired the services of lawyers, notaries, and *papelistas*. These judicial practitioners wrote letters and petitions according to legal standards and brought them before the appropriate authorities. Papelistas usually took small cases or restricted their work to writing up petitions. Functioning as poor people's jurists, these legal agents abounded throughout the Spanish-speaking world.[32] Those who hired papelistas usually lived in urban centers, but in rural areas it remained quite difficult to bring any verbal, let alone written complaints before the magistrates.[33]

However, some jurists in Mompox and at the Santa Fe tribunals stood up for slaves during litigation, taking the role of tribunes of the plebs. Slaves in Mompox must have taken note of jurists who believed masters should not enjoy unlimited power over the enslaved. Some magistrates even insisted that judges should always decide cases "in favor of freedom." Others thought that slavery should eventually disappear altogether. Many of these opinions were expressed as early as the 1770s, usually as variations on more general themes of jurisprudence. Such themes included whether judges should make decisions applying the written laws alone instead of relying on opinions by glossators and commentators, and whether the realm of nature in the end trumped all stipulations found in the written laws.

The lawyer José Ignacio de San Miguel, the highest magistrate in Mompox, believed that "all laws conspire" to protect slaves, those "wretches" with their "freedom lost." Even though legal codes protected slaves, San Miguel complained in 1777 that masters in Mompox treated them "with little humanity," providing them with scant food. He even tried to determine how much food slaves should receive every day to comply with "the laws of humanity and good government." Like Restrepo in Popayán, but about a decade earlier, San Miguel expressed the notion that magistrates had a basic obligation to better the lot of the enslaved, and that this would reflect well on the body politic. Moreover, San Miguel, possibly a slaveowner himself, believed that mistreated slaves were entitled to request a change of master, though he knew that many "judicious jurists" argued that this privilege did not exist.[34] As a magistrate appointed from Santa Fe, San Miguel might have used his jurisdiction to harass local slaveholders who opposed his authority by helping their slaves. It is likely that whatever he said or wrote over the course of litigation caught the attention of expectant slaves and papelistas.

When Gregorio José Cevallos, and enslaved master potter at José Antonio de Bros y Arango's brickworks, filed a complaint against his owner, San Miguel gave the master three days to provide him with papel. Cevallos complained that his master imposed too much work on him, providing him with little food and clothing. Moreover, the master was allegedly cruel and beat his slaves for the slightest of mistakes, though this was a charge that remained difficult to prove. San Miguel's authorization for Cevallos to search for a new master in effect forced Bros y Arango to sell his property. Compelled to sell his most skilled slave, the master appealed to the Real Audiencia in Santa Fe.[35]

Pablo Sarmiento, Arango's proxy in Santa Fe, argued that compelling a master to sell his slave had no legal basis. Sarmiento stated that this issue had been carefully examined by a famous judge from the Real Audiencia in Lima. Although not mentioned by name, we can establish that Sarmiento was referring to Pedro Bravo de Lagunas y Castilla, whose famous legal opinions circulated both in print and handwritten copies.[36] In a 1746 disquisition, Bravo de Lagunas argued that ordering masters to sell their property contravened the law. Such a compulsion, the Lima magistrate insisted, could only take place when masters prostituted or otherwise cruelly treated slaves, as stated in the *Partidas*. Bravo de Lagunas, moreover, asserted that masters should not be compelled to sell their slaves simply "in favor of freedom," as glossators and commentators argued – and as jurists such as San Miguel and Restrepo later proposed. Only when masters willed their slaves to be sold or emancipated could their value be paid, and manumission achieved. This was what existing law mandated according to Bravo de Lagunas and his followers. They proposed that judges should make their decisions adhering to nothing but the written law.[37] In their opinion, nature and custom, which slaves and their legal aides also cited as sources of law, had no role to play in adjudication. But the legal forum was open to divergent interpretations.

With the aid of a lawyer or papelista and with the confidence of the initial positive ruling by the highest magister in town, Cevallos skillfully turned to a more favorable interpretation involving the idea of custom as a source of law. Besides the written laws, slave litigants also took custom to be an important measure of obligations and privileges. Understood as a remembered or current practice, the concept of custom in this case recalled unwritten pacts and reciprocal understandings between masters and slaves. Such transactions could be construed as formally binding commitments.[38] The people of La Honda raised a similar point, maintaining that their former master's oral promises must have legal consequences (though they also knew his promise had been written into his last will and testament). In his allegations, Cevallos argued that it was a "custom" for masters to pay slaves when they were sent to work on holidays. However, his master had failed to do so. According to custom, Cevallos also claimed, slaves sent to gather firewood could distribute the task between two individuals, one who did the cutting and one who carried the fuel to the brickworks. Despite this arrangement and Cevallos' old age (he said he was sixty), his master required him to perform both tasks at once.[39]

José Antonio Maldonado, *procurador* for the poor, took up the cause of Cevallos in Santa Fe, making a broader argument about slavery and natural law. Maldonado had no formal legal training but litigated this case under the supervision of the lawyer Francisco González Manrique, a modern philosophy sympathizer whose wife Manuela Sanz de Santa María hosted the famous Buen Gusto tertulia in Santa Fe. According to Maldonado and González, adding insult to the injury of slavery by cruelly treating slaves contravened "natural law." Taking steps to help slaves was thus important, particularly in "Christian republics" where religion fostered "confraternity." These brotherly polities, they claimed, tolerated slavery but without the rigors proper to slavery "induced by the law of war." Magistrates, therefore, had to prevent anything that inhumanly affronted a slave's body and his "nature" as a "rational individual," including food deprivation and overwork. In this way, Maldonado and González rejected the idea that slaves were originally war captives whose lives had been pardoned on the condition that they remain in their victor's captivity. By rejecting this premise, they also rejected the idea that slaves should be treated as domestic enemies. After all, no Spanish war in Africa had led to the enslavement of people like Cevallos.[40]

Maldonado and González's oblique rejection of the law of war as the crucial source of the right to own persons relied on a specific understanding of slavery in light of natural law. As college students and jurists began to study natural law in the mid-1770s, Pufendorf's doctrines gained prominence in the New Kingdom. Pufendorf, alongside other natural law theorists of the seventeenth century, admitted that a victor could either kill the vanquished or enslave them. Historically speaking, however, Pufendorf viewed the law of war as only a secondary source of slavery. War did not create slavery; it only multiplied slaves, but it did so contractually, since prisoners of war had their lives pardoned only after they agreed to live under the dominium of their victors who became their masters. Nevertheless, the masters had no absolute power over the slaves because their natural right to kill a person in self-defense ceased to exist once the opponent was defeated, disarmed, and rendered incapable of causing harm. Because helpless prisoners-turned-slaves were also humans, moreover, "natural equality" forbade that they be treated like beasts or objects. Masters had to properly feed and clothe them.[41]

For Maldonado, González, and other jurists such as Restrepo, every discussion of natural law implied a wider set of principles. They believed in certain natural drives and rights, common to all humankind and inherent to the universe rather than the product of history, custom or social convention. These included the drive for self-preservation, the imperative not to harm others, the urge to live in peaceful society, and the inclination to freedom and love of liberty. Some magistrates thus imagined people in an abstract, out-of-society state in which all individuals shared the same essence and standing granted by nature that made everybody equal.[42] Mompox's cultural elites held similar ideas. Around the time San Pedro College began operations, philosophy professor José María Gutiérrez de Caviedes told his students that the "Laws of nature" had gifted humans with a propensity to discernment and enlightenment. He had likely read Filangieri's detailed plan for public education, which called for future magistrates and soldiers to study the principles of natural law in their fifth year of schooling.[43]

For some magistrates versed in the critical scrutiny of the natural law doctrine, these principles could be expanded into a wholesale rejection of slavery. Building on natural law and the equal standing of Christians, some advanced the proposition that slavery was entirely unjustifiable, even if sanctioned by written legislation. They favored the cause of slave emancipation and, furthermore, the total abolition of slavery. In their view, this was an unnatural institution, founded on the power of some humans over others rather than an expression of the divine order of the universe. They thus agreed with Montesquieu and Filangieri, who critically assessed seventeenth-century theories on slavery like Pufendorf's. For Montesquieu, slavery and the law were mutually exclusive because slaves occupied an unnatural, extra-social status that violated the right to self-preservation and the right to do anything allowed by the laws. For Filangieri, in turn, slavery was an abomination because it violated the universal rights equally granted by nature to all individuals.[44]

In Mompox, Melchor Sáenz de Ortíz articulated an outright condemnation of slavery, suggesting that it should disappear altogether. In 1804, as procurador for María Magdalena Soto, a slave, he quoted from José Marcos Gutiérrez. A Spanish jurist with a bent for natural law, Gutiérrez argued that it would be easy to prove that no one was a slave "except in the legal codes, and in the [in]humanity and insensibility of other free men."[45] On his annotations to a popular handbook for notaries, Gutiérrez further remarked that nature itself rejected the wrong of slavery. Sáenz shared Gutiérrez's wish to "see the vile and shameful words serf, serfdom, slave, slavery banished from legal codes."[46] A few years later, Antonio de Villavicencio, who may have read Gutiérrez and who shared his plan to reform slavery with Restrepo, expressed a similarly worded desire. In his view, the government had to destroy "even the very name of slavery."[47] Like Montesquieu, they maintained that there was no room for slavery in civil society and that slaves existed only beyond the law; and like Filangieri, they believed lawgivers had to actively work for the dismantling of slavery.

While some magistrates aired their hopes for the abolition of slavery during litigation, slaves' struggles against abuse remained challenging, and their aspiration to freedom difficult to articulate and even harder to realize.[48] Masters, overseers, inheritors, creditors, and officials with an interest in maintaining slavery often resorted to violence and intimidation to achieve their goal – especially when they knew a slave had legally sound arguments against them. This was demonstrated in the case of La Honda, south of Mompox, where, as we have already seen, in 1802 and early 1803 the master's heirs, with the help of officials, waged war against the inhabitants of the hacienda and ultimately re-enslaved many of them. The former slaves knew, as did their opponents, that their late master had provided for their emancipation in his last will and testament, but even in such cases, the prospect of freedom remained elusive. Still, the hope of legal recognition of their emancipation and formal sub-municipal incorporation was kept alive almost to the end.[49]

Despite the continuing difficulties for slaves, Mompox's early political innovation, natural law speculations and egalitarian impulses would later be expanded into more radical endeavors with the coming of revolution. Although the provincial capital became the epicenter of revolutionary activity, crucial political operatives emerged from Mompox. They led Cartagena to experiment with a new form of government that promoted equality before the law and promised to undermine slavery by facilitating manumission. The Piñeres brothers, supported by people of color from Mompox and Cartagena, became outspoken defenders of autonomy for their villa, independence from Spain, and the end of the stigmas and restrictions associated with enslaved ancestry. Such goals, they would declare in a written constitution, were not only just but natural.

The Revolution of Cartagena

Vicente, Germán, and Gabriel Gutiérrez de Piñeres grew up hearing that a better, more prosperous, maybe even egalitarian world was possible. Their father and his friends believed it, and people like the philanthropist Pinillos and the priest Sotomayor worked to make this ideal a reality. Some Mompox leaders and magistrates believed that slaves and their descendants could aspire to a future without discrimination and free of bondage. These critical aspirations undermined the tenet of legal inequality as an immovable principle. They also questioned the conviction that the economic and social health of the realm hinged on the continuation of slavery. Expectations of change in Mompox also included the hope that this prosperous town would ascend from villa to the lustrous and more independent rank of *ciudad*, thus enjoying the formal autonomy and the prestige required to further other aspirations.

Local elites achieved some autonomy, keeping at bay provincial and viceregal administrators seeking to place Mompox under close fiscal and political oversight. The most distinguished patrician families controlled legal trade and got away with constant and robust illegal commerce, they kept a firm grip on the cabildo, exercised influence over the surrounding rural districts, and largely controlled a royal treasury branch with an annual revenue of more than 100,000 pesos. Further, they achieved astounding leeway for the operations of their San Pedro College.[50] Mompox's achievements, its hope to ascend in the municipal hierarchy, and its reputation as a contraband heaven did not sit well with high bureaucrats in the viceregal capital.

Political tensions between Mompox and Santa Fe increased in late
1808. Between November 20 and 22 the Magdalena broke over its
banks, dramatically flooding the town. Movable property was swept
away, and the foundations of many buildings were undermined.
Because the cabildo had collected taxes for the construction of a levy,
the viceroy quickly asserted that failure to complete the project proved
negligence and possibly fraud on the part of local aldermen. He seized
the opportunity, sending an assertive engineer (with a military rank by
definition) to oversee construction of the levy. This engineer was also
meant to keep an eye on the locals, who were now deemed to be intent
on taking advantage of the ambiguous situation created by Napoleon's
invasion of Spain earlier that year. The engineer sided with the hypoth-
esis that the viceroy and all other representatives of the king should
remain in their posts, and he was promoted to royal treasury sub-
delegate for Mompox in August 1809. Afraid that this official would
charge local merchants for smuggling, members of the cabildo
opposed the promotion. They saw the move as a ploy to prevent them
from making any further assertion of autonomy, or to answer to the
growing crisis on their own terms. They accused the officer of treating
local inhabitants "like slaves."[51]

Despite the opposition, the engineer stayed in town and continued
to report to the viceroy, insisting that the Piñeres clan stood on the
brink of revolutionary action. As soon as they heard of the deposition
of the Quito authorities, he informed his boss, cabildo members had
begun to conspire to set up their own independent government in
Mompox. A few months later he further reported that the Piñeres
brothers were spreading news about the collapse of the Spanish military before the French invaders, telling people that the viceroy and the
governor of Cartagena were in cahoots with Napoleon. Unless
deposed, the Piñereses allegedly implied, those officials would deliver
their jurisdictions to the French just to keep their offices and salaries.[52]

The engineer's estimation of the situation might not have been
altogether exaggerated. Anxiety for political change was widespread.
With his reported harsh treatment of locals, the engineer also elicited
pushback from free people of color in town. As rumors swirled in
Santa Fe that the viceroy himself might be a partisan of Napoleon, the
engineer prepared to travel to the viceregal court to support the high
authorities there, but before his planned departure, the townsfolk

came out to demonstrate their discontent with the official. Led by Estanislaa Barón, and likely in concert with Vicente Gutiérrez de Piñeres, a crowd of women, former slaves, and other people of humble background stormed the engineer's house on June 25, 1810. This crowd action forced him to flee. En route to Santa Fe, he learned that yet another crowd of humble folk had helped depose high authorities in the capital on July 20.[53] The coup against the viceregal court, we must remember, had taken place after the deposition of the governor of Cartagena, which deprived the viceroy of his authority over the strongest military garrison on the land.

Anxious for greater autonomy from Madrid and Santa Fe, leading merchants in the city of Cartagena had formed a coalition led by the rich patrician José María García de Toledo. Toledo's group gradually took over provincial administrative business. The Spanish governor did not hesitate to call these developments a "revolution," and Toledo and his allies finally deposed the official on June 14, 1810. Also known as *toledistas*, this faction was now at the head of a new local junta in Cartagena, laying claim to jurisdiction over the entire province. Toledistas espoused a home rule approach, hoping to maintain allegiance to the Regency Council, keep their social and political privileges as people of Spanish descent, obtain authorization for free trade with foreign powers, and continue to receive an annual subsidy for military defense purposes – hundreds of thousands of pesos largely pocketed by merchants who sold goods to soldiers and craftsmen on the king's payroll.[54]

To back up his legal and political maneuvers against the governor, Toledo turned to commoners and their leaders for support. Pedro Romero, a highly skilled master blacksmith working for the royal navy post and reputed to be of African ancestry, staged a mutiny against the governor with the help of his artisan allies and poor city dwellers. Moreover, on June 19, 1810, Toledo presided over the organization of these commoners into an armed force known as the Patriotic Volunteers, with Romero taking the rank of colonel.[55] Romero and others understood that Toledo and his "aristocratic" allies cared little about equality for people of color, however. The Piñereses, on the other hand, had a different reputation. An unsympathetic observer would later scorn Gabriel as someone who "everywhere preaches absolute equality...always seen surrounded by blacks and mulatos who had no education, and he desired the rest of

citizens to do the same, under the penalty of being deemed aristocrats."[56] Scores of commoners would soon abandon the toledistas to
join the so-called *piñeristas*.

The Piñeres clan already had an important presence in the provincial
capital. Germán and Gabriel became official residents of the city, while
Vicente remained in Mompox (where he joined the San Pedro fac-
ulty).[57] The Cartagena contingent courted assertive artisan leaders and
militiamen of African descent who hoped to remove, even if on a case-
by-case basis, the legal limitations preventing free men of color from
holding royal posts or joining colleges, the legal professions, and the
priesthood. Friendly to the proposition that an egalitarian society was
possible, the brothers seemed ideal allies for those seeking to do away
with the stigma of enslaved ancestry. The growing crisis would solidify
this alliance.[58]

In Mompox, most people celebrated the fall of the governor and the
deposition of the viceroy, though they seemed less excited about the
toledistas' aspirations to uphold allegiance to Spain and claim authority over Mompox. By mid-August, the Piéñereses, other radical patricians, and their commoner allies publicly declared that, with the
viceroy's deposition, Mompox too had become free to choose its
own government. Gutiérrez de Caviedes, teacher of the doctrines of
natural law at San Pedro and a former participant in Santa Fe's Buen
Gusto tertulia, publicly claimed that the people of Mompox had to
recognize that "we are no longer slaves, we are free." With the fall of
the viceroy and Audience judges in Santa Fe, he believed, sovereignty
had reverted to the people, and the links with the Regency had been
dissolved. Mompox, he insisted, had "no other sovereign than itself,"
for all men had received from "nature" a holy patrimony of rights,
including natural freedom and "sacred equality."[59]

Mompox radicals broke away from the provincial capital and
declared independence from the Regency (though not from the
deposed king). They set up a junta in October 1810. Presided by
Vicente Gutiérrez de Piñeres, the new government had the support of
popular leaders like José Luís Muñoz, Luis Galván, José de los Santos
Iglesias, and the carpenter José María Vides, all free men of color.
They approved seceding from the province of Cartagena but formally
upholding allegiance to the imprisoned monarch. This bold step
elicited a strong response from the toledistas, who aspired to control

Mompox's important location and resources, and disliked the egalitarian, pro-independence leanings of their rivals. Toledo sent troops to occupy the town. After three days of fighting, the defenders of Mompox evacuated on January 23, 1811. The toledistas dissolved the junta, expatriated its members, and confiscated their properties. Vicente fled and some of his associates were thrown in jail.[60]

The aggression against Mompox and developments in Spain radicalized piñerista sympathizers led by Gabriel, who remained free in the provincial capital. The Spanish Cortes, a reforming Spanish parliament that had finally convened, decreed that no person of African ancestry was worthy of Spanish citizenship or the right to vote. News of this arrived in late August, further galvanizing pro-independence sentiments. The Cortes, moreover, denied political equality to Spain's overseas territories, making it more difficult for Spanish families of high social standing to defend the old order. These families thought of themselves and their jurisdictions as integral members of the monarchy. Now, however, they were denied equal political standing with their peninsular brethren, and their provinces and kingdoms were treated as colonies. With a growing number of allies, the piñerista coalition now openly supported absolute independence from Spain. Pedro Romero, Gabriel Gutiérrez de Piñeres, and hundreds of commoners from the city pressed for full independence and full equality before the law. The popular demands would be met over the following months.[61]

On November 11, 1811, the re-grouped radicals staged a crowd action against the Toledo government and declared independence from Spain. After marching on the governor's palace where the Cartagena junta was in session, the piñeristas successfully forced the government to declare Cartagena, by right and in fact, a "free State, sovereign and independent."[62] Toledo and his allies ended the military occupation of Mompox and set the prisoners free. In January 1812, the revolutionaries formed a constitutional Convention for their new country, the State of Cartagena. Mompox's influence was palpable in the Convention: the prefect was Remigio Márquez, a man of color from the villa; the Mompox curate Fernández de Sotomayor and the three brothers Piñeres were members of the Convention; the main drafter of the constitution project, Father Manuel Benito Rebollo, had also exercised his priestly duties in Mompox. Pedro Romero was also one of the leading members. To give better shape and lasting meaning to their convictions, these revolutionaries designed a new legal framework for their independent polity, drawing on natural law generally and on specific considerations by Montesquieu, Filangieri, and the US federal and state constitutions.[63]

On June 14, 1812, the Convention completed an egalitarian constitution for the State of Cartagena. The old province was now a "representative republic" with division of powers which recognized no corporate, inherited, or aristocratic privileges. The idea of "legal equality," the constitution stated, was "right, just and natural." All free male adults would now be equal before the law.[64] The odious distinctions between Spaniards and people of color should now disappear. A few days before approval of the constitution, the local revolutionary gazette announced that the treatment of "don," traditionally the prerogative of the high patricians, would be extinguished. All free inhabitants would enjoy the treatment of "citizen." The "titles, and badges proceeding from the abolished government of Spain, mean nothing in the estimation of the government of this State." The radical Gabriel Gutiérrez de Piñeres was elected vice-president of the State and president of the senate. Mauricio Romero (Pedro's son), recently barred from attending college in Santa Fe because of his African ancestry, now became a member of the new legislature.[65]

This promise of equality did not, however, automatically gain the trust of all people of color. Free individuals of African or mixed descent were subject to deep-seated prejudices. They had slave ancestors, slave relatives and made a living from mechanical occupations, and therefore, in the eyes of many, they bore the stigma of presumed illegitimacy, bodily pollution, and reprovable conduct. But different people reacted to the challenges of prejudice and discrimination in different ways. People made their political choices in answer to, not as a logical consequence of their genealogical backgrounds. Better-off craftsmen from the city worked to overcome the consequences of their stigmatized history. Before the revolution, Romero and other up and coming artisans lobbied officials to have some legal restrictions lifted for their children. They would later support the principle of equality before the law.[66] Poor rural dwellers seemed less persuaded by the idea of legal equality, however. Peasants and other rural workers of mixed African and Indigenous ancestry in the Sinú and Tolú river plains (see Map 4), for example, revolted against the new Cartagena government in September 1812. Though moral prejudices and legal restrictions also limited their life choices, scores of rural folks joined Toledo in a dramatic counter-revolution. Their mobilization was stopped by force and at the cost of yet more blood.[67]

Still, radical political leaders in Cartagena publicized their conviction that people of African descent had equal, if not greater, merit. They even described people of color as the exact opposite of cruel Europeans, who were responsible for all manner of crimes throughout the world. The Spanish Constitution of 1812 sanctioned by the Cortes, an article in the local gazette insisted, excluded men of color from political representation, giving them the useless label of "españoles" and imposing on them fiscal, military, and civic obligations while preventing them from becoming full "ciudadanos." The prejudices against African origin undergirding this exclusion appeared ridiculous considering the history of Spain itself: because "the Arabs owned the country for eight hundred years, there is barely anyone who can boast of not having something of African origin." In Cartagena, the article recalled, no difference was recognized to exist between "pardos" (men of color) and those who descended from the European nations.[68]

Even people who would have fallen under the nebulous category of French blacks (accused of conspiring to destroy the city and liberate the slaves back in 1799), were now admissible for political belonging in the new State. Between 1813 and 1815, the State of Cartagena enacted a robust privateering policy to attack Spanish shipping in the Caribbean, undermining Spanish power while securing a desperately needed source of income. Most sailors manning the ships outfitted as Cartagena privateers were former slaves and free people of color from places like Saint-Domingue and Guadeloupe. Hoping that their maritime warfare would adhere to international law, Cartagena's leaders allowed these and other foreigners to obtain naturalization letters, officially recognizing them as citizens of the State.[69]

Alongside these emerging spaces of political belonging for some people of African ancestry, Cartagena espoused a tacit critique of slavery and the slave trade. Unlike leaders in Popayán, Cartagenan revolutionaries directly answered to the expectations of those who anticipated the end of slavery. The Constitution outlawed the slave trade to the State. It stipulated that authorities had to guarantee masters would not treat slaves with excessive cruelty. But Toledo (who owned around fifty slaves) and other slaveholders with positions in the Convention managed to fend off attacks on their right to own other human beings. Indeed, the Constitution stated that no official would "emancipate slaves without the consent of their masters, or with no compensation for their value." Nevertheless, the Constitution called for the legislative power to consider a manumission project. Referred to as a "manumission fund" in the document, we may surmise that the project required the State to collect taxes to pay for the liberation of individual slaves.[70] But almost no evidence about this project seems to have survived, and it is unlikely that it was ever even partially enacted.

In the end, Cartagena revolutionaries did little on behalf of mistreated slaves or to end the slave trade and promote slave emancipation. Continuing factional struggle and the threat of pro-Regency invasion from Panama or the province of Santa Marta to the north led to the virtual suspension of several constitutional guarantees. Further, there is sufficient evidence to suggest that slaves introduced from overseas by Cartagena privateers continued to be traded in the local slave market, and that this happened with the blessing of the State's tribunals and notaries. Some of the many foreigners coming to newly independent Cartagena participated in these transactions, including people from the French Caribbean and the English-speaking world. Santiago Capurro, from Genoa, also sold slaves on behalf of a local priest.[71]

And yet the radical patrician-plebeian coalition from Mompox and Cartagena propelled antislavery sentiments and the idea of legal equality to a new stage of politics. As they put into practice the doctrine of natural law, the plight of the enslaved and their free relatives became a matter of State, an issue to be taken up by the government, as Restrepo had theorized. The old prejudices against slaves or individuals with enslaved African ancestry remained widespread, and not all free people of color supported the new doctrines, but some of them came to play crucial roles in the revolution. As they participated in the construction of the new State of Cartagena, they built their antislavery and egalitarian positions into the emerging independent, constitutional order. Though only in theory, republican Cartagenans stood for ending domestic slavery as consubstantial with the ending of political enslavement by Spain. Slave emancipation was formally bound up with emancipation from the metropole and the restitution of the natural and sacred rights of individuals.

***

An alliance that included free people of color at the leadership and rank and file levels led revolutionary Cartagena to declare independence and ratify an egalitarian constitution. These Cartagena leaders also proposed that a republican government devoted to equality before the law and independence from Spain should question the yoke tying the slaves to the masters in perpetuity. Slavery, and the stigmas of African, enslaved ancestry, were nothing but the unjust, unnatural legacies of Spain, and were comparable to the illegitimate power exercised by Spanish officials over the province of Cartagena.

The intellectual background of these propositions can be partially traced in litigation and politics in Mompox. In the judicial forum and over the course of social reform projects, Mompox magistrates, litigants, and local leaders had long debated the potential social consequences of natural law and egalitarian convictions. This included critical assessments of the relationships between masters and slaves, criollos and free people of color, priests and their parishioners, villas and cities. Many took up the doctrine that despite the hierarchical, unequal nature of these relationships, all humans shared an equal standing, independent from legal and social differences. They developed the conviction that all people were endowed with equal potential and equal rights. Some believed that this natural equality extended to the slaves, who also had natural aspirations to liberty, prosperity, and happiness. A magistrate even spoke of ending bondage, annihilating the very term "slavery," an odious, undesirable, unnatural condition.

With the outbreak of civil war and revolution, the possible implications and applications of these propositions became even more imperative. If Spain could be identified as a cruel mistress, and the king's ministers accused of treating vassals like slaves, domestic slaveholding had to be critically assessed as well. Cartagena revolutionaries outlawed the slave trade, declared legal equality for former slaves and their offspring, and anticipated that their now independent State would take steps to begin to manumit slaves with public funds. Nevertheless, independent Cartagena did little to translate these legal achievements into meaningful social change. Slavery and the slave trade continued. Still, a set of doctrines that litigants had typically applied on a case-by-case basis became overarching legal principles with the potential to encompass an entire polity, particularly a newly liberated country.

This emerging conceptual link between antislavery and independence took different forms and was built on different experiences through this period of atomized, provincial revolutions. Slaves in Popayán argued that the breaking of the chains imposed by Spain on their masters should be extended to their own situation, but circumstances there delayed the formation of a revolutionary government. The powerful slaveholding elite would prove committed to keeping slavery for years to come. In Antioquia, as we shall see, slaves would legally and forcefully request that the newly formed government revisit its founding doctrines of liberty, thereby seeking to extend freedom to the enslaved.

With all its shortcomings, revolutionary Cartagena did embrace the idea (shared by Félix José de Restrepo, Antonio de Villavicencio and others) that any prudent legislator and every forward-looking government should favor the cause of the slaves. Though Juan del Corral, who was also steeped in Mompox's reformist environment, soon joined forces with Restrepo to legislate in favor of slaves in Antioquia, they would do so only under pressure from expectant and collectively organized slaves. Antioquia's "free womb" anti-slavery legislation, an act of legal reform deemed worthy of a free polity, would lift the obstacles on the way to freedom for all slaves in a limited form.

5

Antioquia: Free Womb, Captive Slaves

By 1810, the province of Antioquia produced almost as much gold as the governorate of Popayán. Unlike in Popayán's Pacific mining districts, however, Antioquia gold was mined by slaves in small gangs, typically less than ten per group. Mining operations often included both free workers as well as slaves. The small-scale free prospectors known as mazamorreros even worked side by side with their slaves. Collectively, these small, mixed workforces were responsible for the largest share of Antioquia's gold production. Large slaveholders were rare. While merchants and magistrates kept a few household slaves, slaveholding did not make-or-break the riches or status of the Antioquia patriciate.[1]

Like their Popayán counterparts, however, Antioquia's masters had a firm grip over their slaves. Notarial records from Medellín and the city of Antioquia, the provincial capital, reveal that only a few slaves received manumission every year. Manumitted slaves typically obtained their freedom only after paying their masters to "rescue" them. Those willingly manumitted by their masters usually had to wait for their owners to pass away before receiving their freedom papers; others remained bound in servitude to their masters' family even after obtaining formal emancipation. Many slaves officially emancipated by the "grace" of their owners had taken steps to convince or pressure their masters to set them free.[2]

Yet in Antioquia, slaves enjoyed a comparatively remarkable level of autonomy: they moved about the province more easily and often than slave miners in the Pacific or slave rural workers on the Caribbean plains of Cartagena. Antioquia slaves traveled to pan for gold, on errands, or followed their masters along the short distances separating the main provincial towns and rural districts (Antioquia, Medellín, Rionegro, and Marinilla) (see Map 2). They experienced the constant tension between captivity on the one hand, and geographic mobility and social communication on the other. Many Antioquia slaves easily and constantly talked to other slaves and to free people, even across jurisdictional borders. Through this grapevine, some of these slaves shared their hopes that an end of slavery was possible and a better life after bondage achievable. This vibrant culture of expectation incorporated legal leitmotifs and tactics.

Building on the relatively autonomous travel and communication across districts, some slave leaders tried to organize collectively to press for the end of their enslavement. Already by the year 1781, authorities worried about slaves' cross-district collaboration, insisting they were out to destroy the masters along with the entire social order. In fact, many slaves remained convinced that their enslavement could be ended by legal rather than violent means. They hoped to press authorities to finally bring to light the rumor of a royal decree liberating them and turning them into free vassals who paid taxes "like Indians" or mazamorreros after emancipation. Similar hopes surfaced in 1798 and again in 1806.[3]

Expectant Antioquia slaves were particularly well positioned to listen to, share, and interpret information concerning the unprecedented political developments that followed the 1810 crisis. Whether they had lived through previous episodes or heard the stories from their elders, slaves shared expectations about, and mobilized to take advantage of the shifting circumstances in their home province. After Antioquia's peaceful revolution and its transformation into a republic devoted to individual freedom in 1812, slave leaders would emerge as the first critics of the founding documents and legal principles of this new polity.[4]

When Antioquia's revolutionary Constitution of 1812 announced that "liberty" and "equality" had come to end "slavery" and "chains,"[5] a robust cross-district slave alliance filed a collective petition before the new

State's high justice tribunal requesting to know whether these statements in the Constitution were "true."[6] Ever attentive and increasingly organized, Antioquia's slave leaders scrutinized the legal logic of a republic that gained independence from Spain and maintained domestic slavery. They pressed political leaders to abide by their own convictions, further highlighting the tension between slavery and independence from Spain that was also identified by slaves in other provinces. Building on earlier ideas expressed in the judicial forum, they voiced their aspirations for the freedom of all slaves and for political belonging in the new republic.

Mompox's Juan del Corral and Popayán's Felix José de Restrepo, now leading members of Antioquia's newly independent government, would eventually listen to the logic of the 1812 slave petitioners. Amalgamating the experiences and perspectives they had first begun to develop in Cartagena and Popayán, they invited their revolutionary colleagues to consider that prudent legislators and truly forward-looking governments had a supreme obligation to favor freedom over slavery. They proposed that aspiring to emancipation from Spain, an aspiration supported by natural law, would be incompatible with denying slaves their own liberation. Corral and Restrepo thus used the image of Spain as a cruel mistress beyond its metaphoric uses, though only after pressure from slaves and in the context of rising counter-revolutionary challenges.[7] In 1814, they crafted an antislavery law based on the free womb principle. It categorized slaves as "captives" to be redeemed by pious benefactors.[8] With an elite whose material life and sense of purpose did not pivot exclusively on slaveholding, Antioquia's initiative partially incorporated the slaves' own political propositions and was peacefully accepted by patrician families.

Based as it was on the free womb principle, and thus promising only gradual slave emancipation instead of the long-hoped for abrupt end to slavery, the law was correctly understood by slaves as a legal act with acute limitations and ambivalences. They held on to their conviction that nothing but finishing slavery altogether could remedy their unfair captivity, interpreting the limited legislation as just another liberation decree thwarted by the masters. For many slaves, the immediate end of slavery, rather than gradual slave emancipation, was the only coherent way forward.

Free people as well as slaves had a bearing on Antioquia's antislavery positions, though their exchanges of opinions were unequal and often mediated by force. Masters and slaves lived cheek by jowl in tightly packed Antioquia, and this gave some slaves the chance to directly gather political information from high places. Slaves ruminated on this information and what it might portent for their own future. Gregorio, Antonio, and Joaquín, Restrepo's slaves, signed the petition in 1812 and stood in intimate, servile proximity to the provincial revolutionary elite, acting as part of a larger collective. Jose María Martínez, a restive slave who had already embarked on an individual quest for autonomy and freedom, would also serve the elite families who referred to themselves as slaves of Spanish tyranny. Directly and indirectly, everyday rebels and slave legal activists pressured revolutionary leaders to envision domestic slavery as part and parcel of Antioquia's political transformation.

Everyday Rebels

José María Martínez was born around 1789 in the Sacaojal hamlet, not far from the city of Antioquia on the farmstead of Bacilio and Salvadora Jaramillo (see Map 2). When he was about sixteen years old, José María did the heavy farm-work alongside two other young male slaves. They tended ten pigs, four goats, one mare, and the crops. An adult female slave oversaw the household tasks and cared for several slave children. The Jaramillos also owned a small property in the cool highlands of the Los Osos plateau. The older slaves traveled back and forth between the properties, often without the supervision of the masters, and sometimes defying their orders. Like most slaves in Antioquia, José María worked on a small estate, shared his duties with only a handful of other workers, and traveled and communicated across valleys and mountains with relative ease.[9]

Building on this relative autonomy, José María sought to defy his enslavement: by the time his master Bacilio died in 1805, he had already run away on at least one occasion. After Bacilio's death, José María and his nineteen year-old brother Gabino became more assertive and defiant.[10] They turned the death of the master into an opportunity to increase their own autonomy and achieve freedom. In 1806, as rumors circulated that a black Queen had arrived in Antioquia to set the slaves free, José María ran away.[11] The widow Jaramillo paid someone to hunt for and bring back José María, who had reached the

Magdalena River on the eastern border of the province. José María, she wrote, was likely to cause damage to the estate of her deceased husband for "whoever completes six leagues has no problem completing one hundred."[12] She was referring to his passage along the harsh roads during his escape and to her fear that José María would not rest until he had escaped. Little did she know that her words would prove premonitory. In later years, José María would see places that most people born in Antioquia could never imagine.

José María and Gabino recruited allies and resorted to litigation in their quest to get away from their master's widow. Gabino, if we believe the widow's account, sought refuge from slavery with a married woman, moving in with her in early 1807.[13] But he also sought legal advice, scoring an important judicial coup. A magistrate declared him *depositado* – legally placed with another master pending a final decision. José María left the farm again and requested that he be similarly placed with another master.[14] The siblings moved from informally defying their mistress to legally challenging her. Unfortunately, the only surviving evidence of Gabino and José María's legal quests is a letter written by the widow requesting the help of a magistrate in the provincial capital. Nevertheless, there remains some evidence that another slave from the Jaramillo farmstead brought complaints of mistreatment before the authorities. This third slave was placed with another owner on account of being "punished with excess by the widow."[15]

In her letter to the local magistrate, the widow Jaramillo declared she could no longer keep the slaves under subordination. She requested that the magistrate send José María and Gabino to prison, "with a shackle," offering to pay for their arrest and confinement with funds from the estate's probate. She also told the magistrate that the brothers should be sent to work at the main parish church of the city of Antioquia, now under construction. The arrests had to happen quickly, she advised, "to avoid scandals and robberies and to avoid having their idleness and lack of subordination lead them to do things damaging to the estate and for I fear that they may take to the road and be lost as was their brother."[16] It appears that yet another one of the Jaramillo slaves had also run away.

The magistrate or some other official listened to the widow's request, and José María and his brother were sent as laborers to the church construction site. While they remained enslaved, the two brothers had nonetheless escaped their abusive mistress. Their absence left the Jaramillo farm in disarray. By late 1807, the pigs were gone, the goats had been stolen, and the mare was nowhere to be found. Floodwaters had also damaged the land. To sell what little remained to fend off poverty, the widow searched for potential buyers, with no success. Despite her distrust of José María, who was now in the provincial capital working on the church construction, she convinced him to help her find a buyer. José María swiftly found someone willing to purchase the property at a discount.[17]

José María himself was also sold at a discount to a family of high standing in the provincial capital. On March 4, 1808, the patrician lawyer Faustino Martínez bought José María for just over 66 pesos, a low price for a young slave.[18] José María's new master was a patron of the parish construction project. Later that year, Faustino also purchased the royal post of *alguacil mayor* in Antioquia's cabildo, becoming the chief enforcer of the local government's authority. He alone could enter town council sessions while bearing arms.[19] His father, Juan Esteban Martínez, directed the construction of the parish church and served as *mayordomo* of the Blessed Sacrament brotherhood. He also administered the affairs of other brotherhoods. A devout man who was directly linked with important corporations and families in Antioquia, Juan Esteban was a stern and respected spiritual and political leader.[20] José María was now enslaved by a clan with influence in politics. By year's end, he would have overheard his masters' discussions about current affairs – the absent king, the usurper Napoleon, the invasion of the Peninsula. José María saw the imminent political crisis up close, and he would witness the unfolding of revolution firsthand.

The Revolution of Antioquia

Alarming news arrived in Antioquia in August 1810: Santa Fe had formed a junta in July, and the viceroy and Audiencia judges had been thrown out of office. The New Kingdom of Granada lacked a visible head, and the constituent members of the body politic were pulling apart. Antioquia elites would manage to fend off civil war, even though they were as internally divided as Cartagena or Popayán patricians.[21] In spite of an old rivalry pitching the city of Antioquia and the *villa* of Medellín against each other, the leading criollo families coordinated a unified response to the crisis, bringing together leaders from the four urban centers with functioning cabildos. Delegates from Medellín, Rionegro, and Marinilla arrived in the city of Antioquia on August 30. Local notables, including Francisco and Manuel María Martínez, also members of the Martínez clan, hosted the meeting of this "Provincial Alliance."[22] This rare display of unity laid the foundations for the peaceful and original initiatives that would follow.

José María must have caught a glimpse of the Alliance's proceedings, maybe even heard his master's friends assuring each other about their loyalty to the deposed monarch – though not to the Regency or the deposed viceroy. Antioquia leaders planned to take full control of the provincial government. This measure would help them prevent a Napoleonic invasion, internal division, and a potential power grab from Santa Fe. Indeed, members of the old viceregal capital's junta claimed to possess the government privileges of the deposed viceroy. Arguing that Santa Fe was no longer the head of a now atomized Kingdom but only the head of its own province, Antioquia patricians established a Provincial Congress, seeking to lead their own public affairs on behalf of the absent king.[23]

The Provincial Congress transformed itself into a Provincial Junta, which in turn further changed Antioquia's form of government and formalized its autonomy. This junta published a set of rules that some people referred to as a "constitution" meant to govern provincial affairs until either the king was restored to the throne, or the "people" were duly represented in a Spanish parliament. The door to independence was thus subtly left open. Unless they obtained parliamentary representation in the metropole, Antioquia leaders reserved the right to maintain their autonomy. Other steps were less subtle, however. The new authorities pressured the king-appointed governor to resign in February 1811. Furthermore, the junta now adopted a formal but temporary constitution, the "Rules of Provisional Constitution for the State of Antioquia," ratified on June 27. Naming Antioquia a "State" instead of a province and establishing separation of powers, the Provisional Constitution openly embraced republican principles. Despite pushback from a pro-Regency faction in Medellín and some reluctant members of the Martínez clan in the city of Antioquia, the establishment of an autonomous government had been peacefully achieved. In the process, public allegiance to the monarchy had begun to give way.[24]

Mompox's Juan del Corral became an important participant in this revolutionary process. Born in 1778 and raised in the reformist environment of his hometown, he was an early supporter of the transformation of Antioquia's government. Like other merchant families in Mompox, Corral's family had strong connections with Antioquia: his father was a business associate of the rich merchant Juan Pablo Pérez de Rublas, and soon after settling down in Antioquia at the end of the eighteenth century, Corral married Pérez de Rublas's daughter. He became a member of the provincial capital's cabildo, and quickly achieved prestige as an active trader, cacao grower, and land speculator. His mother-in-law was Rita Martínez, a sister of Faustino Martínez, José María's master.[25]

Corral, alongside the lawyer José Manuel Restrepo (a relative of Felix José de Restrepo's and a former habitué of the tertulias in Santa Fe), helped design the new institutions and a new permanent constitution. These and other budding revolutionaries steeped in modern philosophy and natural law set up an Electoral and Constituent College. Elections for representatives to this assembly took place in November 1811. The College debated a constitutional project authored by Corral and José Manuel Restrepo. Unanimously supported by the constituents, the new Constitution of the State of Antioquia went into effect in May 1812. Juan Esteban Martínez and his brother Manuel Antonio were signatories of the new charter.[26]

While it did not declare formal independence from Spain, Antioquia's Constitution made no declaration of loyalty to the king. It stated that all monarchs are "equal to the rest of men," stipulating that the people of Antioquia had every right to elect their own king, or to do away with monarchy altogether, choosing a form of government that would better suit their aspirations for peace, justice, and happiness. The Constitution guaranteed the separation of powers and held equality before the law as one of the fundamental "rights of man." From now on, no privilege could be inherited, and the notion that a man could be born "King, Magistrate, Legislator, or Judge" was declared "absurd and contrary to nature." The Constitution also protected other "natural rights," including the defense and preservation of one's own life and the search of security and happiness. Roman Catholicism continued to be the official and sole religion of this State.[27]

Corral now sought to further enact the egalitarian sensibility promoted by his father and other leaders in Mompox. Like his forbears, he believed equality had to be practiced. In a most telling example, he planned to bring legal equality to the local militias. When he drafted the general rules for a reformed militia for Antioquia, he introduced an egalitarian innovation. To avoid "division" and foster "homogeneity" among militia personnel, Corral eliminated the genealogical and color distinctions that had ordered military service under the Spanish regime. Instead of units segregated according to their ancestry and closeness to slavery, the new militias would be divided by municipal jurisdictions. They would simply be called "Patriotas de Defensa," identified collectively with their respective towns as opposed to any of the old hierarchical rankings.[28]

Nevertheless, the Antioquia elite's remarkable show of political unity partially stemmed from their fear of "anarchy," by which they meant any challenges to their power and prestige. Unlike many of their Cartagena counterparts, they sought no explicit alliance with people of color. Their commitment to equality was tempered by the masters' worries of a world turned upside down. Rival families came together not only to prevent foreign threats to their autonomy but also to defuse a potential plebeian uprising at home. José Manuel Restrepo warned his colleagues about the constant threat of a "slave rebellion."[29] Among the slaves of Medellín's Restrepo clan, discussions about legal emancipation and divine punishment for the masters had been reported as early as 1798. Fearful that slaves might strike for their freedom and that social climbers flush with gold might join forces to push for radical equality, Antioquia families of Spanish stock came together to preserve their positions of power.[30] Slaves would be given no new hopes and no political belonging in the new republic. They were meant to remain denizens rather than become members of the new polity.

Furthermore, Antioquia's Constitution offered no new avenues to slave emancipation. Among the "natural" rights protected by Antioquia's Constitution was the right to property – which tacitly included the property of other human beings. Constitutional rights, moreover, only extended to *patres familias* – free citizens over twenty-five who headed a household and were economically independent. Women and slaves were left out. The Revolution of Antioquia had been successfully managed by people who feared slave uprisings and simultaneously aspired to keep their slaves in bondage, and yet, like patricians elsewhere, Antioquia's emerging republican elite saw themselves as the undoers of Spain's cruel and illegitimate mastery.

Unsurprisingly, slaves noticed this tension between declarations of liberation from Spain based on natural rights and their own continuing enslavement. News that the Constitution's language included a rejection of "slavery and chains" spread fast among expectant slave communities.[31] Although the Constitution only referred to rejecting the chains imposed by Spain on Antioquia, many slaves argued that such rejection should be meant to include domestic slavery. Soon after the Constitution went into effect, the newly established Supreme Tribunal of Justice in Medellín received a collective petition from about 200 slaves from the municipalities of Antioquia, Medellín, Rionegro, and Marinilla.[32] The type of cross-district collaboration among Antioquia slaves, suspected, misrepresented, and thwarted by masters and magistrates since the times of the Comunero Revolution, now seemed more robust than ever.

Finally, a group of slave activists had been able to enter the judicial forum on their own terms, filing a *representación*, a collective petition on behalf of all slaves. The petition implied that their liberty was consubstantial with their humanity. They represented their captivity as an illegitimate act of force, particularly under the newly independent legal order. The slaves wrote in their petition that news had arrived long ago that their freedom had been granted, something they even knew directly from the "words of our own masters." They claimed to have learned from the Constitution that "God our lord made us free and independent from slavery." Moreover, they had heard from the authorities that everybody was "equal." Their petition had one goal only: "to know if this is true."[33] Straightforward and deceptively simple, the slaves' goal nonetheless reflected a complex political stand.

In 1812 the petitioners understood that a written republican Constitution, unlike the unwritten and venerable constitution of the monarchy, was within the reach of people and that the charter was open to political exegesis. The revolutionary imperative to write constitutions indeed rested on the idea that a constitution did not have to

pre-date the social compact. In other words, if the patrician revolutionaries believed they were constituting a new society on the explicit and
free will of the associates, the constitution guaranteeing this new pact
had to be made from scratch and could be modified according to
political developments and the test of time. The slave petitioners saw
the ongoing revolution as an opportunity to instate a new community,
one that would finally offer them explicit political belonging and equal
legal protections. A written constitution, they clearly understood, was
a fundamental law adopted by a people rather than imposed upon it.[34]
Their quest was to press the authorities to see them as part of this
people, and to decide whether slavery was compatible with this new
society in the making.

Despite the slaves' recourse to legal channels, high magistrates
treated these petitioners as criminal conspirators. Several slaves from
the Restrepo clan figured among the leaders of this legal quest. These
included Gregorio, Antonio, and Joaquín, Félix José de Restrepo's
slaves. The slave José María Martínez did not formally support the
petition, but his master Faustino was now a magistrate in the Supreme
Tribunal. Although Faustino and the other judges accused slave
leaders of planning to take their freedom with violence, there is no
evidence of this. Instead, Antioquia slaves, like their counterparts in
Popayán during the challenges to governor Tacón, set out to highlight
the contradictions and conflicts of interest of the slaveholders-turned-
revolutionary leaders, and the tensions of their constitutional regime.
Their masters' new Constitution denounced "despotism" and "tyranny," but it simultaneously kept thousands in chains; it called for
equality while giving no citizenship rights to slaves. The organizers of
this legal challenge were thrown in jail, and some were sentenced to
forced labor or were banished to other jurisdictions.[35] Antioquia's
leaders had kept "anarchy" at bay.

By mid-1813, alarming developments in the south threatened
Antioquia's peace. Spanish pro-Regency troops had re-occupied the
city of Popayán. They looted towns and countryside as they marched
north, and their advance on Antioquia seemed imminent. Lacking
military resources and experience, the State of Antioquia was not
ready to face battle. Desperate, political leaders decided to partially
suspend their new constitutional regime, naming a Rome-inspired
"dictator" to swiftly prepare the defense of the land. They chose

Corral, whose revolutionary spirit and talent in statecraft were now famous. He assumed dictatorial powers at the end of July.[36]

With full powers, Corral was free to to protect Antioquia with zeal. He energetically moved on staunch monarchists who revealed their true colors by actively making plans against the new government. He confiscated their property and banished them from the State. Through these measures, well over 60,000 pesos were transferred to the government's coffers. Among the expelled royalists was José María's master, Faustino Martínez. The now deposed magistrate departed for Cartagena, en route to Jamaica, taking José María with him.[37] Although he would later return, the slave José María would not witness the further radicalization of the Revolution of Antioquia. This new stage in the political transformation would even include a partial answer to the organized slaves who had robustly questioned whether slavery was compatible with the new form of government.

Free Womb

Escaping civil war and political uncertainty, Félix José de Restrepo had left Popayán in 1812, arriving in Antioquia by year's end. Corral and other Antioquia revolutionary leaders were pleased to see the famous magistrate and professor return to his native land. They invited him to advise the new government, which he did while teaching modern philosophy in Medellín. Restrepo closely collaborated with Corral, and they were further radicalized in their anti-Spanish sentiments by August 1813. Following the news from Europe that Napoleon's armies had been finally defeated in Spain, these and other leaders throughout the old viceroyalty now anticipated that a direct clash with re-grouping Spanish peninsular forces was inevitable.[38]

Corral and his closest advisers decided that an absolute and formal declaration of independence from Spain was needed. With the threat of invasion from Popayán and the possibility that Spain might finally be able to send reinforcements, the idea gained momentum. On August 11, 1813, the State formally ceased to recognize Ferdinand VII as its absent monarch, rejecting any authority "not emanating directly from the people, or its representatives." Antioquia broke "the political union of dependence with the Metropole," declaring itself "forever separated from the Crown and government of Spain." Like other peoples now liberated from the "yoke" of Spain, Antioquia embraced its liberty as a "gift from Heaven and from nature." Antioquia's "Act of Independence" was crafted using the idiom of slave emancipation that had proved so useful before: Antioquia was portrayed as an abject slave redeemed by Corral. In a turn of phrase reminiscent of Restrepo's early propositions about slavery, Antioquia's declaration of independence was deemed an ideal avenue for the people through which they might reach the "summit of their dignity."[39]

The argument that independence led to dignity had consequences for slavery in Antioquia, since Restrepo had previously argued that dignity should extend to the slaves as well. In a partial response to slave pressure and given the shifting political circumstances, antislavery arguments that first began to develop in the judicial forum now became entangled with revolutionary politics. Antioquia's new government, Restrepo insisted, had to improve the conditions of the slaves. Corral agreed. The Citizen Dictator was no stranger to the slaves' struggles and expectations of freedom. As an in-law of the Martínez clan, he might have been aware of José María's previous struggle to get away from the widow Jaramillo. Most importantly, Corral and Restrepo had been alarmed by the petition presented in 1812 by organized slaves demanding coherence from those who spoke of a natural right to freedom while keeping people in chains. Slavery should be reformed, Corral and Restrepo now openly argued, and the sooner the better.[40]

By the end of 1813, Corral implicitly but publicly provided an initial answer to the slaves who questioned why the new government's rejection of slavery and chains did not include a repudiation of their own enslavement. Claiming liberty from Spain, Corral told his peers, was incompatible with keeping people in slavery. The "love of freedom," he wrote, is as present in the heart of a slave "humiliated" under the will of a master as it is in the heart of free patricians devoted to their "original rights" and "independence." Unless the new government was willing to fall back under the authority of Spain or be the victim of a long-touted slave uprising, revolutionary leaders had to better the lot of the slaves. Freedom from Spain, he insisted in a report to Antioquia's legislature in early 1814, would not be consolidated until freedom from slavery was realized. Even the "shadow" of slavery had to disappear.[41]

In practice, however, Corral's commitment to slave emancipation proved less radical than suggested in principle. Corral understood that immediate and complete abolition – the unconditional liberation of all the slaves from the power of their masters – was a distinct possibility. He referred to it as "general slave manumission" and "universal manumission," but he claimed that this approach would have "mortal" consequences for the republic. "Drunk" with "sudden emancipation," he asserted, freed people would abandon any restraint on their criminal behavior. In other words, he continued to rely on long-held stereotypes about slaves, using the same kind of canards and apprehensions typically used by masters to paint slaves as a dangerous, conspiratorial lot bent on turning the world upside down. Corral would not consider the slaves as members of the body politic who had to be freed on account of their human dignity, as the petitioners in 1812 and other Antioquia claimants and some magistrates suggested even before 1810. Instead, Corral and Restrepo came together to develop a legislation project that would theoretically end slavery over time. Based on Antonio de Villavicencio's plan, which Restrepo had read in Popayán, this project hinged on the application of the free womb principle and the creation of mechanisms for the "successive emancipation" of adult slaves.[42]

On April 20, 1814, just a few days after Corral died unexpectedly, Antioquia's legislature passed the "Law on the Manumission of the African Slaves' Offspring and on the Means to Successively Redeem their Parents." This was the only antislavery law ever passed during this early revolutionary period in the old viceroyalty. It was also the model for the manumission law that would be passed by Colombia's General Congress in 1821. Antioquia's manumission law declared the children of enslaved women to be free at birth, discarding the legal principle that slavery was transmitted from mother to child. The legislation, however, left standing the hierarchical relationship of power binding together masters and slaves: in short, slaves were to remain enslaved. The law categorized them as "captives," calling for manumission boards to collect funds to pay for their progressive liberation. While it also called for masters to support the free children of their slaves for the first sixteen years of their lives, these children had to reciprocate by working for the masters and respecting them as patriarchs. This attrition tactic would theoretically bring an end to slavery in the future, "leveling the classes" to secure stability for the new republic.[43] Those who sympathized with immediate, general slave emancipation must have been disappointed.

For the State's leaders, Antioquia's antislavery legislation achieved other immediate goals. First, the manumission law allowed them to partially fend off the charge of political incoherence articulated by slaves in 1812, resolving somewhat the tension between liberty from Spain and domestic slavery. The legislation stated that freedom from Spain was incompatible with slavery, and that facilitating slave emancipation would perfect the work of independence. Bringing liberty to the "peoples of America" had no other goal than to turn vassals into virtuous, just citizens, worthy of enjoying their natural rights. Even slaves would thus be brought, through republican law, into the "class of citizens" to enjoy a "just and equitable" government, one that could never be achieved "under the barbaric laws of Spain." Political emancipation and slave emancipation were thus legally recognized to be irrevocably bound. The link between the two was no longer metaphorical but literal – a point made by the slave petitioners in 1812.

Second, Antioquia's manumission law established the bona fides of revolutionaries like Corral and Restrepo as prudent legislators who followed the doctrines of modern philosophy. They revered Filangieri, who believed the end of slavery was an enterprise that concerned not only the slaves themselves but wise legislators and the whole of humanity. They read Montesquieu, who had declared slavery incompatible with a "prudent" form of government. Antislavery legislation was thus interpreted as the most sublime exercise of the prudent, forward-looking legislator, whose goal was to bring into harmony revelation, law, and the principles of nature to improve the human condition.[44] As a crime against the "imprescriptible rights of the liberty of men" and the "inviolable rights of humanity and reason," slavery seemed the ideal field through which to exercise a new approach to legislation that would propel humankind toward a brighter future.[45]

This idiom of humanity permeated Antioquia's antislavery legislative experiment. Corral had called on Antioquia's lawmakers to build the "most sumptuous monument to humanity" – an antislavery law. The fate of the slaves was, in his estimation, an affair that interested "the whole of humankind."[46] Manumission boards established in

Antioquia to gradually emancipate slaves with public funds were fittingly called *Juntas de amigos de la humanidad* – Boards of Friends of Humanity. Any citizen who willingly freed at least sixteen slaves (excluding the old and infirm) would be graced with official recognition as "Meritorious Citizen of the Republic and Friend of humanity."[47]

However, old prejudices against slaves and their descendants continued to influence slaveholders, and these pre-existing stereotypes were even built into the new legislation. Unlike Cartagena, with its radical egalitarian leaders, independent Antioquia did not publicly denounce such prejudices and stereotypes. Antioquia leaders' commitment to equality proved less central to their politics and more cautious in its scope. Antislavery magistrates thus presumed that freeborn children of slaves would hardly be able to surpass their parents' supposed low moral caliber and naturally bad inclinations. Though freeborn and potential citizens, they were still deemed deserving of unequal treatment. The manumission law anticipated that some of those children would grow to be "immoral and depraved" adults or would "abuse" their freedom. In such cases, the offenders would be sent back to the custody of the manumission boards. Antioquia's gradualist approach also stipulated mechanisms to prevent the freeing of adults considered to be unworthy of emancipation by the manumission boards.[48] Even as they increasingly rejected the Spanish regime, early republican, slaveholding leaders were less assertive against the kinds of essentialist assumptions inherent in the old hierarchical order.

And yet the State of Antioquia also created clear and practical enforcing mechanisms for its antislavery legislation. On the death of every slaveholder with legal heirs, the law mandated, one in every ten slaves would be freed. If no heirs existed, a fourth of the slaves would be manumitted. Masters had to report the number of their captives to census takers, and they would lose any slave not accounted for. Unreported slaves would be granted freedom without compensation for the masters. Funds for the liberation of slaves would be collected from donations as well as from taxes on slaveholding. Masters had to pay two pesos a year for every adult male slave and one peso for every woman. Moreover, the State tapped *mandas forzosas*, long-standing compulsory donations for the "redemption of Christian captives, upkeep of the Holy Places of Jerusalem, and for wedding orphan women."[49] These testamentary contributions, allocated by the king of Spain for the liberation of Christians captured by Muslims in the Mediterranean, would now be used to "redeem" Antioquia slaves from their captivity. Slave manumission was thus ingeniously presented as a traditional religious obligation, and an old tax was cloaked in new garb.[50]

The State gave further teeth to its manumission law through an executive decree in September 1814. This decree established six Boards of Friends of Humanity throughout the autonomous republic, and Félix José de Restrepo joined the Medellín Board. Public notaries and judges were ordered to participate in the antislavery effort. Charged with collecting taxes on slaveholding, these and other agents also had to take a census of the enslaved population within a month and would select the slaves to be publicly manumitted every year over Easter, starting with elderly captives.[51] Because only fragments of the documents produced by the State are extant, it is difficult to ascertain how many slaves obtained emancipation in this way. However, the surviving evidence suggests that the Boards were quite diligent, especially if compared with the later boards called for by Colombia's manumission law of 1821, which took several years to begin their work and largely failed in their mission.[52] Moreover, the fiscal pressure on small slaveholders led some Antioquia masters to simply free a few of their slaves instead of paying the annual tax. Even a wealthy master emancipated eighty slaves in exchange for recognition as "friend of humanity."[53]

Between mid-1814 and March 1816, some slaves also achieved emancipation through other means facilitated by the revolutionary government. Even before the passing of the manumission law, authorities offered slaves paid jobs at Antioquia's new saltpeter facilities. They were expected to save their salaries to purchase their own emancipation, but once on the work site they were already deemed freed from bondage – able, for example, to freely marry. Some may have also taken jobs at the newly established mint and armory as an avenue to freedom, and others were sent to the army instead of their master's children in exchange for their freedom after military service.[54]

But even in the relatively effervescent antislavery environment of this State, the tensions between slavery and freedom, and the hierarchical power of the masters over slaves, would not be easily solved. The State of Antioquia's initiatives left most existing slaves in captivity. Restrepo, at least since he had read Villavicencio's plan, had sided with the idea that the rights of the "proprietors" had to be respected in the process of ending slavery.[55] With the exception of some slaves, like the petitioners in 1812, few seemed willing to consider, let alone commit, to abolition. Thus, although antislavery became a trademark of the ongoing revolutionary process, the end of slavery remained beyond reach. When Antioquia sent copies of its manumission law to neighboring autonomous provinces, including Popayán, the expected emulation of its antislavery initiative failed to materialize. To many slaves, however, even Antioquia's efforts looked moderate and incoherent.

Less than pleased with Antioquia's gradual approach, groups of slaves gathered again to discuss the situation. Some remembered expectations of general emancipation dating back to the 1780s, as well as the rumor that a higher power had legally decreed general emancipation, but the masters and local magistrates illegally withheld the decree. Now many interpreted the manumission law as solid evidence that the abolition of slavery had finally arrived. Masters and magistrates, slaves believed, were simply continuing to withhold the benefits granted them by a higher authority. The old rumor had a somewhat more visible basis this time: the manumission law had been passed in April 1814, but it was meant to be kept secret until August. Even after the actual contents of the law became public, some slaves continued to discuss the imminent end of their captivity with the assumption that the antislavery law had already fully emancipated them. Others believed the end of slavery would only materialize on Easter (the annual holiday on which Boards were expected to enact collective emancipations). Still others revived the familiar narrative that all they had to do to gain freedom was pay the government. Three pesos was the fee, was the report that circulated this time.[56]

Between 1812 and 1815, some slaves' long-standing expectations for the end of slavery and their incorporation as members of the body politic rose to the surface of Antioquia politics. Though rejected as a criminal act by the magistrates, the slaves' petition of 1812 partially shaped Antioquia's subsequent antislavery initiatives. Born from a peaceful political transformation, led by revolutionaries who identified as prudent and humanitarian legislators, and with its autonomy increasingly threatened by the looming Restoration, independent Antioquia took the most serious antislavery stance of this early revolutionary period. Besides pressure from slaves, the masters' economic and social circumstances may have also played a role in the process. Slaveholders whose income, identity, and sense of purpose did not rest heavily on ownership of slaves did not resist the limited intrusions of the new government on their privileges – including the imposition of new taxes and the expectations that they would liberate some slaves. Nonetheless, these antislavery projects ended early. The independent government was dissolved in 1816, and subsequent events set the broader revolutionary process on a different path.

The Colombian Path

The anticipated invasion of Antioquia from the south never took place. A bigger threat, however, began to form with the return of Ferdinand VII to the Spanish throne in the spring of 1814. By September, Antioquia inhabitants learned that the monarch had set out to restore "shameful despotism." After dissolving the relatively liberal regime that had formed in his absence in Spain, the restored monarch set out to quash the revolutionary movements in the Spanish Indies. The task, the king's strategists decided, had to commence by defeating the State of Cartagena and bringing under control the New Kingdom of Granada. Once superficially hailed as the absent lord of Spain's New World domains, the king was now firmly denounced as a "crowned monster" ready to re-enslave the free Americas, becoming once again a "chief of slaves." Formed by personnel seasoned in the Napoleonic wars, Spain's Expeditionary Army besieged and defeated Cartagena. The port city fell to General Pablo Morillo in early December 1815. The independent State ended, and the king was restored.[57] The process was repeated in all the remaining autonomous states.

Unlike in Spain, the Spanish Restoration came with harsh and violent measures in some regions of the New Kingdom. Cartagena put up a fierce fight, and triumphant Spanish troops executed several of the revolutionary leaders. The group included José María García de Toledo, who had led an "aristocratic" effort to come to terms with Spain. His "popular" rivals, the craftsman Pedro Romero and the Piñeres brethren, escaped to the Antilles. As they advanced inland,

Morillo and his officers ordered more executions throughout the restored viceroyalty. The general arrived in Santa Fe on May 26, 1816. Camilo Torres, who had been an early and ardent supporter of independence while his family struggled to keep the slaves of San Juan under their power, was executed in Santa Fe.[58]

News of the fall of Cartagena arrived in Antioquia in January 1816. On March 16, advanced Spanish troops attacked Antioquia's northernmost military detachment on the Magdalena.[59] The revolutionary government was dissolved by the end of the month. The high magistrates and their supporters tried to escape. Some were arrested; others gave themselves up. The Restoration in Antioquia was completed by March 24. To avoid the fate of their Cartagena colleagues, Antioquia's leaders used subterfuges to elicit sympathy from Spanish officers, and gold to bribe them. Some Medellín patricians alleged Juan del Corral, a tyrant inspired by French revolutionary principles, had forced them to follow his lead. José Manuel Restrepo facilitated the delivery of 20,000 pesos to the restored authorities, and Spain's leading officer in the region pocketed a portion of the money. Félix José de Restrepo claimed he had been forced to support the revolutionary government. He had rejected administrative positions, he told the restored authorities, and had only taken on certain responsibilities under pressure. Included in an amnesty extended by the new viceroy, Restrepo swore allegiance to Ferdinand VII in 1817. Many other leaders did the same, thus escaping the firing squad.[60]

The re-establishment of the viceroyalty sparked hopes for the exiled royalist Faustino Martínez, who set sail for the New Kingdom after three years of exile in Jamaica, bringing along his slave José María Martínez.[61] Although he had caused headaches for his owners on the Jaramillo farmstead, José María claimed he had behaved as a "loving servant" during his years in Jamaica.[62] However, a report was made that José María's disrespect for his master and other free people had been already evident in their journey out of Antioquia in 1813. Apparently, the master kept José María around but was unable to fully control him. Although no master had ever seemed able to gain unconditional obedience from José María, he had also never fully escaped the reach of those who claimed him as property.[63]

Now José María was ready to take that final step to freedom. As his master's political position shifted unexpectedly, the opportunity finally presented itself. As early as January 1816, Faustino offered his lawyerly services to General Morillo, who named him *auditor de guerra* – legal adviser to the Expeditionary Army.[64] Faustino participated in the tribunal that executed dozens that year, and José María, still under his master's orders, witnessed this repression at close range. By year's end, the General dismissed Faustino,[65] placing him in a vulnerable position for a while, short of money and with no job. José María seized his chance and ran away. As he would later recall in a petition to formalize his freedom, he "deserted" his master and proceeded to "wander" about the country for the next three years.[66]

As he roamed throughout the restored New Kingdom, José María would have seen that all important towns and most roads were back under Spanish control. But he probably also learned that some surviving revolutionary leaders had retreated to backcountry areas, supporting from time to time a guerrilla war against Spanish forces, both in the New Kingdom as well as in neighboring Venezuela. In their efforts to feed the army, stabilize the situation, and make money from their expedition, Spanish troops executed people, plundered, and requisitioned from patricians and plebeians alike. While revolutionary authorities had been lenient with those who opposed them, Restoration officials proved unforgiving. Spanish forces, which included scores of local troops, were also plagued by internecine strife. The Expeditionary Army found it difficult to enact a coherent policy, at times facing opposition from Spanish civil administrators. Meanwhile, anti-Spanish guerrilla fighters gained military experience, popular support, and unity of purpose.[67]

A small but popular and mobile armed uprising was now crystallizing, its leaders increasingly concentrating on defeating Morillo. Led by men with military backgrounds who called themselves *libertadores*, this revolution took a new approach. Under the leadership of the Venezuelan Simón Bolívar, an army of *llaneros* (plainsmen on horseback from the Orinoco flatlands), European mercenaries, and soldiers from Haiti climbed the Andes to take Santa Fe from its eastern flank, a demanding maneuver Spanish officers failed to anticipate. Once in the highlands, many people near the capital flocked to Bolívar's forces, strengthening his unlikely move. Following Bolívar's August 7 victory on the field of Boyacá, just north of Santa Fe, Spanish authorities abandoned the capital. Unopposed, Bolívar entered the city on August 9.[68]

Bolívar's revolution also took a different political approach, giving fresh meaning to the enterprise of independence from Spain. In December, Bolívar and his allies met in Congress at Angostura, on the banks of the Orinoco. Rejecting the early drive for provincial sovereignties, so vigorously cultivated by political leaders in Antioquia and Cartagena, the libertadores agreed that a large and centralized republic had to be formed. Together, Venezuela and the old New Kingdom should constitute a single republic. It would be called Colombia. It would be an undivided state with the capacity to extend its liberating influence all over Spanish South America. On December 17, the Angostura Congress passed the "Fundamental law of the Republic of Colombia." To consolidate the Republic, a general legislative congress would follow in 1821, with delegates from all over the new polity's territory.[69]

After Boyacá, Bolívar dispatched a column to re-take Antioquia. The liberating force pushed fast into the province. Spanish colonel Carlos Tolrá fled north along with thirty of the king's soldiers. Royalist civilians followed his escape route. Faustino Martínez, who had become an adviser to officer Tolrá, took to the road with other soldiers a few days later. Faustino became the head of the last royalist faction in Antioquia, but he was the target of an intense pursuit by Colombian soldiers who probably had orders to kill him.[70] Meanwhile, Bolívar's operatives established a new government in Antioquia, appointing José Manuel Restrepo the political governor of the province and Félix José de Restrepo the director of the new printing office.[71]

The new government confiscated the property of many royalists and enforced "voluntary" donations for the "cause of independence." The royalist wing of the Martínez clan was pressed hard, and Faustino's father, Juan Esteban Martínez, contributed 500 pesos. Manuel Antonio Martínez had to pay an equal amount, and Eugenio Martínez was to supply the new government with 200 pesos.[72] At the same time, the army recruited fresh soldiers and welcomed volunteers. With their decisive triumphs, assertive measures, and the force of their growing army, the liberators achieved popular support and political legitimacy. The Restrepos and other survivors of the Restoration, once committed to their provincial polities, now followed the new path of a centralist republic.

Increasing numbers of people of African descent, particularly slaves and escaped slaves, joined the liberators after the battle of Boyacá. Some must have heard that Bolívar would bring the end of slavery to the liberated territories – a promise he had made in 1816 to the Haitian leader Alexandre Pétion in exchange for logistical support. Bolívar had even asked the Angostura Congress to abolish slavery altogether. But these promises never fully materialized. It was only in early 1820 that Bolívar explicitly reiterated the offer of freedom, but only for slaves willing to join his forces.[73] José María Martínez, who had at some point returned to his native Antioquia, had already joined the army in 1819.[74] He was assigned to a military unit under the orders of Lieutenant Buenaventura Correa, who had also rushed to join the new army after Boyacá.[75]

In a remarkable twist of fate, José María's military unit was charged with pursuing the royalists led by his old master, Faustino.[76] Faustino's plan was to reach Cartagena and then set sail for Jamaica. José María and his fellow soldiers marched north after the fleeing royalists. Though they took some prisoners and confiscated military supplies, Faustino and other leading men kept several steps ahead. He made it to Cartagena territory along with four Spanish officers.[77] In the end, Faustino got away. He was probably never aware that his escaped slave, now comporting himself as a free man, was among the pursuing soldiers. With his life now entwined with the nascent Republic of Colombia, José María seemed to have finally overturned his masters' authority over him and taken hold of his destiny.

Following this campaign, José María served as a freshwater sailor in the Magdalena River. As the liberators retook the province of Cartagena, José María saw action again in 1820, worked at a mobile military hospital, and was stationed near Mompox.[78] A long, convoluted decade had passed since he had first witnessed his master's reaction to the political crisis of 1810. Over this decade, he had proved the widow Jaramillo right in her apprehension that he would reach faraway places and slip away from those claiming him as property. Perhaps hoping to turn military service into formal manumission, he had even joined an epochal revolution, but José María left the army before securing his freedom papers, a decision he soon regretted.

On August 28, 1822, the Colombian government formally authorized masters to reclaim their wartime runaway slaves. Some masters moved to re-enslave runways who were not working as soldiers. Martínez, whose informal freedom now seemed particularly fragile, had a choice to make.[79] On January 17, 1823, he re-enlisted in the army, to avoid re-enslavement. He signed up as a soldier "for the duration of the war." The Republic of Colombia continued its fight against Spain on a continental scale, concentrating on the liberation campaign of Perú and Upper Perú (Bolivia). Many of Martínez's fellow combatants from 1819 to 1820 participated in the events. José María Martínez, however, remained stationed in Antioquia, where he would face his final challenge.[80]

A little less than a year after his reenlistment, a Colombian military tribunal charged José María Martínez with murder. He was arrested on December 31, 1823, at the house of the patrician Juan Pablo Arrubla –a member of the Martínez clan. Earlier that day, José María had sought refuge with his former masters after wounding another man in a street fight in the city of Antioquia.[81] On his deathbed, the victim declared that José María had attacked him with premeditation. That afternoon, the dying man also mentioned, José María had robbed him of some silver coins that slipped out of his pocket during a "masquerade party." He went to the authorities and accused José María of theft, which might have motivated the attack. José María mortally wounded his accuser on the left side of the abdomen.[82]

José María was sent to the military tribunal in Medellín. He was tried and found guilty of voluntary homicide during a fight. The crime was punishable by death. On July 10, 1824, at four in the afternoon, José María Martínez was shot by a firing squad.[83] His case was not unique. In the end, José María was another casualty of the everyday violence that had become common around this time. Félix José de Restrepo, now chief magistrate of the new Colombian High Court of Justice in Bogotá (formerly Santa Fe) and the highest martial judge, came across growing evidence of this deteriorating environment. The excesses of army officers, brawls involving unruly soldiers, increasing banditry on the roads, and urban crime were common after 1821. Some of the criminal cases reached Restrepo's desk in Bogotá.[84]

Soldiers like José María, with little money and no prospects in a country devastated by years of conflict, were prone to restlessness and trouble; their lives were often cut short as a result. By contrast, his former commanding officer, Buenaventura Correa, from a family of high standing, went on to become a captain, stayed in the army until 1830, and then returned to his "career of letters." He went back to his books to prepare himself for ordination as a priest, enjoying the property he had inherited from his deceased father and the pension he was later entitled to receive.[85] Both Correa and Martínez had joined the liberators, but the new Republic struggled to place all new citizens on an equal footing, including its citizen-soldiers. And when their visible African ancestry revealed their enslaved background, coming up in the world remained as daunting as ever, even for those lucky enough to obtain formal emancipation.

* * *

Over the course of its political transformation from province of Spain into independent republic, Antioquia witnessed a remarkable, unequal exchange between republican leaders and slave leaders. In 1812, soon after the publication of the Constitution, a cross-district slave coalition took Antioquia's new authorities to task, directly questioning whether it was coherent for the newly freed polity to become a slaveholding republic. Slave leaders pressured the new government to act in accordance with the principles of the Constitution, its mandate for equality and its explicit rejection of enslavement and tyranny. Partly as an answer to this petition, and in the context of a radicalization of Antioquia's anti-Spanish position, Corral and Restrepo wrote a gradual manumission law that was approved by the legislature in 1814.

Strongly articulated by slaves in their 1812 judicial petition, the conceptual link that bound antislavery initiatives and anti-Spanish politics was adopted as one of Antioquia's central political propositions. At first, emerging revolutionaries largely relied on slavery as a metaphor that allowed them to denounce Spanish tyranny. State leaders soon decided to take on domestic slavery and place their antislavery policies front and center in their platform. The manumission law was the first legislative act ever to be published by the gazette of this provincial state, taxes were imposed on slaveholders to fund slave emancipation, and public works employed slaves willing to save their salaries to purchase their freedom. Antioquia's antislavery stance was, moreover, defined as an exercise for the betterment of humanity, not just the benefit of the enslaved population. Heir to the egalitarian sensibilities that had developed in his native Mompox, Corral assured legislators that ending slavery would have a "leveling" effect on society, helping the republic achieve the "equilibrium of wealth" needed to bring about "equality" among its citizens.[86] In practice, however, the road to general slave emancipation and equality remained complicated.

Antioquia elites continued to fear slaves and other supposed social-climbers. Patricians avoided civil war in part to fend off the "anarchy" that they feared would result from manumission, hoping that a peaceful political transformation would prevent slaves from realizing their alleged plans to take their own freedom by force. Moreover, well-off families kept up-and-coming gold miners and merchants (many of them people of color with enslaved ancestry) from achieving positions of power in the emerging representative government. Inter-related families of Spanish stock and patrician standing firmly controlled Antioquia's legislature. Only one person of African descent was allowed to rise to the rank of senator; he owned property, had previously demonstrated his intellectual capacity as a Latin grammar instructor, and was chosen to fill a vacant seat.[87]

The law of 1814 did not end slavery, instead it left the power of the slaveholders over their slaves almost intact and the hierarchy of slavery largely unquestioned. Antioquia's manumission law left most adult slaves in their station as captives waiting to be redeemed by pious friends of humanity. The new State took concrete steps to start the herculean task of redemption. To many, however, it was clear that it would be impossible to end slavery without ending the privileges of slaveholding. Many slaves, especially those who believed that their immediate liberation was feasible, were unconvinced. The law failed to adopt an abolitionist stand to match their own expectations – a possibility that Corral and Restrepo had discarded on account of what they predicted would be its terrible consequences. However, some slaves openly discussed whether Antioquia's 1814 antislavery legislation should be taken to mean the complete end of slavery. The manumission law, they believed, had an abolitionist component, one that would become visible through accurate interpretation. Some would express these positions in the judicial forum, practicing an exegesis of liberty that built on a tradition of legal meditation and action. These individuals were at the vanguard of antislavery politics.

6

An Exegesis of Liberty

In the judicial forum, slaves, former slaves, magistrates, lawyers, and informal legal aides interpreted slavery and freedom. As they discerned the legality of individual enslavement or collective captivity, even suggesting that slaves and their offspring had the potential to become law-abiding members of the polity, some developed antislavery arguments well before the political crisis of 1810. With the early revolutions, however, antislavery propositions took on a more transformative potential. Expectations that God might end slavery and punish the masters, that just monarchs would free all slaves by decree, and that slaves could collectively petition municipal authorities for freedom and political belonging seemed to converge with the revolutionary idiom of liberty from Spain. Provincial revolutionary leaders spoke loudly about a natural right to shake off Spanish bondage, but slaves quickly noted that this liberation would be incomplete unless their own enslavement came to an end.

Some turned their interpretations of slavery and freedom into an exegesis of liberty, explicitly tying the cause of slave emancipation to the cause of emancipation from Spain. Seeking to expand the transformative potential of the representative form of government and the constitutional legal order, the Antioquia slave petitioners emerged as vanguard abolitionists in 1812. They scrutinized the policies, constitutions, and laws of the early provincial revolution, folding critical antislavery conventions from the judicial forum into emerging anti-Spanish, egalitarian, and republican doctrines. The metaphorical rejection of "slavery" and "chains"[1] should be perfected by making the liberation of slaves an immediate purpose of the new republic. Elaborating on the theme of political belonging, the petitioners suggested that slaves (and future freed people) fully belonged in their homeland of Antioquia – a critique of limited citizenship under the Constitution of 1812.

Rather than simply embracing republicanism, some slaves became its first critics.[2] Suggestions that republican liberty and the dignity of independence also encompassed slaves constituted an early critical assessment of the new polity. Evidence of this radical interpretation is not limited to the petition of 1812, since Antioquia's manumission law of 1814 generated comparable criticism. To some slaves, the manumission law must have seemed limited in its reach. They turned, therefore, to the notion that high government decisions (an emancipatory decree by the king or, in this case, a law with the blessing of the State's president) possessed hidden abolitionist potential. Just months after the passing of Antioquia's manumission law, Cornelio Sarrazola, a slave, would be arrested for questioning the limitations of the republican government's antislavery initiatives.[3]

With Colombia's manumission law of 1821 based on the form and logic of Antioquia's earlier legislation, critical observations made by some slaves during the early revolutionary period would remain valid during the Colombian republic of the 1820s.[4] As the leading antislavery legislator during Colombia's first General Congress, Félix José de Restrepo introduced a manumission law that was shot through with the ambivalences that had been scrutinized and criticized by Antioquia slaves. Unsurprisingly, he claimed that the slaves' immediate liberation would bring about the chaos that had been long predicted by the anxious masters. Slaveholders continued to insist that people of African descent inherited unspeakable criminal impulses from their ancestors. In other words, free, propertied, male Colombians deserved equality and citizenship, but slaves must be kept under control and continue to toil for the masters.[5] Congress closed the possibility of immediate abolition. Most of the legislators simply set aside their qualms about a slaveholding representative republic, which Restrepo himself recognized as a dangerous oxymoron.[6]

Some slaves and former slaves continued their efforts to untangle the meanings, true potential, and limitations of antislavery in the new republic. Before his execution, for example, José María Martínez embarked on a legal quest for formal recognition of his informal freedom. This slave, who had run away from his owners as early as 1806 and again in 1816, entered the judicial forum in 1822 with an eclectic and illuminating petition. His own exegesis recalled his services as a loyal slave and later a soldier of Colombia, proposing that even if his enslavement was allowed by law he was "in Justice a free man."[7] This and other litigants in early Colombia insisted on measuring antislavery initiatives (individual, collective, judicial, and legislative) against the overarching principles of natural law, equity, equality, republicanism, and Christianity.

Despite its concessions to the masters, Colombia's manumission law sparked a counter-exegesis, a series of arguments by slaveholders seeking to demonstrate why slaves had to remain in their natural, inferior place. In this counter offensive, even the constitutional principle of equality was openly questioned. In the old governorate of Popayán, where the majority of slaves and the most intransigent slaveholders still lived, alarmist petitions to reform Colombia's anti-slavery legislation were drawn up and sent to the central authorities.[8] Following his last efforts to bring to heel the slaves of San Juan, Gerónimo Torres arrived in Bogotá, where as a senator he represented the interests of Popayán masters, depicting slave liberation as the trigger of a war of "black" against "white" – a disingenuous position that failed to recognize that some people of color, too, owned slaves.[9] A case in point was Pedro Antonio Ibargüen, whose early arguments regarding equality for former slaves now seemed vindicated by the Colombian Constitution.

As he resumed his quest for property and standing in Popayán, Ibargüen celebrated the fall of the "the colossus of aristocracy," and the egalitarian "destiny" of Colombia.[10] He knew all too well, however, that equality was a continuing struggle. Yet considering Colombia's formal commitment to equality and slave emancipation, he now spoke with increased force and clarity, opposing the "greed and monopoly" of patricians who refused to concede that freed slaves could become lawful citizens making their own way in the world.[11] Though a small slaveholder himself, as an ex-slave discriminated against for his African ancestry, Ibargüen recognized that former slaves were fighting for equal opportunity, dignity, and respect – and that this was a fight for political belonging against vestiges of the Spanish hierarchical order rather than a war against whites.

Abolition and Political Belonging

Enslaved people who spoke their minds in the judicial forum often expressed a preoccupation with their political belonging after slavery. An unavoidable corollary to freedom, political incorporation after emancipation was at the heart of many of their legal efforts. Freedom took on a substantial meaning when freed people ceased to be persons who could be bought and sold and began to exercise the privileges and duties associated with membership in the larger community. Some slaves hoped to form their own sub-municipal congregations, to live *en policía* under the authority of a priest and a magistrate, paying taxes "like Indians." The slaves of La Honda in 1799 and Antioquia slaves, as early as the year 1781, stated similar aspirations. This was not, however, an atavistic desire on the part of the slaves.

Cautiously articulated, to be sure, aspirations that lowly slaves could become free and worthy of a better status were nonetheless radical in their political implications. In Popayán, the former slave Pedro Antonio Ibargüen argued that emancipated slaves should be held as "equal vassals."[12] A paradoxical notion in an unequal slave society, this proposition had an affinity with ideas expressed by other slaves well before the notion of equality before the law gained traction following the crisis of 1810. Slaves who suggested that they too could enjoy the benefits of being vassals – that they were worthy of spiritual care by the clergy and justice distribution by the magistrates – were thus palpably forward-looking. They aspired to expand political membership, seeking a practical redefinition and clarification of the boundaries of the moral community under the king and the society of individuals under the constitutions. In effect, they proposed that the stigmas of African, enslaved ancestry should be discarded as politically irrelevant, offering slaves a chance to move from mere denizens to explicit members of the polity.

Slaves expressed these general aspirations through the language of corporate belonging and municipal politics, both before and after 1810. Usually, such aspirations were limited to discrete enslaved communities, as happened with La Honda slaves, who expected to be manumitted while arguing that the estate could be incorporated as a settlement of free parishioners. In other cases, as was typical in Antioquia, some slave leaders aspired to a substantial shift in status for everyone enslaved within the boundaries of their municipal and provincial jurisdictions – the primordial sphere for the practice of political belonging under both the Spanish monarchy and the early republics.[13] Indeed, both spiritual membership in the church as well as a specific position in the social hierarchy remained the foundations of political belonging after 1810. Republican Antioquia held Roman Catholicism as the "religion of the State," and the new category of "citizen" was limited to free men of property and standing within a parish.[14]

The slaves' petition in 1812 elaborated on the importance of municipal membership while questioning the limitations of the new franchise and envisioning a more inclusive alternative. On the one hand, the slaves who led the judicial quest in 1812 reiterated a preoccupation with political belonging after slavery at the municipal level. Declaring themselves "poor little captives" who had longed suffered under the harsh and unjust yoke of the masters, the petitioners complained that slavery tore families apart, for Antioquia masters sold enslaved children to "foreign lands."[15] Selling slaves away from their homeland was unjust because it violated the new principle of equality, the slaves mentioned, but it also undermined the old principle of corporate, municipal belonging, for children sold to foreign lands would be "subject to no one." Individuals with no attachment to a parish, without villa or without city, could not comport themselves as Christians or live under the tutelage of a social superior or a magistrate.

On the other hand, the petition implied the existence of a more abstract level of belonging, explicitly mentioning that the document was filed on behalf of all Antioquia slaves. Slave petitioners powerfully built on municipal politics by presenting all slaves as potential legitimate members of a supra-municipal community – the community of Antioquia citizens, equal under the law. Signed or ghost-signed by dozens slaves from a cross-district alliance, the petition addressed the high magistrates as "we ten thousand and seven hundred slaves." Ten thousand people was the estimated slave population for the old province of Antioquia. Slaves had long communicated across different jurisdictions in this province, typically with the aspiration to press their claims in the judicial forum. Relying on old tactics, in 1812 the leaders expanded their legal strategy with the urgency and possibility brought about by revolution.[16]

To emphasize the condemnation of slavery contained in the petition, the legal activists also mixed old and new sources of meaning. Filed with the State of Antioquia's Supreme Tribunal of Justice, the petition affords a glimpse of the coexistence of different antislavery propositions. The writers of this document clearly referred to Antioquia's Constitution of 1812 as a legal touchstone whose principles, if taken seriously, rendered slavery unjust and illegitimate. They agreed with the new republican, representative principles of individual freedom and rights, but proposed that such principles might extend to the entire population. And they continued to rely on a religious paradigm, writing that "God our lord" had "made us free." Their captivity was thus an affront to Providence itself and therefore a sin in any Christian polity. God and political coherence demanded that the "insufferable yoke of slavery" be abolished in the new Catholic State.[17]

Some slaves constructively criticized representative government and constitutional republicanism. Suggesting that the republic's liberty, the dignity of independence, and the rights of citizens might also include the enslaved constituted a powerful critique of the new order in Antioquia. Such suggestions highlighted substantial limitations and tensions in the region. As we know, republican leaders interpreted this criticism as an illegal act. In 1812, officials alerted military personnel about a conspiracy allegedly lurking behind the petition, referring to the situation as the "movement of the Ethiopians"– an attempt by "wicked" slaves of African descent to take their freedom by force. Secretary of grace and justice, José Manuel Restrepo, who insisted that Antioquia was on the brink of a slave uprising as early as 1811, took immediate measures to stop what he called "this revolution."[18]

If the subsequent manumission law of 1814 was a partial answer to the questions posed by the petition in 1812, as well as an effort to defuse slaves' growing expectations, some slaves would demonstrate their disappointment in this answer. Revolutionary leaders, in turn, would again try to prevent slaves from scrutinizing too closely the ambiguities and true potential of the ongoing political transformation.

The manumission law did not deliver general slave emancipation, which many anticipated. Already in 1812, as slave leaders prepared to file their petition, a man who had saved money to purchase his wife's freedom was advised to suspend the payment on account of the current efforts for the "general freedom of all slaves."[19] In September 1814, five months after the approval of Antioquia's manumission law, the slave Cornelio Sarrazola publicly stated his propositions on the end of slavery. He questioned the limited scope of republican antislavery initiatives, revealing that a fresh collective petition regarding the new law was in the works.

About to be sold to a new master, Sarrazola advised the potential buyer against completing the transaction. The purchaser would lose both the money and the slave, Sarrazola told his prospective new owner, because slaves were now free. "Heaven" itself supported this liberation, he claimed, thus interpreting the manumission law beyond its apparent limitations and proposing that true abolition was the providential righting of a sinful wrong. His idea of providential abolition also implied imminent punishment for those who would oppose the liberation of the slaves. Indeed, Sarrazola was accused of prophesying that within a month the world would dramatically change, and should this change be stopped, "there would be fire." Reminiscent of the slave who had prophesied a divine reckoning for the masters during the Mompox fires, Sarrazola also asserted that the "road had been opened" to the slaves, who would not "remain silent" any longer.[20]

Other slaves also broke their silence to discuss and broadcast their views on the government's antislavery measures. Sarrazola individually expressed his opinion, but he reportedly participated in a "junta" with other slave leaders who collectively discussed the situation. They planned to petition the government, presumably to clarify and expand the scope of the manumission law. Despite the legally tinged label ascribed to the slaves' organization (a junta), authorities saw their collective efforts as a new instance of "suspicious" and "criminal" meetings. Sarrazola was charged with trying to take his own freedom by force, though he had only participated in a collective effort to file a new petition and had openly expressed his ideas on the end of slavery.[21] However, only citizens were allowed by Antioquia's Constitution to "examine the procedures" of the government and "write, speak, and freely print" their political opinions.[22]

By discussing and organizing a new legal effort, some slaves sought to discover the abolitionist potential in Antioquia's manumission law. Specifically, they scrutinized the legislation's free womb principle, asking whether it could somehow apply to adult slaves. The slave Vitorino Garro, a witness in the trial against Sarrazola, declared to have talked to his fellow slave Juan de Dios about potential ways that adult slaves might also be freed, given the liberation of their future children. For these slaves, enslaved parents of freeborn children presented a contradiction. Garro's interrogators asked what he would do if freedom proved impossible to achieve. Answering with tact, Garro said he would continue to "serve his master with love, as he has done so far, and with manly good will."[23] Slaves had to tread carefully in the judicial forum, abiding by the conventions of patriarchy and order while bravely suggesting that a truly free polity was feasible.

Sarrazola further used his unexpected entry into the judicial forum to assert the justice of the cause of general slave emancipation, insisting on his associates' good intentions. Instead of leading a revolt, he oversaw a legal effort to formally ask for the "grace" of freedom. The plan was to plead before the State's president "as though asking Mercy from God." His "junta" associates were even prepared to pay for their emancipations by covering the taxes imposed on slaveholders by the manumission law. His premonition of change within the month, therefore, only referred to the expectation that the petition would be favorably answered by a top official. Sarrazola denied ever mentioning "fire," but only because no such threat was needed given the justice of the claim. Pressed by magistrates, Sarrazola tempered his views, stating that the new petition stemmed from a misunderstanding of the manumission law rather than from its critical interpretation. He understood that only children would be freed, and only with time would all slaves phase out of their captivity; for now, he was forced to agree with the gradualist logic of Antioquia's antislavery legislation.[24] Nevertheless, the magistrates decided that Sarrazola and his colleagues had criminally conspired to "defend their system of liberty by force."[25]

Only a few people seemed willing to recognize the political nature of the slave's critical interpretation of Antioquia's manumission law. Sarrazola's sympathetic legal defender was one of these lone voices in the wilderness. He believed that the slaves soundly understood the official logic of the law; however, he wrote, they had been carried away over the course of their conversations by their enthusiasm and their "hope of LIBERTY." The capitalized word in the defender's handwritten argument suggested the explanatory relevance of this notion. Nothing less than enthusiastic discussions about freedom could be expected from slaves who were everywhere exposed to the revolutionary idiom of liberty from Spain. Slaves were "aware of their dignity as men," he argued. They knew of "many public papers" publishing statements against slavery, and now, in light of the manumission law, they had simply come together to bring a petition before the president. This was clearly not a crime, the defender insisted.[26] José Manuel Restrepo, in his capacity as the State's secretary of grace and justice, intervened. Sarrazola was to be returned to his master, who should ensure that this slave would never try to organize other slaves again. The manumission law, the secretary reiterated, stipulated that all adult slaves were to remain under the authority of their owners.[27]

Despite revolutionary leaders' efforts to curtail the criticism and radical interpretation of the manumission law, the conversation and discussions continued among the enslaved. In March 1815, José Manuel Restrepo reported that slaves continued to organize and hold meetings, and word circulating through the slave grapevine was that the manumission law had ended slavery altogether. Restrepo's report suggested that slaves were disappointed with gradual slave emancipation and planned to pressure for immediate abolition, even if they had to pay some taxes to facilitate the process.[28]

Critical interpretations of Antioquia's Constitution and antislavery law pivoted on the tension between corporate and individual political belonging. The idea that slaves could become free, law-abiding, tax-paying members of society after final and general emancipation drew on aspirations and propositions articulated before 1810. Some, as we know, evoked the corporate status of Indians as a potential blueprint. Many referred to collective membership in parishes and municipalities as a measure of meaningful freedom. After 1810, some hoped that freed slaves could become members of the broader citizenry. However, the idea that single citizens could claim equal rights under law, including former slaves, became a more widely accepted possibility in the wake of Simón Bolívar's successful campaign. The triumph of the libertadores in 1819 and the rise of the Republic of Colombia opened the door to litigation strategies and legal interpretations emphasizing individual accomplishments and the individual franchise.

Servile Freedom

Before his demise at the hands of a firing squad, José María Martínez had set out to finally complete his long quest for autonomy and manumission. After enlisting in the libertador army in 1819 and pursuing his old master the royalist Faustino Martínez, José María joined the campaign to liberate Cartagena. Deployed to Magangué, another riverine port town near Mompox (see Map 4), one day in 1821 Martínez came across other people from Antioquia who were also serving in the army.[29] In the group were three relatives of his former master: Manuel del Corral (Juan del Corral's son, and the husband of María de los Santos Martínez, Faustino Martínez's sister); Celestino Martínez (Faustino's cousin); and Julián Arrubla (Juan Pablo Pérez de Rublas' nephew). The encounter with these men might have alerted José María to the imminent threat to his informal freedom. They informed him that his former master's father, Juan Esteban Martínez, was determined to re-enslave him.[30] To make matters worse, in August 1822 José María learned that the Colombian government had authorized masters to reclaim wartime runaway slaves.[31]

José María left the army and set out for Antioquia, where he hoped to obtain formal freedom once and for all from any would-be masters. In Antioquia, he crossed paths again with Julián Arrubla, who provided him with a letter attesting to his work as a patriot soldier. Along with this document, José María filed a petition for emancipation in September 1822. However, given that he had left the army early, his judicial strategy did not rest on his military service alone. His petition contained a perceptive, multi-layered legal and social interpretation of slavery and freedom written by an aspiring equal citizen under republican law. Crafted with the aid of a papelista, his petition is an example of an old practice that thrived during early Colombia, as slaves and former slaves stepped even more eagerly into the judicial forum.[32]

José María's petition was an ingenious legal take on the ambiguities of slavery as it was experienced by mobile and relatively autonomous slaves in Antioquia since before independence. José María and others had taken advantage of the mobility required by their jobs, sometimes straying from their masters and even defying their authority – these were tactics he had practiced in his early days at the Jaramillo farmstead, and even during his travels with his master Faustino. Because his enslavement had unfolded as a tug-of-war experience, a near-constant back-and-forth with his enslavers, José María now asserted that his legal status was not clear cut. Instead, he presented the idea that he had long enjoyed *libertad servil* – "servile freedom."[33] This proposition blurred the line separating slave from free. It evoked the notion that slavery was not an immutable status.

José María combined two apparently contradictory words to convey that, although legally a slave, the services he had rendered to his master had emanated from his own decision to serve the Martínez family. After all, freedom was legally defined as the natural ability to do whatever a person pleased if his or her actions did not violate the laws or the existing privileges of others.[34] The petitioner had interacted with the members of the Martínez clan in a context of autonomy within slavery, enjoying a wide berth to exercise his free will. He now implied that he could have easily run away for good earlier but had instead decided to remain and serve his owners.

To lend credence to this paradoxical proposition, José María argued that he had willingly provided the Martínez clan with his services without ever fully giving himself up as property. Instead, he had comported himself with the assertiveness of a free person. This was clear during his trip to Jamaica. An eyewitness maintained that the alleged slave had disrespected him en route to the island. Despite the witness's complaint at the time, the putative master proved unable to punish the slave. The witness, therefore, told the supposed master that he would treat the supposed slave as a free man. The master did not object. The witness thus concluded that "José María was a free man." The petition, moreover, claimed that the master Faustino repeatedly claimed to have brought Martínez to Jamaica "as a companion, and not as a slave."[35] While there was no evidence to support this last assertion, there was evidence that José María was treated as free man even by his reputed master.

With the aid of his hired legal helper, José María may have bent the facts somewhat, but this served to illustrate an understanding of slavery and freedom as processes rather than essences. The petition relied on the notion that slavery was an unhappy, unnatural, not necessarily everlasting state of captivity. Slavery could be left behind by running away temporarily, but freedom could also be permanently secured by paying masters for manumission. José María ingeniously expanded on this, proposing that the very work performed by slaves was equivalent to a freedom payment. He had been "humbly born a slave," José María explained, and as a slave he had been later purchased by Faustino Martínez from the widow Jaramillo. But José María argued that Faustino had been duly compensated for his investment by his "loyalty during seven years, in which I accompanied him in long journeys to Bogotá and Jamaica, and a thousand different services, these being so well-known that I choose not to mention them."[36] His loyal, hard work amounted to a return on the master's initial investment and the equivalent of a manumission payment.[37]

Unlike the collectively organized slaves aspiring for abolition, José María seemed willing to concede that a period of work under the tutelage of masters was a fair requisite for freedom. This potential acceptance of the gradualist approach was, again, built on past experiences and on Spanish legal culture. About a decade earlier, José María had sought to emancipate his little godson, also a slave to the Martínez family. After saving Juan Esteban Martínez's life in a street fight, José María had received the gratitude of the family and the promise of freedom for his godson, which was to be delivered upon his acquiring of "a little bit of experience."[38] Whether or not this promise had been made, José María apparently thought of this apprenticeship as an avenue to a particular type of freedom, one that could be earned through labor and bestowed in gratitude.

José María presented work, good deeds, and loyalty to his master as legal grounds for his claim to freedom, obliquely suggesting that his exercise of free will had never trumped the privileges of slaveholders. The street fight episode, in which he allegedly risked his own life to save that of his master's father, was thus recalled as a paramount example of the individual merits supporting his claim to formal manumission. In a grandiloquent turn of phrase, José María asserted that, second only to God, he himself had given life to the old patriarch Juan Esteban.[39] The petition painted the street fight as a true ordeal and José María's actions as heroic and loyal. The surviving criminal records concerning this episode in 1811 reveal that José María accommodated the events to better serve his present legal needs. He had defended Juan Esteban, but Juan Esteban's life seems never to have been at risk. But according to the Spanish *Partidas*, still in use in early Colombia, a slave who saved a masters' life, uncovered their murderer, or avenged the crime became eligible for manumission.[40]

José María recounted his entanglements with his master's family, but his claim to freedom rested heavily on his individual situation. Because he was seriously wounded in the fight, José María presented the episode as evidence of his love for his master's family. This also reinforced his reflection on free will, the idea that he had made his own choices even while legally held as property. The episode was presented as an instance of his "servile freedom" status. The manly display of loyalty had emanated from his deliberate desire to serve the Martínez family well, not from obligation or coercion. His military "services" to the Republic, also mentioned in the petition, rounded up his claim to freedom on individual choice and meritorious work.[41]

And yet the proposition that José María had enjoyed "servile freedom" also relied on the unwillingness or inability of masters to actively exercise authority over the alleged slave. In other words, the 1822 petition tacitly used the principle of prescripción – which Félix José de Restrepo had invoked in Popayán. To claim freedom by prescription, we may recall, litigants had to establish that they had lived as free people for a period of ten years. In this way, the attribution of slave status rested not on the understanding of enslavement as an unchanging "legal fact" but rather as a set of "social relations" and "practices that needed to be interpreted."[42] It was precisely within social relations that José María hoped to find enough leads to make his case. Evidence of his freedom in the world of social relations should lead to his freedom in the world of the law.

This eclectic petition relied on shifting legal concepts intersecting in the nascent republican judicial forum. It would be a threat to "reason," José María claimed, for him to be returned to his "ancient slavery."[43] In other words, it would be unreasonable to consider José María the subject of an outdated system of domination. To decide the case in favor of his former owners would be to irrationally ignore what, in his view, was self-evident: that he should be "in Justice a free man," "emancipated" as "equity" would suggest.[44] By referencing equity, however, the petitioner and his legal aid also recognized that a favorable decision might emanate not just from "reason" alone (a disinterested interpretation of the law in light of supposedly self-evident facts) but from the judge's own sense of fairness (a personal inclination to favor freedom over slavery). Best understood as "judicial compassion," the old principle of equity referred to moderation in law enforcement, a sense of tolerance for discrepancies between written law and specific circumstance. More recently, the notion of equity had even taken on the meaning of a personal quality that magistrates might sometimes possess. Because the facts of the case were not exactly congruent with formal stipulations (he had not lived as a free person for at least a decade, he was in theory a runaway slave, and he had not served long enough in the army to gain manumission), José María hoped to benefit from a lenient, equitable judge.[45]

In the end, José María Martínez seems to have found no magistrate who would adjudicate his case with the equity he expected. He apparently dropped his legal bid before returning to the army, where he likely hoped to find a firmer path to freedom. As we know, however, José María found instead further difficulties, legal trouble, and ultimately – death. Meanwhile, other former slaves resurfaced in the republican tribunals to defend their egalitarian aspirations. The new Republic offered equality as a constitutional mandate, but equal standing would prove elusive for those who took on the old "aristocracy" seeking to realize their aspirations for dignified lives after slavery.

Republicanism and Aristocracy

As early as 1791, the former slave Pedro Antonio Ibargüen and his then legal adviser Félix José de Restrepo argued that even freed people deserved equal protection by the government. Rich and poor alike, Ibargüen further and paradoxically argued, were "equal vassals of His Majesty."[46] Now the Constitution of the Republic of Colombia, sanctioned on August 30, 1821, by Restrepo and other delegates to the first General Congress, timidly but explicitly listed equality, along with liberty, security, and property, as one of the most prized benefits of citizenship. The fruits of revolution and the new emerging republican, representative order should be equally enjoyed by all Colombians.[47]

As its provincial predecessors, however, the new polity offered only limited citizenship. Colombians, the Constitution declared, were the "free men" born in the country and their children – or naturalized free men. This restrictive extension of political belonging excluded free women and all slaves. Moreover, to vote and to be elected to public office, a Colombian citizen had to be literate and possess 500 pesos worth of real estate or 300 pesos in annual income. Citizens with a scientific or professional degree or practice, regardless of income, were also eligible to participate in representative government. Some free people of color held minor administration posts at the local level and some rose to become officers in the army. A few were elected to high office in the Senate and House of Representatives, but they endured deep-seated prejudice against former slaves and their offspring.[48]

Long existing stereotypes about slaves and their descendants under-pinned this political exclusion and the difficulties in enacting the principle of equality. A Cartagena merchant declared in 1806 that he regarded Africans and their descendants as barbarians and as the "natural enemies" of white people.[49] In 1827, a former secretary of foreign affairs would lament that Colombia contained within its borders an "African belt," imagining that the country would be better off without black people – in his view, they were a burden and a danger.[50] Simón Bolivar and José Manuel Restrepo, the first president of the Republic and secretary of the interior respectively, seem to have been convinced all along that recruiting slaves was crucial to the war effort and to "keep the equilibrium among the different races." They sought to prevent the potential growth of the "African" population by sending as many people of color as possible to the battlefields.[51]

More important, the survival of slavery revealed a tension between Colombia's commitment to equality and its tolerance for odious mani-festations of the old hierarchical order. Popayán slaveholding patricians reluctantly threw their lot behind the libertadores' new republic so long as they could keep slavery. Some Colombian officials had envisioned slave recruitment as a tactic to undermine Popayán's elite, but influential and committed slaveholders truncated slave recruitment, shoring up the slavery-based gold economy in the early 1820s.[52] Both Félix José de Restrepo and Pedro Antonio Ibargüen specifically elaborated on this theme, asserting that the existence of an "aristocracy" within a republic of equal citizens constituted a brazen political contradiction. Both men believed that Republicanism was, by definition, incompatible with aris-tocracy, and the aristocracy of the country was constituted by large slaveholders and arrogant patricians.

Restrepo pointed out this tension during the debates on the 1821 manumission legislation. At the General Congress, he stated that slavery contradicted the egalitarian principles of the Colombian Republic. The persistence of slavery would prevent the Republic from reaching its potential as a country under a popular and representative form of government. Comparable to "lords of vassals" and to "little absolute sovereigns," Restrepo asserted, the slave masters made Colombia look more like an "aristocracy" than a "democracy," more like the old Spanish monarchy than a new republic. Preventing rule by the people and instead stimulating rule by a few powerful men, slavery was a despicable inheritance from the tyrannical Spanish past, and tolerating slavery would render Colombia's political system a "feudal government." In practice, masters agglutinated the three powers (legislative, executive, and judicial) which ought to be separated by constitutional mandate.[53] Instead of a society of equal citizens, slavery made Colombia a polity of corporations with unequally distributed privileges. For Restrepo, in a theory he only partially practiced, slavery negated the revolution.

Ibargüen shared this notion of egalitarian republicanism, articulating even more forcefully the proposition that Popayán aristocrats undermined Colombia's egalitarian foundations. As a minor slaveholder himself, Ibargüen paid less attention to the slaveholding practices of his enemy aristocrats. As a free man of color still struggling for property and standing, he focused on the prejudices and discriminatory attitudes of the Spanish-descended patriciate. Ibargüen's vision of egalitarianism had been developing alongside his legal quest to work a gold claim on the Pique River, and litigation pitted him against well-to-do Popayán families. Expelled from Pique, Ibargüen returned to work his gold diggings after obtaining a favorable ruling in 1804. As he would explain in an 1824 petition, he had recovered the mining site with his "sweat" and against the "opulence of arrogant people."[54]

His "arrogant" adversaries, however, kept up their pressure on Ibargüen. In 1818, he traveled once again in serach of justice, making the long trip to Santa Fe. Here he met the seasoned lawyer José Ignacio de San Miguel. Active since 1768, San Miguel had maintained in 1777 (in Mompox) that slaves were simply people who had lost their freedom. He would later become a theorist of Colombian independence, asserting that Colombians of African descent, of better blood than "arrogant" Spaniards, had proved their merit on the battle-fields.[55] San Miguel and Ibargüen co-authored a new petition regarding Pique, but the case was returned to the local authorities. Meanwhile, Ibargüen continued to exploit the mines, valued at over 3000 pesos by 1824. José Ignacio de Castro, who had challenged Ibargüen's right to set up an operation at Pique since the 1790s, now revived his attacks on the former slave. Agents of the Grueso family, most importantly Guillermo Antonio Segura, a younger member of this clan, also sought to take over the rich deposits. In 1825, they successfully expelled Ibargüen from Pique once again.[56]

Almost eighty years old, Ibargüen continued to litigate. Between 1825 and 1827 he traveled several times to Popayán to plead his case. His opponents argued that this was a dispute over landed property, as opposed to mining rights, a take on the situation unfavorable to Ibargüen. Although legally entitled to mine for gold, Ibargüen had never produced notarial documents to prove that he had ownership of land. In June 1827, the Superior Court of Popayán decided that Ibargüen had no property rights over Pique.[57] Still, he spoke his mind in the judicial forum, always painting his case as an episode in the larger drama of political and legal change.

His was a transcendental legal cause. It stood in for the struggle between propertied families and dispossessed individuals, a battle in the war against corporate privileges and the influence that came with high social standing. Over three decades into this fight, Ibargüen reiterated that despite his African ancestry and enslaved past, he was equally entitled to the protection of the law, and to make a living by exploiting resources long monopolized by families of Spanish ances-try.[58] He usually had great difficulties convincing magistrates and officers. Over time, however, his claims on legal equality and the undue power of Spanish ancestry gained crucial currency. Deemed outlandish under the monarchy, such arguments resonated with the new republic's ideology and legal order. After 1819, revolutionaries more cogently articulated the ongoing conflict as a clear-cut struggle of Colombian versus Spaniard. This was now an epochal quest against tyranny, pitching oppressed natives against foreign invaders.[59]

Even though Ibargüen's early, egalitarian arguments now seemed vindicated, he still faced the prejudice that was directed against people of African descent. As a literate, free man with some capital, Ibargüen had a claim to Colombian citizenship and a measure of respectable social standing. His opponents, however, continued to regard him as a person of inferior worth and rebellious inclinations. Vicente Olave, an attorney for Guillermo Antonio Segura, called him a "usurper" and an agitator introducing "disorder" among those "of his color."[60] Defeated in court, he was insulted with the usual slander that was levelled at people of color who were seen as a threat to the social order. However, Ibargüen did not accept this slander quietly.

Unable to find a lawyer who would take on his case, Ibargüen hired a papelista in July 1827. Appealing the Superior Court's ruling, Ibargüen articulated his understanding of legal equality as a safeguard against abuse of power and the vitriol of prejudice. He came from those of the "humiliated color of the Africans," Ibargüen wrote, from people condemned to "horrific slavery" by "greed and monopoly." Though his opponents might not concede that a former slave could be a worthy, peaceful citizen, he wrote, the "wise Laws of Colombia," based on the principles of nature, reason, and philanthropy, would prove them wrong.[61] In light of the new legal order, his fight against those who denied the merits of people of color and opposed their aspirations to property and political belonging had been just all along, even under Spanish rule. Otherwise, he asked, how could a "black," "abject" and "lay" individual have dared to confront powerful lawyers in the royal tribunals? His claims had always been legitimate – and even more so now that "the colossus of aristocracy has fallen, and equality is inscribed in the destiny of Colombia."[62]

Nevertheless, Ibargüen understood that persistant prejudices and hierarchy made it near-impossible to achieve his goals. His rivals prevailed thanks to their "influence" and because they benefitted from the continuing division of society according to ancestry. Influential Popayán families "drowned" his rights and treated him "worse than a donkey" because they were white and rich in a caste society where people of color were meant to be poor and servile. His opponents had power to abuse, Ibargüen insisted, but no sound legal arguments to back their claims. They drew on false information and tendentious interpretations. Even if Pique had legally belonged to others, their property rights had expired by prescription. Since the original owners had not exploited the mines for an extended period, Ibargüen argued that his continuing usufruct of the property made the mine his by rights.[63]

Turning the prejudice of ancestry on its head, Ibargüen painted himself as a virtuous Colombian opposed by wicked Spaniards, a weak mortal "fighting against gods." Ibargüen further described himself as a "sad African" dueling with the "descendants of the Goths." A derogatory term for Spaniards in the parlance of the time, the expression Goth allowed Ibargüen to highlight the wider implications of his case, depicting haughty Popayán families as Colombians only in name. Once again, Ibargüen likened his own struggle against Popayán elites to Colombia's struggle against Spain, equating his fight to that of a Christian against a Sultan and painting his cause as nothing less than a holy war.[64]

Ibargüen again traveled to Bogotá, where he appealed before the High Court of Justice. During the appeal process in 1827 he learned that the chief magistrate of Colombia's highest justice tribunal was his one-time legal counsel Félix José de Restrepo. Almost four decades had passed since their first encounter back in Popayán, and Restrepo could barely remember Ibargüen. By contrast, Ibargüen remembered well that Restrepo had recused himself from the case in 1791 on account of his friendship with the Castro family. Ibargüen now asked that Restrepo recuse himself again.[65] Restrepo did so, and on September 26, the High Court ruled that Ibargüen indeed had mining rights over Pique.[66]

However, weeks away from Bogotá, at the gold diggings in the Pacific region, Ibargüen's enemies prevented enforcement of this final ruling, and local authorities thwarted him from regaining full access to his gold claim. In 1828 and 1829, he traveled again between the Pacific mining districts and the city of Popayán, seeking total control of the gold deposits.[67] From surviving notarial records, we can infer that Ibargüen was unable to become the sole gold miner and formal owner of Pique. Indeed, the Castro family continued to mine the river, and the Segura clan would also exploit the deposits for another forty years.[68] Ibargüen visited a Popayán notary in 1829 for the last time. Squeezed by other miners and unable to translate a court ruling into effective property, he ceded his rights over Pique to his friend Manuel Agustín Varela, free of charge.[69] After this transaction, Ibargüen disappears from the records.

A Seigneurial Counter-Exegesis

Some members of the families Ibargüen called "aristocrats" showed only mild enthusiasm for the representative government of Colombia. In the end, Popayan's elite accepted the libertadores' triumph and supported Bolívar, but leading patricians made every effort to defend the old hierarchies and ensure that slavery remained unchanged.[70] They showed equal zeal in their fight over gold deposits owned by former slaves as in their opposition to Colombia's antislavery initiatives. In the process, they practiced a counter-exegesis of liberty, an interpretation that was, unsurprisingly, founded upon stock accusations made against slaves. These slaveholders relied on the prejudice, censured by Ibargüen, consisting of the long-held idea that slaves were the natural enemies of hierarchy and the principle of authority, and that their liberation would accelerate the ongoing destruction of the mining economy.

Gold production figures reveal the extent of the losses incurred by Popayán gold mining elites during the revolutionary period. Between 1801 and 1810, the Royal Mint forged coins valued at around half a million pesos. By contrast, during the turbulent years between 1811 and 1822, the total came to just over 126,000 pesos.[71] The slaveholding gold economy, alongside Spanish ancestry, underpinned Popayán high patricians' livelihoods and sense of purpose. The sharp economic and political disruption that accelerated after 1810 brought great uncertainty to this seigneurial way of life. Long accustomed to litigation and now represented in the Senate, the upholders and beneficiaries of the old order would not submit to their own decline without a fight. In their view, their survival hinged on keeping slaves working and under their patriarchal watch.

To keep control of mining workers, slaveholders took steps to undermine Colombia's antislavery efforts. Besides successfully opposing slave recruitment by the libertadores' army, they blockaded new avenues to manumission opened by the law of 1821. Moreover, they set out to reform the legislation itself, defending the increasingly dated notion that the unequal order of the world was natural, and its undoing would cause only chaos. To liberate slaves, in their eyes, was to turn the world upside down.[72] Against the backdrop of conflict with their slaves at the San Juan gold mine, the Torres y Tenorio family, particularly Gerónimo Torres, championed the cause of the masters. He publicized his criticism of the law in the city of Popayán, as well as in the Colombian legislative chambers in Bogotá. Above all, he sought to retain the enslaved work force under the hierarchical power of the masters for even longer than the law seemed to anticipate. His pro-slavery politics reveal the seigneurial, anti-egalitarian logic of the efforts to shore up slavery in early Colombia.

At the San Juan gold mine, where slave leaders had long been engaged in a continuing struggle with their putative masters, the years between 1810 and 1818 saw little intervention from Popayán. Slave leaders seemed to have communicated with royalist agents, apparently collaborating with them, but stopped communication with their masters. In 1818, the slave captain Juan Camilo Torres, alongside another twenty male slaves, unsuccessfully filed for their emancipation on account of their support for the king's cause. The San Juan slaves had also openly declared their freedom during the conflict with Spanish governor Miguel Tacón, refusing to collaborate with him, and thus their political inclinations were less than clear-cut. Not all the slaves participated in this legal effort to acquire formal emancipation, however.[73]

Gerónimo Torres, the would-be master of the San Juan community, finally found an opportunity, and the courage, to travel to the mining enclave in 1819. He arrived at the mine hoping to peacefully bring the men and women there back under his formal control. As he recalled later, he did not challenge members of this community in any way. Instead, he claimed to have provided them with fresh tools and medical care, allowing them to remain in possession of their garden plots, and declaring that he would not charge anyone for whatever property might have been lost or destroyed over the previous years. Torres even allegedly said that the slaves could continue to mine for their own gold, and expressed his willingness to grant further concessions. But his position was a tenuous one. It seems that it was the slaves who gave Gerónimo a concession by allowing him to enter San Juan in the first place.[74]

By his own admission, Gerónimo Torres's plans were thwarted. His "indulgent" approach, he had anticipated, would allow him to dispense with "the severity and rigor that have always been deemed necessary for governing the blacks." Nevertheless, he had traveled to

San Juan with a guarantee from the governor of Popayán that, if necessary, authorities would use force to subdue the San Juan community. The slaves, Torres mentioned, had at first clearly faked "an apparent submission to their master's dominion," but they soon showed him their "pride" and "insolence." Pushback from the slaves, in Torres's perception, only confirmed his prejudices. He believed that slaves had an "innate and irreconcilable hatred" against masters. This hatred, Torres wrote, originated as soon as slaves ceased to feel the burden of their master's authority.[75]

In Torres' view, effective enslavement rested on the threat and actual use of force. He specifically mentioned the scare tactics and the violent means available to a slaveholder in the Pacific mining districts. When a particular male slave proved openly belligerent, Torres threatened to send him to Barbacoas, where he would be sold to the infamous slaver Casimiro Cortés. This would scare other members of the San Juan community into submission, Torres expected. Cortés, who enjoyed much influence in the district of Barbacoas, had been accused in 1787 of causing the death of two slaves he severely punished and tortured. In 1798, his slaves brought a legal complaint for cruel punishments.[76] Even under threat to be sold to Cortés, the individual in question remained at San Juan and "considers himself a free man." Unless the government acted to "subjugate" this and the other slaves, Torres believed, his authority as master could not be restored. However, his request to the governor for a commissioner and soldiers to travel to San Juan, arrest the community leaders, and sell them off to Cortés was rejected.[77]

Although the residents of San Juan did not achieve formal emancipation, neither did the Torres family succeed in enforcing their full authority as masters.[78] Apparently the last member of the Torres y Tenorio family to ever set foot on San Juan, Gerónimo Torres left Popayán for Bogotá soon after his failed attempt to bring the autonomous slaves to heel. But he would continue the fight by other means. As elected senator (he was a member of Congress from 1821 to 1828),[79] Torres inaugurated Popayán's campaign to modify the manumission law to reflect even more accurately the masters' needs and perceptions. This campaign rested once again on the propagation of the prejudiced narratives about the alleged "wicked" social and moral condition of the enslaved. This was a counter-exegesis of liberty, a rejection of the propositions that bound labor should end as soon as possible, and that slaves and former slaves were not innate criminals or childish entities but people worthy of political belonging on an equal basis.

Torres's main contribution to this counter-exegesis, a printed pamphlet denouncing the manumission law as an affront to proper social order and hierarchy, evidently drew on his family's failure to fully subjugate the community of San Juan to the yoke of slavery. It also reflected his own personal failure to fully restore the world to its old seigneurial order. Despite the fact that Colombia's antislavery legislation safeguarded the masters' right to hold other human beings as property, Torres insisted that the manumission law undermined the property rights of slaveholders. Moreover, he declared that the law seriously threatened the health of the body politic, the peace of the republic, and the legitimately unequal order of the world. High Popayán patricians defended the old social order both publicly and in private, and they questioned whether fulfilling the constitutional mandate for equality was even feasible in Colombia.[80]

Torres proposed that Congress decree the absolute freedom of all slaves, but with no intention of allowing freed people to simply walk away from their masters. Once the slaves were freed, their monetary value would be recognized as national debt, with the government paying the former masters a 3 percent annual interest until the value of the slaves was paid in full. Torres proposed that the freed people be deemed minors, thereby remaining under the control of their former masters as their legal guardians. As wards of their social betters, the former slaves would remain bound to the mines and haciendas where they labored; they would work for wages, paying an annual tax of eight pesos from their salary. The collected funds would be then redistributed among the former masters as compensation for the liberated slaves – even though these freed people would still be toiling under their old master's authority, and as minors who were not actually emancipated.[81]

Besides ensuring compensation for lost property, keeping former slaves under the control of their former masters was seen as a way to prevent otherwise "inevitable" upheaval, and the final upending of social order. Torres insisted that the sudden liberation of thousands of individuals who had lived on the fringes of society would usher in a violent cataclysm. Their "indolence" and lack of education and property would lead slaves to behave improperly after an abrupt transition from slavery to freedom. Tacitly and inaccurately drawing on the example of San Juan, Torres wrote with no little vitriol that freed slaves would naturally fall into criminal behavior, claiming to have seen it happen with his own eyes. He reported to have witnessed slave gangs avoiding "the dominion of their masters, taking over all the properties, gold sources and mine tools." He had seen how a decade of "complete freedom" among slaves had led them to "a life of leisure, libertinage, and all sorts of vices, robbing, destroying, and killing each other."[82]

Torres even claimed to have witnessed how the libertine slaves, appalled at the horrific consequences of their freedom, willingly returned to the authority of the masters. The libertines he described decided to return to slavery, "frightened by the horrendous abyss of disorders in which they had fallen." The excess of liberty left them "naked, hungry, loaded with misery, corruption, superstition and crime," anxious to return to slavery, imploring "protection and shelter from their masters." Life in slavery, unlike life in freedom, was a peaceful paradise in Torres's estimation. His pamphlet described slavery as an orderly existence in which slaves lived "with affluence, overflowing with basic and even sumptuary food, had many garments, and all had abundant gold jewelry."[83] Torres turned his distorted version of the San Juan episodes into a cautionary tale, a prefiguration of what would happen throughout Colombia unless even liberated slaves were firmly kept in their place.

Keeping manumitted slaves in their place was also a tactic used to prevent the alleged "natural" animosity among blacks and whites from turning into a new kind of war. "The black man will never mix with the white man," Torres explained, and "the black man will forever be the white man's enemy." Visibly and naturally different from each other, blacks and whites were predestined to fight in an epochal struggle for power. Since Colombia's weak government was unable to prevent this conflict, the responsibility of containing the former slaves fell to the masters. They alone could keep those dangerous minors under close watch. This guardianship, moreover, had one final and chilling goal: it was deemed a necessary step toward the gradual dissolution of Colombia's "African belt," to "extinguish the black color." Torres suggested that vagrants and prostitutes be sent to gold mines and haciendas, where they would presumably initiate the work of miscegenation to "whiten" the Republic.[84]

It seems that Ibargüen's assessment of aristocratic sentiment was on point. Members of the Popayán elite despised those of his calidad, and leading patricians of Spanish stock proved unwilling to accept the principle of equality, clinging instead to stereotypes about slaves, former slaves, and people of African descent. Further adding to Torres's counter-exegesis, the newly established Electoral Assembly of Popayán and other Popayán slaveholders joined the effort to undermine the antislavery initiatives. Like Torres, they could not help but reveal the hierarchical ideology, patriarchal sensibility, and essentialist perceptions underpinning their anxieties about slave emancipation. Colombia's manumission law, another senator from Popayán would declare in 1829, "undermines the foundations of society."[85]

The alarmed slaveholders' apprehensions, however, were founded on ideas shared by most Colombian framers and legislators in 1821. Popayán patricians defended a seigneurial order based on the conviction that severing the bonds of dependency tying the slaves to the masters would have fatal consequences on the larger social order. This conviction was built into the manumission law since its early conception in Antioquia. As in 1814, in 1821 Félix José de Restrepo espoused the free womb principle and gradualism on indemonstrable premises. He assumed as a matter of fact that an unconditional, immediate liberation of slaves would bring about "disasters," the "ruin" of the "white" slaveholders, "great inconveniences," and a "violent explosion."[86] Dispensing with his knowledge that people of color also owned slaves, Restrepo adopted the tendentious view of the end of slavery as an inevitable clash of black against white rather than as a matter of politics in the age of republican independence and representative government. Restrepo's own authority over his slaves, after all, was not predicated on his now anathematized Spanish ancestry. It rested, instead, on his continuing legal competence to buy, sell, and hold other human beings as property.[87]

* * *

What revolutionary leaders called Spanish enslavement ended soon after 1821, but domestic slavery continued. Rather than a passive inheritance from the Spanish period, this was a deliberate continuity. Many slaves, former slaves, and some magistrates and legislators cast serious doubts on a limited, gradual approach to antislavery. Liberty from Spain, some argued, would be incomplete without freedom from slavery. For some powerful masters, however, the tension between the two seemed less alarming. For many scions of the Popayán Spanish clans, keeping an enslaved workforce was central to their effort to revive the gold economy and uphold their place in the world. They even offered to end slavery in name only, so long as the freed people remained under their power. Mastering others constituted and made visible their standing as true patricians in a seigneurial, unequal order that they refused to relinquish.

Committed to slaveholding, Gerónimo Torres avoided employing free people of color, preferring to exercise authority over enslaved servants. From Bogotá, he sent to Popayán for an enslaved page and an enslaved cook. He would take a free person as a cook only if there was no other choice. In the end, he grudgingly compromised. The young slave Rafael had recently married a manumitted woman working as a cook. Torres received news in 1827 that the couple was to move to Bogotá to enter his service. Rafael would be his page, but Torres would have to suffer Rafael's free wife cooking his meals. Rafael's wife, though legally free, would enter the household of a severe master, with her husband still enslaved and liable to physical punishment.[88] Freedom from slavery was thus a rare and mixed experience, an ambiguous situation in a new age of limited slave emancipation and complete liberty from Spain.

The Republic of Colombia lasted only about ten years, and its manumission law failed to stimulate slave emancipations. By 1830, only seventy-three slaves had been manumitted in the old governorate of Popayán, where most slaves were still concentrated. Popayán's slaveholding elite systematically undermined and dramatically mismanaged the manumission boards. In the city of Cartagena, 101 slaves were freed by 1831. Even in Antioquia, with its early and more palpable commitment to slave emancipation, only eighty-four manumissions took place between the passing of the Colombian manumission law and 1830. Only four of these emancipations were formalized with no compensation for the masters. Most of these freed slaves paid for their own freedom. The commitment to humanity once expressed by Antioquia's republican leaders had dissipated, at least in practice. Overall, manumissions in Antioquia sharply declined between 1820 and 1830.[89]

Corral expressed his desire to end forced labor altogether and Restrepo painted his 1821 antislavery convictions and actions as an "abolition," the "radical remedy" of slavery. Slaveholding, Restrepo claimed, was an illegal act of force.[90] The voices of many slaves during sundry judicial encounters, however, encourage us to interrogate the place of those assertions in the history of abolition. Slaves developed a radical, complex politics of antislavery. For some, antislavery politics hinged on the possibility of actually and immediately ending slavery. Soon after 1810, moreover, a new conception of what it meant to abolish slavery emerged. Founded on slaves' exegesis of liberty and rooted in the judicial forum, this idea of liberating all the slaves was indistinguishable from liberation from Spain and equality before the law. For vanguard abolitionists, the time was now.

Epilogue: The Slaves Before the Law

The status of enslaved Africans and their offspring in the Spanish Indies remained a legal quandary across the three centuries preceding the Spanish American Revolutions. Present in the Bible, civil law, canon law, natural law theories, the law of nations, and royal jurisprudence, long-existing justifications of, and challenges to slavery were variegated. They were also practically irrelevant unless invoked by someone under specific circumstances. In short, there existed no consistent or single "theory of the source of the property right in persons." "The more closely we examine the problematics of law and slavery…the more clearly we see that law in slaveholding societies did not and could not cohere."[1]

The very word *esclavo* was only one of several Spanish words available to refer to people owned as property, further suggesting the legal ambiguity of enslavement. Men and women under this form of dominion were indistinctly referred to by different labels, archeo-legal terms from a vast history of human bondage rooted in antiquity and the Middle Ages. Someone in slavery could be called *siervo* and described as *sujeto a servidumbre* – subject to servitude. To evoke subjection implied that the slave's condition was not innate but acquired, the result of the absolute power imbalance between master and slave. The same understanding underpinned the expression *bajo la condición de esclavo*, under the condition of slave, also present in the inherited legal vocabulary of enslavement. Spanish-speakers also

referred to slaves as captives (*cautivos*), and to their emancipation as
rescue (*rescate*) or redemption (*redención*).[2]

This legal ambiguity also included the issue of slaves' political
belonging. While slaves could theoretically benefit from the protection
of royal magistrates, they were neither Indians nor Spaniards, and thus
more denizens of the Spanish monarchy than vassals of the king of
Spain. The early republics failed to fully solve this quandary. They
postponed the abolition of slavery, declaring that slaves, as a general
rule, were unprepared to become citizens of the new polities. The anti-
Spanish, antislavery revolutionaries who achieved emancipation from
Spain reserved "the sweets of freedom for those who never tasted the
bitter cup of bondage."[3] Neither citizens nor foreigners, enslaved
inhabitants of provincial states like Antioquia and Cartagena or the
national state of the Republic of Colombia occupied a vague legal
zone. The active exercise of power by a master, rather than any one
cohesive legal doctrine or clearly defined status, effectively made each
slave a person owned by another person.

To facilitate making slaves the subjects of antislavery legal reform,
potential solutions to the legal riddle of slaves' status had to be
considered. Juan del Corral and Félix José de Restrepo tackled crucial
questions. Who or what, exactly, was a slave before the law? Were
slaves "captives," as Antioquia's petitioners claimed in 1812? Were
they "serfs," as medieval law and notarial formulae called them? How
could legislators incorporate slaves in the legal regime of a republic of
free citizens? The answers were clever and retained all the ambiguity of
the issue. They exposed both the legal intricacies of slave emancipation
as well as the limits of revolution. Even as they set out to undo their
ancien régime society, pro-independence leaders facilitated the continuation of the most feverishly denounced of all pre-existing
hierarchies.

Relying on the concept of "serf," Corral proposed a solution.
Slavery, he suggested, could be replaced with a more flexible "servitude of the glebe." This expression, which he gleaned from
Montesquieu and the French *Encyclopédie*, evoked Roman colonists
and European serfs. Corral thus imagined that slaves could officially
be granted the new status of serfs of the glebe, meaning serfs of the
land. Workers straddling captivity and freedom, serfs would be
attached to their former masters' estates but not to the masters

themselves. The masters' power over the serfs would be partially limited, as bonded labor would no longer rest on personal servitude. Serfs would not be bought and sold, and in this way they would cease to be persons traded as property.[4] Everything else would remain unchanged.

In the end, Restrepo and Corral turned to the concept of "captive." They settled on regarding slaves of African descent in the Americas as Christian captives crying for physical deliverance and spiritual redemption rather than as individuals denied access to citizenship. To think through the tension of a slaveholding republic devoted to liberty, legislators reached for a seasoned European conceptual framework. This approach left slaves in legal limbo. Evoking Mediterranean captivity, Antioquia's manumission law called for the "redemption" of as many adult slaves as possible. Slaves would continue to live in slavery, but they were also categorized as unfortunate captives whose fate was now in the hands of pious Christians and "friends of humanity" willing to redeem them.[5] Colombia's manumission law called the emancipation of individual slaves a "pious goal."[6]

This language of spiritual captivity and redemption recalled the holy war experiences of Christians and Muslims. Between 1500 and 1800, millions of European Christians experienced slavery throughout the Mediterranean world, particularly on the northern African coast.[7] People in the Spanish Indies and the early Spanish American republics remained acutely aware of this. Captivity narratives figured prominently in oral and written traditions. Moreover, those who wrote last wills and testaments had to pay *mandas forzosas*, a tax to fund the redemption of captives back in Spain. The semantic stock of slavery and emancipation thus included physical but temporary forms of enslavement at the hands of Ottomans and their allies. However, this also implied the subsequent possibility of either slippage into spiritual captivity through apostasy, or redemption by ransom or escape and return to Christendom. The key concept was captive, and the rescuing of captives was an obligation of faith – a pious and redemptive act.

Corral and Restrepo thus agreed with those slaves who saw themselves as Christian captives. When Antioquia's slave petitioners suggested in 1812 that it would be logical to expand the constitutional definition of "liberty," they claimed to speak "on behalf of all the unhappy captives." The slave leaders called for the lifting of the "insufferable yoke of slavery" throughout the State, making room for the liberated slaves to become members of the new republic. God, they insisted, was "on our side."[8] Monolingual in Spanish, up to date on the revolutionary developments, and indoctrinated in the rudiments of Christianity, the slave leaders understood the implications of their vocabulary. Continuing enslavement defied the logic of a Catholic polity built on the idea of liberty and devoted to individual rights. When it came to matters of freedom, the voices of the unfree were the most critical and universal.

Antislavery legislation relied on the idiom of captives' redemption because its mechanics facilitated the gradual approach to slave emancipation. Officials would continue to collect taxes originally established for the redemption of Mediterranean captives, but they would now use the funds to pay for the manumission of local slaves. In Antioquia, those whose liberty was paid for with this money would be publicly manumitted every year on Resurrection Passover (Easter Sunday) – the most solemn feast of the Lord, a mystical commemoration of redemption, of passage from death to life, from light to darkness, from captivity to freedom.[9] Following the dissolution of the bonds of political dependence with Spain, the convictions and obligations of captive redemption could be mobilized to liberate Christians from their domestic captivity. The redemption of captives, however, was a spiritual commitment with no single beginning or clearly identifiable end. It was an ongoing, gradual process rather than a sudden change.

By reading litigation as a sphere of politics, however, we have been able to see how some slaves struggled (conceptually and legally) to propose alternatives to continuing captivity. Typically hostile and riddled with silences, judicial records nonetheless contain important clues on slaves' antislavery propositions. Between the 1780s and the 1820s, enslaved legal activists made important efforts to articulate the idea that slavery could and should end by legal means. As the Spanish monarchy collapsed and independent, representative republics began to form, some slaves proposed that their own emancipation should take place without delay and without excuse. Some free people agreed. Demonstrating whether the new doctrine of liberty and equal rights was "true," and by extension defining the scope of revolutionary politics, rested on the fate of captives. Crucially, the implication was that male slaves and former slaves, regardless of their alleged sinful African origin, criminal inclinations, and stained background as manual workers should be incorporated as equals into the new body politic.[10] Common litigants demonstrated a vanguard abolitionist political stand and supported equality before the law for ex-slaves. For many, ending slavery altogether was not simply a just concession to the slaves but a crucial step forward for the broader society.

Over the last five centuries, slaves and their descendants have had to meditate carefully on what it means to belong or to be excluded. When considering who they were before the law and how best to define their rights and shift their status, they reflected, by necessity, on transcendental issues of liberty and freedom, natural and civil law, kings, queens, and constitutions. In this process, often slaves and their free descendants stood at the forefront of legal change. Their vital and complicated engagements with magistrates and legislators have reframed, expanded, refined, and even defined citizenship for entire nations.[11] By engaging with those with the greatest legal authority, people with the least legal standing actively shaped the scope and meaning of freer, more open societies in the Americas.

Notes

Prologue: Antislavery, Abolition, and the Judicial Forum

1 José Félix de Restrepo [sic], "Discurso sobre la manumisión de esclavos, pronunciado en el soberano Congreso de Colombia reunido en la villa del Rosario de Cúcuta en el año de 1821," Rosario de Cúcuta, June 28 and July 5, 1821, *Obras completas de José Félix de Restrepo* (Medellín: Bedout, 1961), 297–298; Acta 56 and Acta 64, June 28 and July 5, 1821, *Congreso de Cúcuta 1821. Libro de Actas* (Bogotá: Banco de la República, 1971), 177–179, 201–202 (a handwritten copy of Restrepo's speeches is available at BNC, Fondo Antiguo, RM 223). On slaves and free people of color during the Age of Revolutions in Colombia, see Alfonso Múnera, *El fracaso de la nación: Región, clase y raza en el Caribe colombiano (1717–1821)* 1st ed. 1998 (Bogotá: Planeta, 2008); Aline Helg, *Liberty and Equality in Caribbean Colombia, 1770–1835* (Chapel Hill: The University of North Carolina Press, 2004); Marixa Lasso, *Myths of Harmony: Race and Republicanism during the Age of Revolution, Colombia 1795–1831* (Pittsburgh, PA: University of Pittsburgh Press, 2007); Peter Blanchard, *Under the Flags of Freedom: Slave Soldiers and the Wars of Independence in Spanish South America* (Pittsburgh, PA: University of Pittsburgh Press, 2008); Roger Pita Pico, *El reclutamiento de negros esclavos durante las guerras de independencia de Colombia. 1810–1825* (Bogotá: Academia Colombiana de Historia, 2012); Marcela Echeverri, *Indian and Slave Royalists in the Age of Revolution: Reform, Revolution, and Royalism in the Northern Andes, 1780–1825* (New York: Cambridge University Press, 2016); Edgardo Pérez Morales, *No Limits to Their Sway: Cartagena's Privateers and the Masterless Caribbean in the Age of Revolutions* (Nashville, TN: Vanderbilt University Press, 2018).

2 José Félix de Restrepo, "Discurso," 311–312, 335.
3 Acta 84, July 19, 1821, *Congreso*, 266–269; Law of July 21, 1821, *Gazeta de Colombia* (Rosario de Cúcuta), September 9, 1821.
4 José Félix de Restrepo, "Discurso," 337.
5 Harold A. Bierck, Jr., "The Struggle for Abolition in Gran Colombia," *Hispanic American Historical Review* 33.3 (1953): 365–386; Jaime Jaramillo Uribe, "La controversia jurídica y filosófica librada en la Nueva Granada en torno a la liberación de los esclavos y la importancia económica-social de la esclavitud en el siglo XIX," *ACHSC* 4 (1969): 63–86; John V. Lombardi, *The Decline and Abolition of Negro Slavery in Venezuela* (Westport: Greenwood, 1971); John Kitchens, "The New Granadan-Peruvian Slave Trade," *Journal of Negro History* 64:3 (1979): 205–215; Pablo Rodríguez J., "La manumisión en Popayán, 1800-1851," *Revista de Extensión Cultural* 9–10 (1980): 77–85; Jorge Castellanos, "The Failure of the Manumission Juntas in the Colombian Province of Popayán, 1821-1851," *Michigan Academician* 14.4 (1982): 427–443; Russell Lohse, "Reconciling Freedom with the Rights of Property: Slave Emancipation in Colombia, 1821–1852, with Special Reference to La Plata," *The Journal of Negro History* 86.3 (2001): 203–227; Jorge Andrés Tovar Mora and Hermes Tovar Pinzón, *El oscuro camino de la libertad. Los esclavos en Colombia, 1821–1851* (Bogotá: Universidad de los Andes, 2009); Jason McGraw, *The Work of Recognition: Caribbean Colombia and the Postemancipation Struggle for Citizenship* (Chapel Hill: The University of North Carolina Press, 2014); Rocío Rueda Novoa, "Desesclavización, manumisión jurídica y defensa del territorio en el norte de Esmeraldas (siglos XVIII–XIX)," *Procesos. Revista Ecuatoriana de Historia* 43 (2016): 9–35; Marcela Echeverri, "Esclavitud y tráfico de esclavos en el Pacífico suramericano durante la era de la abolición," *Historia Mexicana* 69.2 (2019): 627–691.
6 José Félix de Restrepo, "Discurso," 341–342.
7 Harold A. Bierck, Jr., "The Struggle;" John V. Lombardi, *The Decline*; John Kitchens, "The New Granadan-Peruvian"; Jorge Andrés Tovar Mora and Hermes Tovar Pinzón, *El oscuro*, 90; Rocío Rueda Novoa, "Desesclavización;" Marcela Echeverri, "Esclavitud;" Daniel Gutiérrez Ardila, "El coronel Concha en el Cauca o la gestación de un vórtice político, 1821–1824," *Historia Crítica* 78 (2020): 65–86.
8 Law of July 21, 1821; Harold A. Bierck, Jr., "The Struggle;" Jaime Jaramillo Uribe, "La controversia;" Jason McGraw, "Spectacles of Freedom: Public Manumissions, Political Rhetoric, and Citizen Mobilization in Mid-Nineteenth-Century-Colombia," *Slavery & Abolition* 32.2 (2011): 269–288. For examples of publicized manumissions, see *Gaceta de Colombia* (Bogotá), February 24, 1822, January 5,

1823, February 9, 1823, April 6, 1823, May 25, 1823, December 14, 1823, January 4, 1824, January 25, 1824, February 15, 1824, April 25, 1824, January 9, 1825, January 16, 1825, January 30, 1825, February 6, 1825, February 27, 1825, September 18, 1825, February 12, 1826, February 26, 1826, March 5, 1826, March 12, 1826, January 18, 1829, March 1, 1829, March 15, 1829, June 7, 1829, June 14, 1829, March 21, 1830, April 25, 1830, May 2, 1830, June 27, 1830, July 11, 1830, August 15, 1830, January 16, 1831, January 23, 1831, February 13, 1831, March 20, 1831, and March 27, 1831. For a citizen privately manumitting an enslaved woman "in celebration of the national festivities commemorating the most important events and glorious triumphs of Our Republic of Colombia, for the Independence of its Peoples," see the manumission act by Antonio Arboleda, Popayán, January 12, 1824, ACC, Notaría primera, vol. 79 1824-I, f. 2r–3r.

9   Acta 63, July 4, 1821, *Congreso*, 195.

10 Acta 63, July 4, 1821, Acta 80, July 16, 1821, and Protesta No. 29 by Juan Bautista Estévez, *Congreso*, 195, 254, 706–707.

11 I borrow the notion of antislavery as a complex web of values, sentiments, opinions, and practices "critical of some or all aspects of the Atlantic slave system" from Christopher Leslie Brown, *Moral Capital: Foundations of British Abolitionism* (Chapel Hill: The University of North Carolina Press, Omohundro Institute of Early American History and Culture, 2006), 17–18. On antislavery as a sensibility and an intellectual field independent from slavery itself and not necessarily committed to abolition, see Alessandro Tuccillo, *Il commercio infame. Antischiavismo e diritti dell'uomo nel Settecento italiano* (Naples: Università degli Studi di Napoli Federico II, 2013); Edgardo Pérez Morales, "Félix José de Restrepo, las ambigüedades de la esclavitud y la sensibilidad antiesclavista. Popayán, 1783–1808," *ACHSC* 48.1 (2021): 45–67.

12 Simón Sáenz de Vergara and Felipe Grueso Rodríguez to Miguel Tacón, Tumaco, December 7, 1811, AGI, Quito, 386; María Eugenia Chaves Maldonado, "El oxímoron de la libertad. La esclavitud de los vientres libres y la crítica a la esclavización africana en tres discursos revolucionarios," *Fronteras de la Historia* 19.1 (2014): 174–200. On the provincial states of 1810–1816, see Armando Martínez Garnica, *El legado de la "patria boba"* (Bucaramanga: Universidad Industrial de Santander, 1998); Daniel Gutiérrez Ardila, *Un Nuevo Reino. Geografía política, pactismo y diplomacia durante el interregno en Nueva Granada (1808-1816)* (Bogotá: Universidad Externado de Colombia, 2010); Isidro Vanegas, *El constitucionalismo fundacional* (Bogotá: Ediciones Plural, 2014); Edgardo Pérez Morales, *No Limits*.

13 *Constitución del Estado de Antioquia sancionada por los representantes de toda la provincia. Y aceptada por el pueblo en tres de mayo del año de*

1812 (Santa Fe de Bogotá: Imprenta de D. Bruno Espinosa, Por D. Nicomedes Lora, 1812), tit. 1, sections 1 and 2, 4–5; We ten thousand and seven hundred slaves to the Supreme Tribunal of Justice, Medellín, August 25, 1812, "Contra varios de los Etíopes, por haber intentado su liberated con violencia," ACCR, Gobierno, vol. 93, f. 3r–v, 7r.

14 "Ley sobre la manumisión de la posteridad de los esclavos africanos y sobre los medios de redimir sucesivamente a sus padres, extendida y propuesta para su sanción a la Cámara de Representantes del Pueblo, por el Excelentísimo Dictador Ciudadano Juan B. del Corral," *Gazeta Ministerial de la República de Antioquia* (Medellín), October 2, 1814.

15 "Criminal contra Cornelio Sarrazola esclavo de Manuel Herrón por pretender su libertad a fuerza," AHA, Criminal, B-84, 1820–1840, doc. 14; Daniel Gutiérrez Ardila, "La politique abolitionniste dans le'État d'Antioquia, Colombie (1812–1816)," *Le Mouvement social* 252 (2015): 70.

16 On the rich tradition of legal struggle and claims-making by slaves and former slaves in the Spanish-speaking world, see, for example, Rebecca J. Scott, "Reclaiming Gregoria's Mule: The Meanings of Freedom in the Arimao and Caunao Valleys, Cienfuegos, Cuba, 1880–1899," *Past & Present* 170 (2001): 181–216; Alejandro de la Fuente, "Slave Law and Claims-Making in Cuba: The Tannenbaum Debate Revisited," *Law & History Review* 22.2 (2004): 339–369; Michelle A. McKinley, *Fractional Freedoms: Slavery, Intimacy and Legal Mobilization in Colonial Lima, 1600–1700* (New York: Cambridge University Press, 2016); Ricardo Raúl Salazar Rey, *Mastering the Law: Slavery and Freedom in the Legal Ecology of the Spanish Empire* (Tuscaloosa: University of Alabama Press, 2020); Richard Lee Turits, "Slavery and the Pursuit of Freedom in 16th-Century Santo Domingo," *Oxford Research Encyclopedia, Latin American History* (Oxford University Press, 2020), oxfordre.com/latinamericanhistory.

17 Aline Helg, *Slave No More: Self-Liberation before Abolitionism in the Americas* (Chapel Hill: University of North Carolina Press, 2019).

18 I draw theoretical inspiration from Carlo Ginzburg, *The Cheese and The Worms: The Cosmos of a Sixteenth-Century Miller* 1st ed. 1976 (Baltimore, MD: The Johns Hopkins University Press, 2013); Carlo Ginzburg, *Clues, Myths, and the Historical Method* 1st ed. 1986 (Baltimore, MD: The Johns Hopkins University Press, 1989). For the law as a field of politics and culture (rather than just an imposition from above) underpinned by changing moral, religious, and social convictions and expectations, see Alberto Flores Galindo, *Aristocracia y Plebe. Lima, 1760–1830 (Estructura de clases y sociedad colonial)* (Lima: Mosca Azul Editores, 1984), 18; Antonio Manuel Hespanha, *La gracia del derecho.*

Economía de la cultura en la edad moderna (Madrid: Centro de Estudios Constitucionales, 1993), 14; Tamar Herzog, *A Short History of European Law: The Last Two and a Half Millenia* (Cambridge: Harvard University Press, 2018), 4–5; Ariela Gross, "Beyond Black and White: Cultural Approaches to Race and Slavery," *Columbia Law Review* 101.3 (2001): 640–690, and the special issue on "Law, Slavery, and Justice," *Law & History Review* 49.4 (2011): 915–1095.

19 Fifteen known constitutional texts were drafted and debated within the borders of current-day Colombia between 1810 and 1821, with the first four preceding the Spanish Constitution of Cádiz (1812). See Isidro Vanegas, *El constitucionalismo*. See also Victor M. Uribe-Urán, *Honorable Lives: Lawyers, Family, and Politics in Colombia, 1780–1850* (Pittsburgh, PA: University of Pittsburgh Press, 2009); James E. Sanders, *The Vanguard of the Atlantic World: Creating Modernity, Nation, and Democracy in Nineteenth-Century Latin America* (Durham, NC: Duke University Press, 2014), and the special issue "Ecos atlánticos de las aboliciones hispanoamericanas," *Historia Mexicana* 69.2 (2019): 613–835.

20 DRLJ, 724, 965. On Spanish American litigation and what I call the judicial forum as practices of dialogue, debate, and political creativity, see Bianca Premo, *The Enlightenment on Trial: Ordinary Litigants and Colonialism in the Spanish Empire* (New York: Oxford University Press, 2017). On the interdependencies between oral and written cultures, and on the politics of writing, legal and otherwise, among all sorts of people (men, women, rich, poor, free, enslaved, literate, illiterate) across Latin America, see Ángel Rama, *The Lettered City* 1st ed. 1984 (Durham, NC: Duke University Press, 1996); Serge Gruzinski, *La colonización de lo imaginario. Sociedades indígenas y occidentalización en el México español, siglos XVI–XVIII* (Mexico City: Fondo de Cultura Económica, 1995); Judy Kalman, *Writing on the Plaza: Mediated Literacy Practice among Scribes and Clients in Mexico City* (Cresskill: Hampton Press, 1999); José Ramón Jouve Martín, *Esclavos de la ciudad letrada. Esclavitud, escritura y colonialismo en Lima (1650–1700)* (Lima: Instituto de Estudios Peruanos, 2005); Sandra Lauderdale Graham, "Writing From the Margins: Brazilian Slaves and Written Culture," *Comparative Studies in Society and History* 49.3 (2007): 6 11–636; Kathryn Burns, *Into the Archive: Writing and Power in Colonial Peru* (Durham, NC: Duke University Press, 2010); Frank Salomon and Mercedes Niño-Murcia, *The Lettered Mountain: A Peruvian Village's Way with Writing* (Durham, NC: Duke University Press, 2011); Joanne Rappaport and Tom Cummins, *Beyond the Lettered City: Indigenous Literacies in the Andes* (Durham, NC: Duke University Press, 2012); Gabriela Ramos and Yanna Yannakakis, ed., *Indigenous Intellectuals: Knowledge, Power and*

Colonial Culture in Mexico and the Andes (Durham, NC: Duke University Press, 2014); Cristina Soriano, *Tides of Revolution: Information, Insurgencies, and the Crisis of Colonial Rule in Venezuela* (Albuquerque: University of New Mexico Press, 2018).

21 Bianca Premo, *The Enlightenment*.

22 Pedro Antonio Ibargüen to the governor, Popayán, February 16, 1793, "Pedro Antonio Ibargüen contra Manuel José Grueso por despojo de una mina de Iscuandé," ACC, sig. 11367 (Col. JI-17mn), f. 18r; Pedro Antonio Ibargüen to Corte del Cauca, Popayán, July 7, 1827, "Posesorio promovido por Pedro Antonio Ibargüen contra Guillermo Segura por despojo de un terreno en 'Pique,'" ACC, sig. 5624 (Ind. C II-24mn), f. 105v–106r.

23 On judicial practice and jurisdictional conflict as exercises of politics, see Margarita Garrido, *Reclamos y representaciones. Variaciones sobre la política en el Nuevo Reino de Granada, 1770–1815* (Bogotá: Banco de la República, 1993); Jean-Frédéric Schaub, *Le Portugal au temps du comteduc d'Olivares (1621–1640). Le conflit de juridictions comme exercice de la politique* (Madrid: Casa de Velázquez, 2001); Pilar López Bejarano, "'Empapelar al enemigo.' El recurso a los procesos judiciales como estrategia de la acción política (Nueva Granada entre colonia y república)," Elisa Caselli, ed., *Justicias, agentes y jurisdicciones. De la Monarquía Hispánica a los Estados Nacionales (España y América, siglos XVI–XIX)* (Madrid and Mexico City: Fondo de Cultura Económica, 2016), 79–102. On legal matters spilling out of judicial proceedings, see Michael C. Scardaville, "Justice by Paperwork: A Day in the Life of a Court Scribe in Bourbon Mexico City," *Journal of Social History* 36.4 (2003): 987–991; Bianca Premo, "Before the Law: Women's Petitions in the Eighteenth-Century Spanish Empire," *Comparative Studies in Society and History* 53.2 (2011): 279–280. On elections during the Spanish period, see Isidro Vanegas Useche, "Elecciones y orden social en Nueva Granada, de la monarquía a la república," *ACHSC* 48.1 (2021): 69–93.

24 Alexis de Tocqueville, *The Old Regime and the Revolution* (New York: Harper & Brothers, 1856); Malick W. Ghachem, *The Old Regime and the Haitian Revolution* (New York: Cambridge University Press, 2012).

25 Bianca Premo, *The Enlightenment*, 15. See also Margarita Garrido, *Reclamos*; Victor M. Uribe-Urán, *Honorable*.

26 Antonio Manuel Hespanha, *La gracia*; Bianca Premo, *The Enlightenment*; Federica Morelli, "Esclavos, alcaldes y municipios. La justicia local en una región de frontera," Elisa Caselli, ed., *Justicias*, 373–396; Geneviève Verdo, "¿Una revolución del derecho? Cultura y reformas jurídicas en tiempos de revolución. El ejemplo de Manuel Antonio de Castro," Pilar González Bernaldo de Quirós, ed., *Independencias iberoamericanas. Nuevos problemas y aproximaciones* (Buenos Aires: Fondo de Cultura Económica, 2015),

199–2016; Isidro Vanegas, "Justicia y ley en el Nuevo Reino de Granada, periodo Borbónico," *Historia y Espacio* 16.54 (2020): 47–72.

27 José Antonio Maldonado (with Francisco González Manrique) to Real Audiencia, Santa Fe, *ca.* August 8, 1777, "Don José Antonio Ambrosi [sic] de Arango sobre la venta que se le quiere precisar de un negro esclavo," AGN, C, NEA, vol. 1, doc. 23, f. 716r–717r; Pedro Antonio Ibargüen and Félix José de Restrepo, Popayán, *ca.* April 29, 1791, "Pedro Antonio Ibargüen," f. 2r.

28 On the study of natural law and eighteenth-century publicists by lawyers and other members of the turn-of-the-century intelligentsia, see Daniel Gutiérrez Ardila, *Un Nuevo Reino*, ch. 2; Isidro Vanegas, *El constitucionalismo*, 165–190; Renán Silva, *Los ilustrados de Nueva Granada, 1760-1808. Genealogía de una comunidad de interpretación* (Medellín: Banco de la República, Universidad EAFIT, 2002).

29 Criticisms of slavery emerged early in the Spanish-speaking world. While the Spanish Abolitionist Society was founded only in 1865, building blocks for a case against the enslavement of sub-Saharan Africans and their offspring date to the sixteenth and seventeenth centuries in the writings of Spanish and Portuguese clergymen. At the turn of the nineteenth century, however, expressing hostility toward slavery, and even the desire to end it, relied on modern philosophy and judicial practices rather than exclusively on earlier Catholic discourses. Christopher Leslie Brown, *Moral Capital*, 38–40, 228–231; Bianca Premo, *The Enlightenment*, ch. 6; Emily Berquist, "Early Anti-Slavery Sentiment in the Spanish Atlantic World, 1765–1817," *Slavery & Abolition* 31.2 (2010): 181–205; María Eugenia Chaves, "The Reason of Freedom and the Freedom of Reason: The Neo-Scholastic Critique of African Slavery and its Impact on the Construction of the Nineteenth-century Republic in Spanish America," Ivonne del Valle, Anna More, Rachel Sarah O'Toole, ed., *Iberian Empires and the Roots of Globalization* (Nashville, TN: Vanderbilt University Press, 2019), 183–205.

30 Federica Morelli, "Filangieri e l'"altra America:' storia di una recezione," *Rivista Storica Italiana* 119.1 (2007): 88–105; Juan Camilo Escobar Villegas and Adolfo León Maya Salazar, *Ilustrados y republicanos. El caso de la "ruta de Nápoles" a la Nueva Granada* (Medellín: Universidad EAFIT, 2011); Genviève Verdo, Federica Morelli, Élodie Richard, ed., *Entre Nápoles y América. Ilustración y cultura jurídica en el mundo hispánico (siglos XVIII y XIX)* (Medellín: La Carreta, Instituto Francés de Estudios Andinos, 2012).

31 Gaetano Filangieri, *La scienza della legislazione* 1st ed. 1780–1791 (Venice: Centro di studi sull'Illuminismo Europeo "G. Stiffoni," 2003), vol. 1; Alessandro Tuccillo, *Il commercio*, 283–293; Vincenzo Ferrone,

The Politics of Enlightenment: Constitutionalism, Republicanism, and the Rights of Man in Gaetano Filangieri (New York: Anthem Press, 2012).

32 José Félix de Restrepo, "Discurso," 312–323; Acta 64, July 5, 1821, *Congreso,* 201–202; Gaetano Filangieri, *La scienza,* vol. 1, 61–72.

33 José Félix de Restrepo, "Discurso," 315–316, 319.

34 José Félix de Restrepo, "Discurso," 337.

35 José Félix de Restrepo, "Discurso," 335.

36 The words *negro* and *mulato,* typically used by others to refer to slaves and their offspring, evoked these supposedly inherent moral and spiritual failings. See María Elena Martínez, "The Black Blood of New Spain: Limpieza de Sangre, Racial Violence, and Gendered Power in Early Colonial Mexico," *The William & Mary Quarterly* 61.3 (2004): 479–520 and Armando Martínez Garnica, "Prejuicio moral e instrucción: dos obstáculos para la incorporación de los pardos a la Nación," *Revista Colombiana de Educación* 59 (2010): 14–32. Instead of assuming these labels have explanatory value and denote unchanging realities, I focus on explaining the social tensions and relationships of power for which they served as shorthand. See Steinar A. Sæther, *Identidades e independencia en Santa Marta y Riohacha, 1750–1850* (Bogotá: Instituto Colombiano de Antropología e Historia, 2005), 199, 202, and his "Independence and the Re-Definition of Indianness around Santa Marta, Colombia, 1750–1850," *Journal of Latin American Studies* 37:1 (2005): 55–80. For approaches to "race" as processes of power and politics, see Norbert Elias and John L. Scotson, *The Established and the Outsiders* 1st ed. 1965 (Dublin: University College Dublin Press, 2009); Marion A. Kaplan, *Between Dignity and Despair: Jewish Life in Nazi Germany* (New York: Oxford University Press, 1998); Rebecca J. Scott, *Degrees of Freedom: Louisiana and Cuba after Slavery* (Cambridge, MA: Harvard University Press, 2005); Rebecca J. Scott and Jean M. Hébrard, *Freedom Papers: An Atlantic Odyssey in the Age of Emancipation* (Cambridge, MA: Harvard University Press, 2012); Joanne Rappaport, *The Disappearing Mestizo: Configuring Difference in the Colonial New Kingdom of Granada* (Durham, NC: Duke University Press, 2014); Jean-Frédéric Schaub, *Pour une histoire politique de la race* (Paris: Éditions du Seuil, 2015); Jorge E. Delgadillo Núñez, "The Workings of *Calidad*: Governance and Social Hierarchies in the Corporations of the Spanish Empire," *The Americas* 76.2 (2019): 15–239; Alejandro de la Fuente and Ariela J. Gross, *Becoming Free, Becoming Black: Race, Freedom, and Law in Cuba, Virginia, and Louisiana* (New York: Cambridge University Press, 2020).

37 Orián Jiménez Meneses, "Esclavitud, libertad y devoción religiosa en Popayán. El Santo Ecce Homo y el mundo de la vida de Juan Antonio de Velasco, 1650–1700," *Historia Crítica* 56 (2015): 13–36.

38 Fr. Joaquín de Finestrad, *El vasallo instruído en el estado del Nuevo Reino de Granada y en sus respectivas obligaciones ca.* 1789 (Bogotá: Universidad Nacional de Colombia, 2000); David Brading, "La Monarquía Católica," and Ramón María Serrera, "Sociedad estamental y sistema colonial," A. Annino, L- Castro Leiva, F.-X. Guerra, ed., *De los imperios a las naciones: Iberoamérica* (Zaragoza: iberCaja, 1994), 19–43 and 45–74; Isidro Vanegas, "Vínculo social, poder y revolución. Nueva Granada de la monarquía a la república, 1780–1816," François Godicheau and Pablo Sánchez León, ed. *Palabras que atan. Metáforas y conceptos del vínculo social en la historia moderna y contemporánea* (Madrid and Mexico City: Fondo de Cultura Económica, 2015), 181–209.

1 Raynal in the New Kingdom?

1 RCD, esp. 2, 884–915; John Leddy Phelan, *The People and the King: The Comunero Revolution in Colombia, 1781* (Madison: University of Wisconsin Press, 1978); Katherine Bonil Gómez, "De 'un Rey Nuevo en Santa Fe' y otros 'cismas.' Negros, mulatos y zambos en la Rebelión de los Comuneros (1781)," *ACHSC* 47.1 (2020): 87–112.

2 John Leddy Phelan, *The People*, 3–35; José Antonio Maravall, *Las Comunidades de Castilla: una primera revolución moderna* (Madrid: Alianza, 1979); John Lynch, *Bourbon Spain 1700–1808* (Oxford: Basil Blackwell, 1989); Anthony McFarlane, *Colombia Before Independence: Economy, Society, and Politics under Bourbon Rule* (New York: Cambridge University Press, 1993); Mark A. Burkholder, "Spain's America: From Kingdoms to Colonies," *Colonial Latin American Review* 25.2 (2016): 125–153; Francisco A. Ortega, "The Conceptual History of Independence and the Colonial Question in Spanish America," *Journal of the History of Ideas* 79.1 (2018): 89–103.

3 *Representaciones*, often filed on behalf of entire communities or corporations, played an important role in political life. See Margarita Garrido, *Reclamos y representaciones. Variaciones sobre la política en el Nuevo Reino de Granada, 1770–1815* (Bogotá: Banco de la República, 1993).

4 DA, vol. 1, book 2, 464; John Leddy Phelan, *The People*.

5 Antonio Caballero y Góngora, archbishop of Santa Fe and later viceroy, believed that the people of the viceroyalty had lost their original innocence during the 1781 uprising. With the vassals' loyalty now in doubt, he claimed that political stability had to be kept through military and policing means. Antonio Caballero y Góngora, "Relación del estado del Nuevo Reino de Granada, que hace el Arzobispo Obispo de Córdoba a su sucesor el excelentísimo señor don Francisco Gil y Lemos," Turbaco, February 20, 1789, Germán Colmenares, ed., *Relaciones e informes de los gobernantes de la Nueva Granada* (Bogotá: Biblioteca Banco Popular, 1989), vol. 1,

484–485. For the sense that loyalty to the crown was alarmingly thin among vassals in the New Kingdom, and the military vulnerable, see, for example, Pedro de Becaria y Espinoza to José de Gálvez, Popayán, September 17, 1784, AGI, Quito, 238, and "Informe del Conde de Torre Velarde, oidor de la Audiencia de Santafé," Santa Fe, July 19, 1797, Sergio Elías Ortíz, *Colección de documentos para la historia de Colombia. Segunda serie* (Bogotá: Academia Colombiana de Historia, 1965), 18–21.

6 Katherine Bonil Gómez, "De 'un Rey."

7 Fr. Joaquín de Finestrad, *El vasallo instruído en el estado del Nuevo Reino de Granada y en sus respectivas obligaciones ca.* 1789 (Bogotá: Universidad Nacional de Colombia, 2000), 42, 45, 62–64, 384, 398, 401, 405; Guillaume-Thomas Raynal, *Histoire philosophique et politique, des établissemens & du commerce des Européens dans les deux Indes* (Geneva: J. L. Pellet, 1780), vol. 7, 220–221.

8 See Daniel Gutiérrez Ardila, *Un Nuevo Reino. Geografía política, pactismo y diplomacia durante el interregno en Nueva Granada (1808–1816)* (Bogotá: Universidad Externado de Colombia, 2010), ch. 2; Juan Camilo Escobar Villegas and Adolfo León Maya Salazar, *Ilustrados y republicanos. El caso de la "ruta de Nápoles" a la Nueva Granada* (Medellín: Universidad EAFIT, 2011); Genviève Verdo, Federica Morelli, Élodie Richard, ed., *Entre Nápoles y América. Ilustración y cultura jurídica en el mundo hispánico (siglos XVIII y XIX)* (Medellín: La Carreta, Instituto Francés de Estudios Andinos, 2012).

9 Vicente Restrepo, *Estudio sobre las minas de oro y plata en Colombia* (Bogotá: Imprenta de Silvestre y Compañía, 1888); Robert C. West, *The Pacific Lowlands of Colombia: a Negroid Area of the American Tropics* (Baton Rouge: Louisiana State University Press, 1957); Jaime Jaramillo Uribe, "Esclavos y señores en la sociedad colombiana del siglo XVIII," *ACHSC* 1 (1963): 63–66; Germán Colmenares, *Historia económica y social de Colombia II: Popayán, una sociedad esclavista, 1680–1800* 1st ed. 1979 (Bogotá: Tercer Mundo, 1997); Anthony McFarlane, *Colombia*, 31–95.

10 Antonio Caballero y Góngora, "Relación," 442–443; José Manuel Restrepo, *Memoria sobre amonedación de oro i plata en la Nueva Granada. Desde 12 de julio de 1753 hasta 31 de agosto de 1859* (Bogota: Imprenta de la Nación, 1860); Jaime Jaramillo Uribe, "La controversia jurídica y filosófica librada en la Nueva Granada en torno a la liberación de los esclavos y la importancia económica-social de la esclavitud en el siglo XIX," *ACHSC* 4 (1969): 63–86; Frank Safford, "Significación de los antioqueños en el desarrollo económico colombiano," *ACHSC* 3 (1967): 49–69; Frank Safford, *The Ideal of the*

Practical: Colombia's Struggle to Form a Technical Elite (Austin: University of Texas Press, 1976); Anthony McFarlane, *Colombia*, 71–95.

11 Cayetano Buelta Lorenzana to Juan José Callejas, Medellín, December 19, 1781, "Don Alonso Elías Jaramillo Capitán a Guerra del valle de Río Negro dando cuenta con testimonio de lo actuado en asunto del levantamiento que proclamando libertad, tenían proyectado los negros, y demás esclavos de aquel valle coligados con los de las Ciudad de Antioquia, y Villa de Medellín," 1781–1782, BNC, Comuneros, rm 376, f. 2r–3r.

12 On the implications of this approach, see Laurent Dubois, "An Enslaved Enlightenment: Rethinking the Intellectual History of the French Atlantic," *Social History* 31.1 (2006): 1–14; Ada Ferrer, "Speaking of Haiti: Slavery, Revolution, and Freedom in Cuban Slave Testimony," David Patrick Geggus and Norman Fiering, ed., *The World of the Haitian Revolution* (Bloomington and Indianapolis: Indiana University Press, 2009), 223–247.

13 Casamayor to Manuel Antonio Flores, Rionegro, April 8, 1781, and Manuel Antonio Flores to José de Gálvez, Cartagena de Indias, August 22, 1781, RCD, 2, 538 and 424; John Leddy Phelan, *The People*, 195–196; Anthony McFarlane, "Civil Disorders and Popular Protests in Late Colonial New Granada," *The Hispanic American Historical Review* 64.1 (1984): 17–54.

14 Beatriz Patiño Millán, *Riqueza, pobreza y diferenciación social en la provincia de Antioquia durante el siglo XVIII* (Medellín: Universidad de Antioquia, 2011), 217–237.

15 Robert C. West, *Colonial Placer Mining in Colombia* (Baton Rouge: Louisiana State University Press, 1952); Ann Twinam, *Miners, Merchants and Farmers in Colonial Colombia* (Austin: University of Texas Press, 1982), 19–21; Beatriz Patiño Millán, *Riqueza*, 189–268.

16 Alonso Elías Jaramillo to Manuel Antonio Flores, Rionegro, September 15, 1781, BNC, Comuneros, rm 372.

17 Manuel Antonio Flores to José de Gálvez, Cartagena de Indias, August 22, 1781, and Salvador Plata, Antonio José Monsalve, and Francisco Rosillo to Manuel Antonio Flores, Socorro, September 17, 1781, RCD, 2, 455, 733. Comparable rumors were present among communities of unfree workers in societies as disparate and distant from each other as Venezuela (1749), Martinique (1768), Russia (1796–1797), and Barbados (1815). See Linda M. Rupert, *Creolization and Contraband: Curaçao in the Early Modern Atlantic World* (Athens: University of Georgia Press, 2012), 204; Julius S. Scott, *The Common Wind: Afro-American Currents in the Era of the Haitian Revolution* (London: Verso, 2018), 78–80; Wim Klooster, "The Rising Expectations of Free and Enslaved Black in the Greater Caribbean," Wim Klooster and Gert

Oostindie, ed., *Curaçao in the Age of Revolutions. 1795–1800* (Leiden: KITLV Press, 2011), 62–69; Laurent Dubois, *A Colony of Citizens: Revolution and Slave Emancipation in the French Caribbean, 1787–1804* (Chapel Hill: The University of North Carolina Press, Omohundro Institute of Early American History and Culture, 2004), 90–92; Roger Bartlett, "The Russian Peasantry on the Eve of the French Revolution," *History of European Ideas* 12.3 (1990): 407; Peter Kolchin, *Unfree Labor: American Slavery and Russian Serfdom* (Cambridge, MA: Harvard University Press, 1987), 322; *Report from a Select Committee of the House of Assembly Appointed to Inquire into the Origins, Causes, and Progress of the Late Rebellion* (Barbados: W. Walker, Mercury and Gazette Office, 1818), 27.

18 "Don Alonso," BNC, Comuneros, rm 376; "Testimonio del expediente formado sobre las inquietudes de los naturales de Guarne, y La Mosca, en la jurisdicción de Río Negro y el pueblo de Sopetrán de la de esta ciudad; de las providencias tomadas sobre dichas inquietudes, y sobre las noticias que a este gobierno se han dado, de intentarse invadir esta provincia," 1781, BNC, Comuneros, rm 372; "Testimonio de un expediente relativo al levantamiento o insurrección de esclavos en la provincia de Antioquia," 1781, *Documentos para la historia de la insurrección Comunera en la provincia de Antioquia. 1765–1785* (Medellín: Universidad de Antioquia, 1982), 441–588. On Sancho Londoño Piedrahíta, see Beatriz Patiño Millán, *Riqueza*, 244–245.

19 Cayetano Buelta Lorenzana to Juan José Callejas, Medellín, December 19, 1781, "Don Alonso," BNC, Comuneros, rm 376, f. 2r–3r.

20 Depositions of Miguel and José Ignacio, Rionegro, December 30, 1781, deposition of José Ignacio, Rionegro, January 1, 1782, "Don Alonso," BNC, Comuneros, rm 376, f. 6v–8r, 10r–v.

21 *Tercera Partida* (Salamanca: Andrea de Portonariis, 1555), Tit. XXIX, Laws XXIII–XXV, f. 170v; *Qvarta Partida* (Salamanca: Andrea de Portonariis, 1555), Tit. X, preamble, Tits. XXI and XXII, esp Tit. XXI, Law VI, f. 15r, 54v–59r; Alejandro de la Fuente, "Slave Law and Claims-Making in Cuba: The Tannenbaum Debate Revisited," *Law & History Review* 22.2 (2004): 339–369; Michelle A. McKinley, *Fractional Freedoms: Slavery, Intimacy and Legal Mobilization in Colonial Lima, 1600–1700* (New York: Cambridge University Press, 2016).

22 Deposition of Pelayo, Antioquia, December 21, 1781, "Testimonio de un expediente," 456, 459.

23 Constantino Bayle, *Los cabildos seculares en la America Española* (Madrid: Sapientia, 1952); Isidro Vanegas, "Justicia y ley en el Nuevo Reino de Granada, periodo Borbónico," *Historia y Espacio* 16.54 (2020): 47–72.

24 Deposition of Pelayo, Antioquia, December 21, 1781, "Testimonio de un expediente," 456; deposition of Miguel, José Ignacio, Rionegro, December 30, 1781, deposition of José Ignacio, Rionegro, January 1, 1782, "Don Alonso," f. 6v–8r, 10r–v.

25 Deposition of Pelayo, Antioquia, December 21, 1781, and Rectificación of Pleayo, Antioquia, April 2, 1782, "Testimonio de un expediente," 558–459, 536–537; Petición by Luis María Pastor, Antioquia, March 25, 1782, "Testimonio de un expediente," 527–531. On the legal "parallels and connections" between Indians and slaves in Popayán, see Marcela Echeverri, *Indian and Slave Royalists in the Age of Revolution: Reform, Revolution, and Royalism in the Northern Andes, 1780–1825* (New York: Cambridge University Press, 2017). For the cases of Santa Marta and Riohacha, north of Cartagena, see Steinar A. Saether, *Identidades e independencia en Santa Marta y Riohacha, 1750–1850* (Bogotá: Instituto Colombiano de Antropología e Historia, 2005).

26 AHA, Escribanos de Medellín, 1781 to 1810.

27 Some historians warn against acritically relying on accusations and reports by bureaucrats, military officers, and masters claiming that slaves and free people of color were bent on replicating violent actions by slaves elsewhere (especially in in the French Antilles after 1791), or more generally accusations that slaves were out to destroy the world around them. See, for example, Philip D. Morgan, "Conspiracy Scares," *The William and Mary Quarterly* 59.1 (2002): 159–166; Bernardo Leal, "Los esclavos del Chocó, vistos a través de documentos judiciales del siglo XVIII," *150 años de la abolición de la esclavización en Colombia. Desde la marginalidad a la construcción de la nación* (Bogotá: Aguilar, 2003), 330–388; Ada Ferrer, "Speaking;" Ramón Aizpurua, "Revolution and Politics in Venezuela and Curaçao, 1795–1800," and Han Jordaan, "Patriots, Privateers, and International Politics: The Myth of the Conspiracy of Jean Baptiste Tierce Cadet," Wim Klooster and Gert Oostindie, ed., *Curaçao*, 97–122 and 150–169; Jason T. Sharples, "Discovering Slave Conspiracies: New Fears of Rebellion and Old Paradigms of Plotting in Seventeenth-Century Barbados," *American Historical Review* 120.3 (2015): 831–833; Aline Helg, *Slave No More: Self-Liberation before Abolitionism in the Americas* (Chapel Hill: University of North Carolina Press, 2019), ch. 4.

28 Real Audiencia to Manuel Antonio Flores, Quito, December 14, 1781, DRC, 2, 519; Acta capitular, Barbacoas, April 17, 1782, "El cabildo de la ciudad de Barbacoas da cuenta de lo acaecido en ella el día dieciséis de abril del presente año, con motivo de la escasez de tabaco y de la mala conducta del administrador de este ramo," BNC, reel 106, mss. 379, f. 38r–39r.

29 Cabildo de Barbacoas to Manuel Antonio Flores, Barbacoas, n.d., DRC, 2, 533–535; Acta capitular, Barbacoas, April 17, 1782, "El cabildo de la ciudad," f. 38r–39r.

30 Real Audiencia to Manuel Antonio Flores, Quito, December 14, 1781, DRC, 2, 519; Acta capitular, Barbacoas, April 17, 1782, "El cabildo de la ciudad," f. 38r–39r.

31 Jean Pierre Minaudier, "Pequeñas patrias en la tormenta: Pasto y Barbacoas a finales de la colonia y en la Independencia," *Historia y Espacio* 3.11–12 (1987): 142–145; Oscar Almario García, *Los Renacientes y su territorio. Ensayos sobre la etnicidad negra en el Pacífico sur colombiano* (Medellín: Universidad Pontificia Bolivariana, Concejo de Medellín, 2003), ch. 1 and 2.

32 Cortés received news on Peru from his nephew in Lima. Marcos Cortés to José Tenorio, Quito, March 18, 1781, RCD, 1, 161–163. On the Cortés clan, see "Expediente formado con motivo del denuncio que se dio a este gobierno de que Don Casimiro Cortés ha dado muerte a dos esclavos de la mina de su padre Don Marcos Cortés ambos vecinos de la ciudad de Barbacoas," 1787–1788, ACC, Sig. 8833 (Col. J II -3 cr); ACC, Notaria 1ra., vol. 54 (1786-IV), f. 21r–23r; "Recurso de Cortés Narcisa, esclava de don Ruiz José, sobre don Cortés Casimiro, para que, previa tasación, reciba el valor de hijos de dicha Narcisa y les de libertad," 1795, ANE, Popayán, box 240, "Autos seguidos por Dn. Casimiro Cortés con su negro nombrado Andrés sobre libertad," 1798, ANE, Popayán, box 257; Marcela Echeverri, *Indian and Slave*, 92–97, 107–109, 114–116. On the anti-colonial character of Andean insurrection in the early 1780s, see Sinclair Thomson, *We Alone Will Rule: Native Andean Politics in the Age of Insurgency* (Madison: University of Wisconsin Press, 2002).

33 The sacred bonds of subordination were embodied by individuals when they requested blessings from their superiors: slaves from masters, parishioners from priests. The practice is still current among devout people. Some godchildren, for example, ask for their godparent's blessings. A trustworthy nineteenth-century chronicler of Santa Fe, with family roots in Popayán, reminded his readers that slaves would greet their masters with their eyes fixed on the ground while pronouncing the sacred formula "Bendito y alabado sea el santísimo sacramento del altar." José María Cordovez Moure, *Reminiscencias de Santafé y Bogotá* (1893; Madrid: Aguilar, 1957), 469. On the sacred nature of the Spanish political and legal order, see Germán Colmenares, "La ley y el orden social: fundamento profano y fundamento divino," *Varia. Selección de textos* (Bogotá: Tercer Mundo, 1998), 209–229; Isidro Vanegas, "Justicia."

34 Fr. Joaquín de Finestrad, *El Vasallo*, 42.

35 Fr. Joaquín de Finestrad, *El Vasallo*, 42, 375–379, 380, 387.

36 "Embargo en el convento de Capuchinos," Santa Fe, 1794, Guillermo Hernández de Alba, ed., *Proceso contra don Antonio Nariño por la publicación clandestina de la declaración de los derechos del hombre y del ciudadano* (Bogotá: Presidencia de la República, 1980), 219–234; Abbé Raynal, *Histoire philosophique et politique, des établissemens & du commerce des Européens dans les deux Indes* (Amsterdam: 1770), vol. 3, 192–216; Renán Silva, *Los ilustrados de Nueva Granada, 1760-1808. Genealogía de una comunidad de interpretación* (Medellín: Banco de la República, Universidad EAFIT, 2002), 292–297.

37 Laurent Dubois, *Avengers of the New World: The Story of the Haitian Revolution* (Cambridge, MA: Harvard University Press, 2004); Laurent Dubois, *A Colony of Citizens: Revolution and Slave Emancipation in the French Caribbean, 1787–1804* (Chapel Hill: The University of North Carolina Press, Omohundro Institute of Early American History and Culture, 2004); Michel Rodigneaux, *La guerre de course en Guadeloupe. XVIIIe–XIXe siècles. Ou Alger sous les tropiques* (Paris: L'Harmattan, 2006); Edgardo Pérez Morales, *No Limits to Their Sway: Cartagena's Privateers and the Masterless Caribbean in the Age of Revolutions* (Nashville, TN: Vanderbilt University Press, 2018).

38 "Providencias dictadas por el señor don Juan Doroteo del Postigo y Valderrama, del consejo de Su Majestad oidor honorario de la audiencia de Guadalajara, caballero de la Real y distinguida orden española de Carlos III, y asesor general del Virreinato, en 12 de enero de 1793 en conformidad de la comisión a su servicio conferida por el excelentísimo señor virrey del reino de que de los mismos, para que haga efectiva la Real Orden de Su Majestad en punto de la expulsión, y extrañamiento de estos reinos, a los extranjeros que voluntariamente no hagan juramento de fidelidad y vasallaje," AGN, AAI, Historia, vol. 3, No. 59; Sergio Elías Ortíz, *Franceses en la independencia de Colombia* (Bogotá: Academia Colombiana de Historia, Editorial ABC, 1971), 85–99; Anthony McFarlane, *Colombia*, 285–291; Rodrigo García Estrada, "Los extranjeros y su participación en el primer período de la independencia en la Nueva Granada, 1808–1816," *Historia Caribe* 16 (2010): 60–61.

39 Luis de Rieux to Antonio Nariño, Honda, April 12, 1794, Guillermo Hernández de Alba, ed., *Proceso*, 157–158.

40 Sergio Elías Ortíz, *Franceses*, 129–130; Renán Silva, *Los ilustrados*, 292–297, 312–324, 334–340. In 1767, the Jesuit library in Santa Fe had 2,353 titles. In Popayán, the Seminary College had 819 and the Missionary College had 1,066. José María Cabal, known as an avid book reader, owned 126 titles (288 volumes) in 1817. José María Serrano Prada, *Apuntes al catálogo sistemático de la biblioteca del Colegio de Misiones de Popayán, siglos XVI–XVIII. Historia y evaluación de la colección* (Popayán: Universidad del Cauca, 2016), 22, 31, 72.

41 Incomplete letter draft, n.a., *ca.* 1794, AGN, ACH, Camilo Torres, box 1, f. 95r; Fr. Joaquín de Finestrad, *El Vasallo*, 42, 375–379, 380, 387.

42 *Papel periódico de la ciudad de Santafé de Bogotá* (Santa Fe), December 5, 1794.

43 *Papel periódico de la ciudad de Santafé de Bogotá* (Santa Fe), August 29, 1794 and September 19, 1794; Renán Silva, *Prensa y Revolución a finales del siglo XVIII. Contribución a un análisis de la formación de la ideología de Independencia nacional* (Medellín: La Carreta Editores, 2004), 136–141. On the Flour Wars, see Jean Nicolas, *La Rébellion Française. Mouvements populaires et conscience sociale (1661–1789)* (Paris: Éditions du Seuil, 2002), 251–258.

44 John Lynch, *Bourbon*, 254.

45 *Papel periódico de la ciudad de Santafé de Bogotá* (Santa Fe), July 22, 1796 and July 29, 1796.

46 *Papel periódico de la ciudad de Santafé de Bogotá* (Santa Fe), October 10, 1794. The Count of Torre Velarde also believed that the events of 1781 were linked to the current "revolution," as the spirit of rebellion had only grown after what he considered to be a lenient treatment of the comunero leaders. "Informe del Conde," 14.

47 Fr. Joaquín de Finesrad, *El Vasallo*, 115–130, 175–195.

48 Fr. Joaquín de Finestrad, *El Vasallo*, 194.

49 Francisco Tomás y Valiente, *El derecho penal de la Monarquía absoluta (Siglos XVI–XVII–XVIII)* (Madrid: Tecnos, 1969), 317–330.

50 Renán Silva, *Los ilustrados*, 99–118. Pasquinades were commonly used as means to communicate political critique, often targeting visiting authorities with special powers. See Natalia Silva Prada, "Pasquines contra visitadores reales: opinión pública en las ciudades hispanoamericanas de los siglos XVI, XVII Y XVIII," James S. Amelang et al., ed., *Opinión pública y espacio urbano en la Edad Moderna* (Gijón: TREA, 2010), 373–398; Natalia Silva Prada, "Cultura política tradicional y opinión crítica: los rumores y pasquines iberoamericanos de los siglos XVI al XVIII," Riccardo Forte and Natalia Silva, ed., *Tradición y modernidad en la historia de la cultura política: España e Hispanoamérica, siglos XVI–XX* (Mexico City: Universidad Autónoma Metropolitana, Unidad Iztapalapa, 2009), 89–143.

51 Guillermo Hernández de Alba, ed., *Proceso*, esp. 11–37. *Oidor* Joaquín de Mosquera y Figueroa led the prosecution of Nariño. Armando Martínez Garnica, "El caso Antonio Nariño y Álvarez: 'itinerario histórico' de la experiencia de la revolución y vivencia de un historiador 'patriota' adverso al paladín de los chisperos santafereños," paper delivered at *Primer Encuentro Nacional sobre "Itinerarios Históricos,"* Medellín, June 9–10, 2011, Universidad Nacional de Colombia. Paper cited by courtesy of the author.

52 Armando Martínez Garnica, "El caso Antonio Nariño"; Anthony McFarlane, *Colombia*, 285–291; Rodrigo García Estrada, "Los extranjeros," 60–61; Sergio Elías Ortíz, *Franceses*, 85–99.

53 Thomas Gomez, "La République des *cuñados*: familles, pouvoir et société à Santafé de Bogotá, (XVIIIe siècle)," *Caravelle* 62 (1994): 218–223.

54 "Las capitulaciones de los comuneros," 1781, RCD, 1, doc. 36, 88; Thomas Gomez, "La République."

55 "El virrey de Santafé da cuenta de la actitud de rebeldía asumida por el cabildo de la ciudad," Santa Fe, September 19, 1795, Guillermo Hernández de Alba, ed., *Proceso*, 471–473; Sergio Elías Ortíz, *Franceses*, 132; John Leddy Phelan, *The People*, 3–17; Anthony McFarlane, *Colombia*, 285–291.

56 Examples are not hard to come by. Finestrad, for one, believed that "Americans" and "Spaniards," though vassals of the same king and members of the same nation, had dissimilar understandings of and links with the New Kingdom. Spaniards were foreign to the land, merely passing "pilgrims." Fr. Joaquín de Finesrad, *El Vasallo*, 90. Pedro Fermín de Vargas, who called for a revolution of independence as early as *ca.* 1790, maintained that the most salient grievance among local elites stemmed from their exclusion from office in favor of *peninsulares*, most of whom aspired to return to Spain after making their fortunes in the Indies. Pedro Fermín de Vargas, "Relación sucinta del estado actual de las colonies españolas en la América meridional," *ca.* 1805, Pedro Fermín de Vargas, *Pensamientos políticos* (Bogotá: Nueva Biblioteca Colombiana de Cultura, 1986), 184–194.

57 A copy of the document in José de Ezpeleta to Duque de la Alcudia, Santa Fe, January 19, 1795, AGI, Estado, 52, N.10. The letter also claimed that Pedro Fermín de Vargas, another associate of Nariño's who had recently defected, had become a revolutionary agent for the United States. Vargas ranked as high as Francisco de Miranda in the Spanish list of dangerous early South American revolutionaries.

58 Luis Muñoz de Guzmán to José Ezpeleta, Quito, October 21, 1794, AGI, Estado, 53, N.55. The main suspect in the Quito events, Eugenio de Santa Cruz y Espejo, may have personally met Nariño a few years earlier. Ekkehard Keeding, *Surge la nación. La ilustración en la Audiencia de Quito (1725–1812)* (Quito: Banco Central del Ecuador, 2005), 578, 597–608. In an essay on the population of the viceroyalty, Pedro Fermín de Vargas expressly referred to the king of Spain as a tyrant. The essay circulated in manuscript form among students and other people with sympathies for modern philosophy and current political debate. Pedro Fermín de Vargas, "Memoria sobre la población del Reino," *ca.* 1790, Pedro Fermín de Vargas, *Pensamientos*, 144, and Notas on 155–164.

59 José de Ezpeleta to Duque de la Alcudia, Santa Fe, January 19, 1795, AGI, Estado, 52, N.10.

60 Nariño later claimed he had burnt all the copies of his translation, a course of action apparently taken by all others who owned copies. Antonio Nariño y Álvarez to Gobierno de Santa Fe de Bogotá, Santa Fe, April 17, 1811, MGO, vol. 13, 91. Even though he regained the favor of metropolitan authorities, Rieux was unable to translate the verdict into good will from viceregal officials. See "Informe de la Audiencia de Santafé sobre el doctor Luis de Rieux," 1799–1807, Sergio Elías Ortíz, *Colección*, 79–90.

61 "Informe del Conde," 17–19. Other judges also possessed information that Nariño had secretly returned to Santa Fe. See Manuel de Mendoza to Juan Hernández de Alba, Santa Fe, July 5, 1797, AGN, ACH, Camilo Torres, box 2, f. 55r–56r. Authorities had a continuing preoccupation about foreign texts entering the viceroyalty. A package for Guayaquil, confiscated in Maracaibo and sent to Santa Fe, contained "French printed materials, gazettes and other publications." Pedro de Mendinueta to Príncipe de la Paz, Santa Fe, August 19, 1797, AGI, Estado, 52, N.57.

62 On French presence in Spanish territories in the age of the French and Haitian Revolutions, see Marial Iglesias Utset, "Los Despaigne en Saint-Domingue y Cuba: Narrativa microhistórica de una experiencia Atlántica," *Revista de Indias* 71.251 (2011): 77–108; Rebecca J. Scott and Jean M. Hébrard, *Freedom Papers: An Atlantic Odyssey in the Age of Emancipation* (Cambridge: Harvard University Press, 2012); Ada Ferrer, *Freedom's Mirror: Cuba and Haiti in the Age of Revolution* (New York: Cambridge University Press, 2014); Graham T. Nessler, *An Islandwide Struggle for Freedom: Revolution, Emancipation, and Reenslavement in Hispaniola, 1789–1809* (Chapel Hill: The University of North Carolina Press, 2016). Intermittent collaboration between Spain and France, and therefore contact, trade, and tension between the French islands and northern South America was a long-existing phenomenon. See Julius S. Scott, *The Common Wind: Afro-American Currents in the Era of the Haitian Revolution* (London: Verso, 2018), 45–47. On the complexities of trans-imperial contact and geopolitical imagination, see Ernesto Bassi, *An Aqueous Territory: Sailor Geographies and New Granada's Transimperial Greater Caribbean World* (Durham, NC: Duke University Press, 2016).

63 The evidence is abundant. See, for example, Deposition of Joaquín Moreno, Cartagena de Indias, August 5, 1797, AGI, Estado, 57, N.17; José de Ezpeleta to Príncipe de la Paz, Santafé, December 6, 1796, AGI, Estado, 52, N.38; Pedro de Mendinueta to Miguel Cayetano Soler, Santa Fe, March 19, 1803, AGI, Estado, 52, N.135; Pedro de Mendinueta to Miguel Cayetano Soler, and Pedro de Mendinueta to Donatien Marie

Joseph de Rochambeau, Santa Fé, March 19, 1803, AGI, Estado, 52, N.135. See also Pedro de Mendinueta to Pedro Cevallos, Santa Fé, June 19, 1803, AGI, Estado, 53, N.15; Pedro de Mendinueta to Pedro de Cevallos, June 19, 1803, AGI, Estado, 53, N.13.

64 Pedro de Mendinueta to Pedro Cevallos, Santa Fe, April 19, 1803, AGI, Estado, 52, N.13.

65 Pedro de Mendinueta to Pedro Cevallos, Santa Fe, April 19, 1803, AGI, Estado 52, N.13; Laurent Dubois, *Avengers*, 287–290; Laurent Dubois, *A Colony*, 402–404.

66 One example among many is Anastacio Cejudo to the viceroy, Cartagena de Indias, June 30, 1799, and enclosed document, AGN, C, Milicias y Marina, vol. 19, doc. 199. On further complexities of the label "French Negroe," see Ashli White, *Encountering Revolution: Haiti and the Making of the Early American Republic* (Baltimore, MD: Johns Hopkins University Press, 2010).

67 I borrow the notion culture of expectation from Julius S. Scott, *The Common*, ch 3.

2 Landscapes of Slavery, Rumors of Freedom

1 For a late seventeenth-century episode and its contrasting interpretations, see Anthony McFarlane, "Autoridad y poder en Cartagena de Indias: la herencia de los Austrias," Haroldo Calvo and Adolfo Meise Roca, ed., *Cartagena de Indias en el siglo XVIII* (Cartagena: Banco de la República, 2005), 221–259, and Sandra Beatriz Sánchez López, "Miedo, rumor y rebelión: la conspiración esclava de 1693 en Cartagena de Indias," *Historia Crítica* 31 (2006): 77–99. On long-standing fears of slave uprising in Cartagena de Indias, see Antonino Vidal Ortega, "Entre la necesidad y el temor: negros y mulatos en Cartagena de Indias a comienzos del siglo XVII," Berta Ares Queija and Alessandro Stella, ed., *Negros, mulatos y zambaigos: Derroteros africanos en los mundos Ibéricos* (Madrid: Consejo Superior de Investigaciones Históricas, 2000), 89–104.

2 Jason T. Sharples, "Discovering Slave Conspiracies: New Fears of Rebellion and Old Paradigms of Plotting in Seventeenth-Century Barbados," *American Historical Review* 120.3 (2015): 831–833; Jill Lepore, *New York Burning: Liberty, Slavery, and Conspiracy in Eighteenth-Century Manhattan* (New York: Vintage, 2005); Aline Helg, *Slave No More: Self-Liberation before Abolitionism in the Americas* (Chapel Hill: University of North Carolina Press, 2019), ch. 4. See also Laurent Dubois, "Avenging America: The Politics of Violence in the Haitian Revolution," David Patrick Geggus and Norman Fiering ed., *The World of the Haitian Revolution* (Bloomington and Indianapolis: Indiana University Press, 2009), 111–124.

3 On corporate society and the law, see Francisco Tomás y Valiente, *El derecho penal de la Monarquía absoluta (Siglos XVI–XVII–XVIII)* (Madrid: Tecnos, 1969), 317–330; Beatriz Rojas, ed., *Cuerpo político y pluralidad de derechos. Los privilegios de las corporaciones novohispanas* (Mexico City: Cide, Instituto Mora, 2007); Jorge E- Delgadillo Núñez, "The Workings of *Calidad*: Governance, and Social Hierarchies in the Corporations of the Spanish Empire," *The Americas* 76.2 (2019): 15–239. On socially transmitted knowledge, including seeming certainties about social groups different from one's own, see Norbert Elias, *Involvement and Detachment* 1st ed. 1983 (Dublin: University College Dublin Press, 2007); Norbert Elias, *The Society of Individuals* 1st ed. 1987 (Dublin: University College Dublin Press, 2010); Norbert Elias, *The Established and the Outsiders* 1st ed. 1965 (Dublin: University College Dublin Press, 2009). The rare occasions when slaves tried to kill their masters were likely seen as confirmation of the general rule that slaves were naturally inclined to murder, rather than as expressions of circumstances. In Antioquia, every ten or twelve years a slave was tried for the murder or attempted murder of a master or mistress. AHA, Criminales, 1680–1780.

4 DA, vol. 3, book 5, 655.

5 Beatriz Patiño Millán, *Criminalidad, ley penal y estructura social en la provincia de Antioquia. 1750–1820* (Medellín: IDEA, 1994); Hermes Tovar Pinzón, *De una chispa se forma una hoguera: esclavitud, insubordinación y liberación* (Tunja: Universidad Pedagógica y Tecnológica de Colombia, 1992); Jill Lepore, *New York*; Ada Ferrer, "Speaking of Haiti: Slavery, Revolution and Freedom in Cuban Slave Testimony," David Patrick Geggus and Norman Fiering, ed., *The World*, 223–247.

6 On rumor and hopeful tales, see the considerations by Georges Lefebvre, *The Great Fear of 1789: Rural Panic in Revolutionary France* 1st ed. 1932 (New York: Vintage Books, 1973); Carlo Ginzburg, *Clues, Myths, and the Historical Method* 1st ed. 1986 (Baltimore, MD: The Johns Hopkins University Press, 1989); Philip D. Morgan, "Conspiracy Scares," *The William and Mary Quarterly* 59.1 (2002): 159–166; Ada Ferrer, "Speaking;" Jason T. Sharples, "Discovering;" Jill Lepore, *New York;* Arlette Farge and Jacques Revel, *The Vanishing Children of Paris: Rumor and Politics before the French Revolution* 1st ed. 1988 (Cambridge, MA: Harvard University Press, 1991), 106.

7 Margarita Garrido, *Reclamos y representaciones. Variaciones sobre la política en el Nuevo Reino de Granada, 1770–1815* (Bogotá: Banco de la República, 1993); Isidro Vanegas, "Justicia y ley en el Nuevo Reino de Granada, periodo Borbónico," *Historia y Espacio* 16.54 (2020): 47–72.

In 1781, some slaves, though these may have been a minority, took justice into their own hands rather than appealing to the magistrates. See Katherine Bonil Gómez, "De 'un Rey Nuevo en Santa Fe' y otros 'cismas.' Negros, mulatos y zambos en la Rebelión de los Comuneros (1781)," *ACHSC* 47.1 (2020): 87–112.

8 Gerardo Reichel-Dolmatoff, ed., *Diario de viaje del P. Joseph Palacios de la Vega entre los indios y negros de la provincia de Cartagena en el Nuevo Reino de Granada. 1787–1788* (Bogotá: Editorial A.B.C., 1955); Marta Herrera Ángel, *Ordenar para controlar. Ordenamiento espacial y control político en las Llanuras del Caribe y en los Andes Centrales Neogranadinos. Siglo XVIII* (Bogotá: Academia Colombiana de Historia, Instituto Colombiano de Antropología e Historia, 2002).

9 "Relación sobre la situación y utilidad de la plaza de Cartagena de Indias," Cartagena de Indias, January 1, 1805, CGE, Archivo Geográfico y de Estudios Cartográficos, Cartoteca, 85(bis); "Noticia de la pacificacion, conquista y poblacion de la Provincia de Cartagena de Indias y de los prelados de su catedral," 1809, Hispanic Society of America (New York), HC 363/709; Haroldo Calvo Stevenson, ed., *Cartagena de Indias en el siglo XVIII* (Bogotá: Banco de la República, 2005); Hermes Tovar Pinzón, Camilo Tovar M. and Jorge Tovar M., *Convocatoria al poder del número. Censos y estadísticas de la Nueva Granada (1750–1830)* (Bogotá: Archivo General de la Nación, 1994), 487–503; Anthony McFarlane, *Colombia before Independence: Economy, Society, and Politics under Bourbon Rule* (New York: Cambridge University Press, 1993), 353.

10 Joaquín de Cañaveral to José de Ezpeleta, Cartagena, January 29, 1793, AGN, C, Milicias y Marina, vol. 84, f. 102r–v. Another fire was reported on March 19. See Matías Ruíz and José Feliciano Cassado to José de Ezpeleta, Mompox, April 19, 1794, AGN, C, Milicias y Marina, vol. 127, No. 105, f. 880r–881r.

11 Anthony McFarlane, Colombia, 40–48, 105–106; Vladimir Daza Villar, *Los marqueses de Santa Coa. Una historia económica del Caribe Colombiano, 1750–1810* (Bogotá: Instituto Colombiano de Antropología e Historia, 2009); Edgardo Pérez Morales, "Manumission on the Land: Slaves, Masters, and Magistrates in Eighteenth-Century Mompox (Colombia)," *Law & History Review* 35.2 (2017): 511–543.

12 n.t., AGN, C, JC, vol. 139, doc. 1.

13 Jill Lepore, *New York*; Jason T. Sharples, "Discovering," 832, 813, 824.

14 Deposition of Damiana González, Mompox, January 16, 1793, AGN, C, JC, vol. 139, doc. 1, f. 3r.

15 Deposition of Damiana González, Mompox, January 16, 1793, and depositions of Juan Santiago Fontalvo, Mompox, January 21 and 22, February 21, 1793, AGN, C, JC, vol. 139, doc. 1, f. 3r–4r, 14v–23v, 40r.

16 The language and practice of prophecy to forecast social and political change was not uncommon in the Spanish Indies. See Natalia Silva Prada, "Los sueños de expulsión o extinción de los españoles en conspiraciones, rebeliones, profecías y pasquines de la América Hispánica, siglos XVI al XVIII," *Chronica Nova* 38 (2012): 44–46.

17 DA, vol. 1, book 1, 86, 118; *Obras de don Francisco de Quevedo Villegas. Poesías* (Madrid: M. Rivadeneyra, 1877), vol. 3, 378, soneto XIX, 131.

18 Pablo Álvarez to Juan Nepomuceno Berrueco, Mompox, March 23, 1793, AGN, C, JC, vol. 139, doc. 1, f. 49r–51r; DRLJ, 1576–1577; Francisco Tomás y Valiente, *El derecho*, 317–330.

19 Juan Nepomuceno Berrueco to Joaquín de Cañaveral, Mompox, January 22, 1793, AGN, C, Milicias y Marina, vol. 84, f. 104r–105v.

20 On the old rivalries, see "Pleito seguido por los presbíteros Florencio Gutiérrez de Salas y Francisco Javier Ibáñez, en su carácter de capellanes de la Villa de Santa Cruz de Mompós, contra doña Damiana González y después con doña Josefa Narcisa González y su hijo político don Andrés Antonio Larios, herederos de doña Damiana, por una capellanía fundada en aquella vía por el doctor don Luis Ascasúa y don Pedro de Lisarmo," and "Pleito seguido ante la vicaría general de Cartagena, por doña Damiana González con don Miguel Baldovino y después con otros sobre la nulidad de la venta de un hato llamado Santa Rosa (a. los Frailes) en el vecindario de las sabanas del Tolú San Benito Abad, el cual tiene una capellanía que fundo el presbítero Felipe Rivero a favor del presbítero Luis José de Luna, como cura y patrono de aquellos lugares," AGN, C, Capellanías de Bolívar, vol. 2, docs. 1 and 3.

21 Mauricio de Cárcamo to Berrueco, Mompox, July 3, 1793, notificación to Josefa González, Mompox, August 11, 1795, Ángel Juan Bautista Trespalacios Mier to Alcalde Ordinario, Mompox, September 21, 1795, and notificación to Ángel Juan Bautista Trespalacios Mier, Mompox, December 3, 1795, AGN, C, JC, vol. 139, doc. 1, f. 63v–64r, 133v–135r, 147r, 150r–151r.

22 José Ignacio de Pombo, "Memoria sobre el contrabando en el virreinato de Santa Fe," Cartagena de Indias, March 12, 1804, José Ignacio de Pombo, *Comercio y contrabando en Cartagena de Indias* (Bogotá: Nueva Biblioteca Colombiana de Cultura, 1986), 88–90. Aline Helg, "A Fragmented Majority. Free 'of all colors,' Indians and Slaves in Caribbean Colombia during the Haitian Revolution," David Patrick Geggus, ed., *The Impact of the Haitian Revolution in the Atlantic World* (Columbia: University of South Carolina, 2001), 157–175; Aline Helg, *Liberty and Equality in Caribbean Colombia, 1770–1835* (Chapel Hill: The University of North Carolina Press, 2004), 100–105; Marixa Lasso, *Myths of Harmony: Race and Republicanism during the Age of*

Revolution, Colombia 1795–1831 (Pittsburgh, PA: University of Pittsburgh Press, 2007).

23 Conde de Floridablanca to Virrey de Santa Fe, San Lorenzo, November 26, 1791, AGN, AAI, Guerra y Marina, vol. 74, doc. 12, f. 823r–v.

24 Anastasio Cejudo to the Virrey de Santa Fe, Cartagena de Indias, April 9, 1799, and Anastasio Cejudo to Francisco de Saavedra, Cartagena de Indias, April 30, 1799, AGI, Estado, 53, N. 77(1) and (1a). Last-minute tips tended to benefit the first informants. The imminence of the threat increased the "value of the information" they offered, possibly strengthening their bargaining position. Jason T. Sharples, "Discovering," 822–823, 840.

25 Anastasio Cejudo to Francisco de Saavedra, Cartagena de Indias, April 30, 1799, AGI, Estado, 53, N. 77(1). Correspondence between Cejudo and the viceroy available at the Lily Library (Indiana University, Bloomington, Manuscript Department, 1797–1803, Latin American mss. Colombia) could shed new light on this, offering grounds for a different interpretation.

26 Anastasio Cejudo to Príncipe de la Paz, Cartagena de Indias, February 20, 1796, AGI, Estado, 53, N.65; *Mercurio histórico y político...Enero de 1776* (Madrid: Imprenta Real de la Gazeta, 1776), vol. 1, 378. "Competencia movida por el tribunal Real del Consulado de esta plaza al señor Gobernador Capitán General de ella, sobre conocer de la demanda que promueve Don Josef Antonio Mosquera contra Don Francisco Antonio Ahumada, por dinero efectivo que le debe por escritura," 1798, AGN, C, Competencias, vol. 1, doc. 10; Joaquín de Cañaveral to Pedro de Mendinueta, Madrid, April 24, 1798, AGN, Residencias de Cundinamarca, vol. 9, doc. 27.

27 Gustavo Bell Lemus, *Cartagena de Indias. De la Colonia a la República* (Bogotá: Fundación Simón y Lola Guberek, 1991), 16–23; Alfonso Múnera, *El fracaso de la nación. Región, clase y raza en el Caribe colombiano (1717–1821)* (Bogotá: Planeta, 2008), 125–152.

28 Manuel González to Anastasio Cejudo, Kingston, May 24, 1798, AGN, AAI, Historia, vol. 4, doc. 7; "El señor gobernador de la plaza de Cartagena acompaña un oficio del cabildo de aquella ciudad en que representa la necesidad que hay de harinas en ella, y pide se dicten por esta superioridad, las correspondientes providencias para su surtimiento," 1799, AGN, C, Abastos, vol. 10, doc. 6, f. 57r–58r, 64v, 67v; AGI, Estado, 53, N. 76 and N. 77; Anastasio Cejudo to the viceroy, Cartagena de Indias, April 9, 1799, and Anastasio Cejudo to Francisco de Saavedra, Cartagena de Indias, April 30, 1799, AGI, Estado, 53, N. 77(1) and (1a).

29 "Don Gabriel Martínez Guerra alcalde ordinario de la villa de Mompós dirige testimonio de la solicitud de Juan Nepomuceno Surmay albacea

testamentario de don Juan Martín de Setuaín, sobre la reducción y pacificación de los esclavos de la hacienda de San Bartolomé de la Honda; para la providencia que haya lugar," AGN, C, NEB, vol. 3, doc. 5; Edgardo Pérez Morales, "Manumission."

30 Deposition of José María Rodríguez, Mompox, July 1, 1799, "Don Gabriel," f. 788v–789r.

31 Edgardo Pérez Morales, "Manumission." See also Marta Herrera Ángel, *Ordenar*; Aline Helg, *Liberty*, 18–41; Hugues R. Sánchez Mejía, "De arrochelados a vecinos: reformismo borbónico e integración política en las gobernaciones de Santa Marta y Cartagena, Nuevo Reino de Granada, 1740–1810," *Revista de Indias* 75.264 (2015): 457–488. More generally, see Richard L. Kagan, *Urban Images of the Hispanic World: 1493–1793* (New Haven, CT: Yale University Press, 2000), 19–44; Tomás A. Mantecón Movellán and Ofelia Rey Castelao, "Identidades urbanas en la cultura hispánica: policía y cultura cívica," Ofelia Rey Castelao and Tomás A. Mantecón Movellán, ed., *Identidades urbanas en la monarquía hispánica (siglos XVI–XVIII)* (Santiago de Compostela: Universidad Santiago de Compostela, 2015), 17–41.

32 Edgardo Pérez Morales, "Manumission," 538–541.

33 Hermes Tovar Pinzón, *De una chispa*.

34 Report on the roads of Antioquia by Pedro Biturro Pérez, 1781, AHA, Caminos, vol. 71, doc. 1971; Francisco Silvestre, *Relación de la Provincia de Antioquia, ca. 1785–1797*, David J. Robinson, ed. (Medellín: Secreteraría de Educación de Antioquia, 1988); Juan Antonio Mon y Velarde, "Sucinta relación de lo ejecutado en la visita de Antioquia," 1788, *Bosquejo biográfico del señor oidor Juan Antonio Mon y Velarde visitador de Antioquia. 1785–1788*, Emilio Robledo, ed. (Bogotá: Banco de la República, 1945), vol. 2, 309–310; Hermes Tovar Pinzón, Camilo Tovar M. y Jorge Tovar M, *Convocatoria*, 115–123.

35 José Manuel Restrepo, "Ensayo sobre la geografía, producciones, industria y población de la Provincia de Antioquia en el Nuevo Reino de Granada," 1809, *Semanario del Nuevo Reino de Granada* (Bogotá: Biblioteca Popular de Cultura Colombiana, 1942, vol. 1, 243–286; Francisco Silvestre, *Relación*; Juan Antonio Mon y Velarde, "Sucinta;" Robert C. West, *Colonial Placer Mining in Colombia* (Baton Rouge: Louisiana State University Press, 1952); Ann Twinam, *Miners, Merchants and Farmers in Colonial Colombia* (Austin: University of Texas Press, 1982); Jorge Orlando Melo, ed., *Historia de Antioquia* (Medellín: Suramericana de Seguros, 1988); Jorge Orlando Melo, ed, *Historia de Medellín* (Bogotá: Suramericana de Seguros, 1998); Beatriz Patiño Millán, *Riqueza, pobreza y diferenciación social en la provincia de Antioquia durante el siglo XVIII* (Medellín: Universidad de Antioquia, 2011).

36 I borrow the notions of "familiar narrative" and a "model fable" from Arlette Farge and Jacques Revel, *The Vanishing*, 106.

37 For evidence of similar fables as a structural regularity among slaves and serfs, see Linda M. Rupert, *Creolization and Contraband: Curaçao in the Early Modern Atlantic World* (Athens: University of Georgia Press, 2012), 204; Julius S. Scott, *The Common Wind: Afro-American Currents in the Era of the Haitian Revolution* (London: Verso, 2018), 78-80; Wim Klooster, "The Rising Expectations of Free and Enslaved Black in the Greater Caribbean," Wim Klooster and Gert Oostindie, ed., *Curaçao in the Age of Revolutions. 1795–1800* (Leiden: KITLV Press, 2011), 62–69; Laurent Dubois, *A Colony of Citizens: Revolution and Slave Emancipation in the French Caribbean, 1787–1804* (Chapel Hill: The University of North Carolina Press, Omohundro Institute of Early American History and Culture, 2004), 90–92; Roger Bartlett, "The Russian Peasantry on the Eve of the French Revolution," *History of European Ideas* 12.3 (1990): 407; Peter Kolchin, *Unfree Labor: American Slavery and Russian Serfdom* (Cambridge: Harvard University Press, 1987), 322; *Report from a Select Committee of the House of Assembly Appointed to Inquire into the Origins, Causes, and Progress of the Late Rebellion* (Barbados: W. Walker, Mercury and Gazette Office, 1818), 27.

38 Cayetano Buelta Lorenzana to Juan José Callejas, Medellín, December 19, 1781, "Don Alonso Elías Jaramillo Capitán a Guerra del valle de Río Negro dando cuenta con testimonio de lo actuado en asunto del levantamiento que proclamando libertad, tenían proyectado los negros, y demás esclavos de aquel valle coligados con los de las Ciudad de Antioquia, y Villa de Medellín," 1781–1782, BNC, Comuneros, rm 376, f. 2r–3r.

39 Rumor is a secret (a whisper, a murmur), a condensed piece of information shared quietly among discrete groups of people. In practice, however, rumor takes on its full shape when it spreads more generally, when it becomes *vox populi*. Rumor only took off when people were pre-disposed to believe its contents, to relay the information to someone else. See DA, vol. 3, book 1, 655; Marc Bloch, "Reflexiones de un historiador acerca de los bulos surgidos durante la guerra," 1st ed. 1921, Marc Bloch, *Historia e historiadores* (Madrid: Akal, 1999), 175–197. See also Georges Lefebvre, *The Great Fear*.

40 Juan Pablo Pérez de Rublas to José de Ezpeleta, Antioquia, December 13, 1794, AGN, AAI, Historia, vol. 3, No 63, f. 649r–653v.

41 *Papel periódico de la ciudad de Santafé de Bogotá* (Santa Fe), June 24, 1791. See also Renán Silva, *Prensa y Revolución a finales del siglo XVIII. Contribución a un análisis de la formación de la ideología de Independencia nacional* (Medellín: La Carreta Editores, 2004), 27–41.

42 Luis Fernando Franco Rodríguez, "Juntos para luchar: prácticas corporativas de los comerciantes de Antioquia y Santafé de Bogotá a finales de la

Colonia," Javier Guerrero Barón and Luis Weisner Gracia, ed., *Visiones multicolores de la sociedad colonial* (Medellín: La Carreta, 2011), 191–212.

43 Juan Pablo Pérez de Rublas to José de Ezpeleta, Antioquia, December 13, 1794, AGN, AAI, Historia, vol. 3, No 63, f. 649r–653v.

44 Hermes Tovar Pinzón, Camilo Tovar M. y Jorge Tovar M, *Convocatoria*, 118–120; Edgardo Pérez Morales, "La sombra de la muchedumbre: vida urbana y reformismo borbónico en la ciudad de Antioquia," *Historia y Sociedad* 10 (2004): 183–199.

45 Juan Pablo Pérez de Rublas to José de Ezpeleta, Antioquia, December 13, 1794, AGN, AAI, Historia, vol. 3, No 63, f. 649r–651v.

46 Luis Fernando Franco Rodríguez, "Juntos," 209–210; Ann Twinam, *Purchasing Whiteness: Pardos, Mulattos, and the Quest for Social Mobility in the Spanish Indies* (Stanford, CA: Stanford University Press, 2015); Mauricio Alejandro Gómez Gómez, "Cerdos y control social de pobres en la provincia de Antioquia, siglo XVIII," *ACHSC* 43.1 (2016): 31–59. On calidad, see Joanne Rappaport, *The Disappearing Mestizo: Configuring Difference in the Colonial New Kingdom of Granada* (Durham, NC: Duke University Press, 2014) and Jorge E. Delgadillo Núñez, "The Workings of *Calidad*: Governance, and Social Hierarchies in the Corporations of the Spanish Empire," *The Americas* 76.2 (2019): 15–239.

47 Ann Twinam, *Miners*, 27–31, 92–100; Anthony McFarlane, *Colombia*, 70–95. See also Vicente Restrepo, *Estudio sobre las minas de oro y plata en Colombia* (Bogotá: Imprenta de Silvestre y Compañía, 1888).

48 Ann Twinam, *Purchasing*, 245–246. Andrés Pardo, another treasury officer and an ally of Visadías, supported the merchant brothers' petition.

49 José Joaquín Gómez Londoño, Auto, Medellín December 27, 1798, and deposition of José Ignacio Posada, Medellín, December 29, 1798, "Expediente seguido en la villa de Medellín, sobre las voces, que se esparcieron en ella de que los negros esclavos, se hallaban impresionados en que habían venido providencias para su libertad, y que intentaban solicitarla, cuyos rumores promovieron la averiguación del origen de ellas," AGN, AAI, Esclavos, vol. 2, f. 1r–4v, 11r.

50 José Joaquín Gómez Londoño, Auto, Medellín December 27, 1798, and depositions of José Ignacio Posada and Teodoro García, Medellín, December 29, 1798, "Expediente seguido," f. 4r–v, 6v and 11r (interspersed), 12v. The old rumor of a royal decree beneficial to slaves may have gained yet a new lease on life thanks to news that an actual 1789 royal document, providing masters and *procuradores* with instructions for the moderate treatment of slaves, had been kept secret by authorities in some jurisdictions. See "R. Instrucción sobre la educación, trato y ocupación de

los esclavos," Aranjuez, May 31, 1789, Richard Konetzke, *Colección de documentos para la historia de la formación social Hispanoamericana. 1493–1810* (Madrid: Consejo Superior de Investigaciones Científicas, 1962), vol. III-2 (1780–1807), doc. 308, 643–652; Julius S. Scott, *The Common*, 99–107, 131–136, 178–180; Laurent Dubois, *A Colony*, 85–123.

51 Deposition of Teodoro García, Medellín, December 29, 1798, "Expediente seguido," f. 12v.

52 Deposition of José Ignacio, Medellín, December 29, 1798, "Expediente seguido," f. 13v.

53 Diligencia by Jacobo Fascio y Lince, Medellín, December 31, 1798, "Expediente seguido," f. 16v–17r.

54 Antonio Viana to Víctor Salcedo, Medellín, December 31, 1798, Víctor Salcedo to the viceroy, Antioquia, February 12, 1799, "Expediente seguido," f. 7r–v, 34r–v; "Oficio reservado del virrey al secretario de Estado de España sobre la asonada que con el nombre de libertad, han causado los negros de la villa de Medellín," 1799, AGN, C, Miscelánea, vol. 99, doc. 8, f. 133r.

55 Margarita Garrido, *Reclamos*.

56 José Joaquín Gómez Londoño, Auto, Medellín December 27, 1798, "Expediente seguido," f. 1v, 4r–v.

57 Candanga might have evoked struggle and trouble. A colloquial "Americanismo" still in use, meaning "the devil" in El Salvador and Honduras, Candanga also implies things that cause nuisance, in Cuba for example. The word is also used in Venezuela to refer to combative, fiery individuals. *Diccionario de la lengua española*, 22nd. ed. (Madrid: Real Academia Española, 2001). Venezuela's Hugo Chávez went by the Twitter handle @chavezcandanga

58 Candice would later appear painted in the Cuban José Antonio Aponte's book of drawings (1812), in which the notion of Ethiopia seems to have been very relevant. See Ada Ferrer, *Freedom's Mirror: Cuba and Haiti in the Age of Revolution* (New York: Cambridge University Press, 2014), 319.

59 Alonso de Sandoval, *De Instauranda Aethiopum Salute* 1st ed. 1627 (Bogotá: Empresa Nacional de Publicaciones, 1956), 178–179.

60 José Mariano Pontón to the governor, Medellín, March 6, 1806, and depositions of José Antonio Quintana, José María Torres and Salvador Correa, Medellín, March 26 and 28, 1806, "Expediente de la Candanga. Criminal contra los esclavos de esta jurisdicción porque se les presumía alzamiento," AHJM, box 171, doc. 3532, f. 2r–v, 6v–7r, 8r–9r.

61 Depositions of Antonio del Valle, José Antonio del Valle, Medellín, March 26, 1806, "Expediente de la Candanga," f. 4v–5v.

62 Deposition of Juan José Porras, Medellín, May 18, 1806, "Expediente de la Candanga," f. 10r. The notion that justice emanated from monarchs

may have been rooted in political cognitive patterns from West Africa, reproduced locally or reinvigorated periodically through the sporadic arrival of individuals from the Antilles, where hundreds of thousands of people born in Africa were kept in slavery. For the case of Popayán, to be examined in the next section, this possibility is suggested by Marcela Echeverri, *Indian and Slave Royalists in the Age of Revolution: Reform, Revolution, and Royalism in the Northern Andes, 1780–1825* (New York: Cambridge University Press, 2017), 170–173. See also John K. Thornton, "'I Am the Subject of the King of Kongo': African Political Ideology and the Haitian Revolution," *Journal of World History* 4.2 (1993): 181–214.

63 Diego Antonio Nieto, "Relación que manifiesta por menor el nombre y número de los pueblos y sitios comprendidos en cada partido de los 16 que componen la provincia y gobierno de Popayán," Popayán, December 5, 1797, Hermes Tovar Pinzón, Camilo Tovar M. y Jorge Tovar M, *Convocatoria*, 325–335; "Estadística," *La Aurora de Popayán* (May 15, 1814); Peter Marzahl, *Town in the Empire: Government, Politics and Society in Seventeenth Century Popayán* (Austin: Institute of Latin American Studies, University of Texas at Austin, 1978); Germán Colmenares, *Historia económica y social de Colombia II: Popayán, una sociedad esclavista, 1680–1800* 1st ed. 1979 (Bogotá: Tercer Mundo, 1997); Martha Herrera Ángel, *Popayán: la unidad de los diverso. Territorio, población y poblamiento en la provincia de Popayán, siglo XVIII* (Bogotá: Universidad de los Andes, 2009).

64 Peter Marzahl, *Town*, 35–53; Germán Colmenares, *Historia*, 215–246; William Lofstrom, *La vida íntima de Tomás Cipriano de Mosquera (1798–1830)* (Bogotá: Banco de la República, El Áncora, 1996), 38–74; María Teresa Pérez, "Hábitat, Familia y comunidad en Popayán (Colombia) 1750–1850" (Doctoral dissertation, Université de Montréal, 2008), 73–100.

65 Alexander von Humboldt to José Celestino Mutis, Popayán, November 10, 1801, Guillermo Hernández de Alba, ed., *Archivo epistolar del sabio naturalista don José Celestino Mutis* (Bogotá: Instituto Colombiano de Cultura Hispánica, 1975), vol. 4, 11–12.

66 ACC, sig. 5903 (Col. CI-10m), sig. 6320 (Col. CI-10m), sig. 7294 (Col. CI-10m), sig. 6131 (Col. CI-10m), sig. 6529 (Col. CI-10m); Fray Juan de Santa Gertrudis, *Maravillas de la Naturaleza, ca. 1775* (Bogotá: Banco Popular, 1970), vol. 2, 132–142; Hermes Tovar Pinzón, Camilo Tovar M. y Jorge Tovar M., *Convocatoria*, 499; Robert C. West, *The Pacific Lowlands of Colombia: a Negroid Area of the American Tropics* (Baton Rouge: Lousiana State University Press, 1957); Germán Colmenares, *Historia*; Germán Colmenares, *Cali: terratenientes, mineros y comerciantes. Siglo XVIII* (Bogotá: Tercer Mundo, 1997); Mario Diego

Romero, *Poblamiento y Sociedad en el Pacífico colombiano siglos XVI al XVIII* (Cali: Editorial Facultad de Humanidades, Universidad del Valle, 1995); Oscar Almario García, *Los Renacientes y su territorio. Ensayos sobre la etnicidad negra en el Pacífico sur colombiano* (Medellín: Universidad Pontificia Bolivariana, Concejo de Medellín, 2003).

67 "Concurso de acreedores de los bienes de José Tenorio," 1782–1791, ACC, sig. 11273 (Col. J III-9su), f. 46v; "Avalúos relativos a la sucesión de José Tenorio. Remate de la hacienda las Huertas de dicho Tenorio para pagar a los acreedores de la testamentaría," 1788–1795, ACC, sig. 10694 (Col. J II-24su); "Autos relativos a la nulidad del nombramiento del albacea de José Tenorio," 1783–1788, ACC, sig. 10592 (Col. J II-22su); "Expediente sobre la administración de la mina de San Juan por dimisión que de ella hizo don Miguel Tenorio: e instancia y reales provisiones presentadas por don Antonio Tenorio sobre que se le restituya dicha administración," 1787, ANE, Popayán, box 246, exp. 7.

68 "Concurso"; "Avalúos," "Autos;" "Expediente."

69 The undated letter is quoted by Renán Silva, *Los ilustrados de Nueva Granada, 1760–1808. Genealogía de una comunidad de interpretación* (Medellín: Banco de la República, Universidad EAFIT, 2002), 106–108. See also Camilo Torres to his mother María Teresa Tenorio, n.p., *ca.* 1794, AGN, ACH, Camilo Torres, box 1, folder 2, f. 12r–15v.

70 "Expediente sobre publicación de guerra contra la nación Británica, y providencias dadas a las poblaciones de la costa del Mar del Sur por el Señor Gobernador; agregadas las del Excelentísimo Señor Virrey," 1796–1797, ACC, sig. 9062 (Col. M I-1c), f. 5r, 6r, 9r, 13r, 25r; "Acuerdos del cabildo de justicia de Barbacoas, sobre la construcción de un cuartel para los veteranos," 1795, ACC, sig. 9677 (Col. M I-1c); Mariano Álvarez y Basconos to Diego Antonio Nieto, Atacames, January 20, 1799, Juan Martínez de Araújo to Diego Antonio Nieto, Iscuandé, February 3, 1799, and Pedro de Mendinueta to Francisco de Saavedra, Santa Fe, May 19, 1799, AGI, Estado, 52, N.75.

71 Camilo Torres to his mother María Teresa Tenorio, Santa Fe, May 20, 1798, AGN, ACH, Camilo Torres, box 1, folder 1, f. 45v.

72 Camilo Torres to dear Pacha (Francisca Prieto y Ricaurte), n.p., *ca.* July 4, 1802 (see also attached note, n.a., n.p., n.d.), and José Camilo Torres y Tenorio and Francisca Prieto y Ricaurte, marriage contract, Santa Fe, December 11, 1802, with annexed documents, AGN, ACH, Camilo Torres, box 1, folder 2, f. 72r, 123r–133r.

73 Camilo Torres to his mother María Teresa Tenorio, Santa Fe, February 20, 1797, AGN, ACH, Camilo Torres, box 1, folder 1, f. 53r–v.

74 Manuel Torres had traveled to San Juan with a plan to introduce new mining practices, replicating a model developed in Barbacoas. Technical

details are scant. Camilo Torres to Ignacio Torres, Santa Fe, June 20, 1810, AGN, ACH, Camilo Torres, box 1, folder 1, f. 32r.

75 Gerónimo Torres to José Concha, San Juan mine, June 20, 1820, ACC, sig. 6596, (Ind. CIII-2g), f. 1r–v.

76 Gerónimo Torres to José Concha, San Juan mine, June 20, 1820, ACC, sig. 6596, (Ind. CIII-2g), f. 1r–v. For an interpretation of the events at San Juan as a "revolt," see Marcela Echeverri, *Indian and Slaves*, 171. It remained quite difficult for most slaves, especially those on remote mining sites, to voice their grievances and appeal to magistrates. Toward the turn of the nineteenth century, it may have become somewhat easier to appeal to the king's justice, but systematic comparison with the earlier part of the Spanish period is still lacking. See Sherwin Bryant, "Enslaved Rebels, Fugitives, and Litigants: The Resistance Continuum in Colonial Quito," *Colonial Latin American Review* 13.1 (2004): 7–46 and Marcela Echeverri, *Indian and Slave*, 92–122.

77 Gerónimo Torres to José Concha, San Juan mine, June 20, 1820, ACC, sig. 6596, (Ind. CIII-2g), f. 1r–v.

3 Popayán: Prudent Legislation

1 Petition by Félix José de Restrepo and Alejandro de la Rosa, Popayán, June 1791, "Alejandro, esclavo de Manuel de la Rosa, pide su libertad en virtud de haber consignado el valor," ACC, sig. 10250 (Col. J II-14cv); petition by Félix José de Restrepo, Popayán, October 12, 1804, "Solicitud de Francisco Rodríguez, para que se le devuelva su esclava Clara, la que fue puesta en prisión," ACC, sig. 10256 (Col. J II-14cv), f. 5v.

2 Petition by Félix José de Restrepo, Popayán, October 12, 1804, f. 5v.

3 "Expediente relativo a la incorporación de Abogado de esta Real Audiencia que solicita el doctor don Félix de Restrepo, abogado matriculado en la Real Audiencia del Nuevo Reino de Granada de Santa Fe," ANE, Incorporación de abogados, box 3, vol. 9, January 9, 1789; "Expediente del doctor don Félix José Restrepo vecino de la ciudad de Popayán en que pide información para España," ANE, Popayán, box 274, exp. 2, June 20, 1793; Félix José de Restrepo, "Oración para el ingreso de los estudios de filosofía, pronunciada en el Colegio Seminario de la ciudad de Popayán, en el mes de octubre de 1791," *Papel periódico de la ciudad de Santafé de Bogotá* (Santa Fe), December 16, 1791; petition by Félix José de Restrepo and Pedro Antonio Ibargüen, Popayán, *ca.* April 29, 1791, "Pedro Antonio Ibargüen contra Manuel José Grueso por despojo de una mina de Iscundé," ACC, sig. 11367, (Col. JI-17mn), f. 2r; Mariano Ospina Rodríguez, *El doctor José Félix de Restrepo y su época* 1st ed. 1888 (Bogotá: Biblioteca Aldeana de Colombia, 1936), 60–62; Edgardo Pérez Morales, "Félix José de Restrepo, las ambigüedades de la esclavitud y la

sensibilidad antiesclavista. Popayán, 1783–1808," *ACHSC* 48.1 (2021): 45–67.

4 "Pedro Antonio Ibargüen;" "José Ignacio de Castro contra varios individuos de Iscuandé por despojo," ACC, sig. 11378 (Col. JI-17mn).

5 HRC, vol. 1, 73–83; François-Xavier Guerra, *Modernidad e independencias. Ensayos sobre las revoluciones hispánicas* (Madrid: MAPFRE, 1992); Renán Silva, *Los ilustrados de Nueva Granada, 1760–1808. Genealogía de una comunidad de interpretación* (Medellín: Banco de la República, Universidad EAFIT, 2002); Daniel Gutiérrez Ardila, *Un Nuevo Reino. Geografía política, pactismo y diplomacia durante el Interregno en Nueva Granada (1808–1816)* (Bogotá: Universidad Externado de Colombia, 2010).

6 Camilo Torres to Ignacio Tenorio, Santa Fe, May 29, 1810, Boletín de Historia y Antigüedades 29 (1905): 260–271; *La Bagatela* (Santa Fe), 38 issues, July 14, 1811 to April 12, 1812.

7 Antonio de Villavicencio, "Delicadísimo punto y plan sobre el comercio de esclavos y la absoluta abolición de la esclavitud en ambas Américas, propuesto por un propietario," Seville, November 16, 1809, BNC, Fondo Antiguo, RM 223, pza 1; J. D. Monsalve, *Antonio de Villavicencio (el protomartir) y la revolución de la independencia* (Bogotá: Academia Colombiana de Historia, 1920).

8 ACC, Notaría 1ra., vol. 56 (1789-IV), f. 13r. On Popayán's slave market, see the rich notarial records kept at ACC, Notaría 1ra., and Germán Colmenares, *Historia económica y social de Colombia II: Popayán, una sociedad esclavista, 1680–1800* 1st ed. 1979 (Bogotá: Tercer Mundo, 1997), 31–48. A slave entrepôt, Cartagena transshipped most slaves sold there to Panama, Peru, the Antilles, and the interior of the New Kingdom, including Popayán. Slaves were sold locally in Cartagena too, but the notarial records have disappeared, making it impossible to fully grasp the long-term trends of the local slave market.

9 ACC, Notaría 1ra., vol. 56 (1789-IV), f. 13r, 516r, 523v–525r; vol. 57 (1791-I), f. 91v–92v, (1791-III), f. 194r; vol. 58 (1792-I), f. 287r–288r; vol. 59 (1792-I), f. 46r–v, 48r, 87v, 89r–v, 203v–204v, (1793-IV), f. 8r–v, 10r; vol. 60 (1794-III), f. 102r–103v, 125v, 127r–v, (1794-VI), f. 76v–77r; vol. 61 (1796-V), f. 91r–92v; vol. 62 (1797-V), f. 104v, 106r–v, (1797-VI), f. 142r–v; vol. 63 (1798-II), f. 83r–v, 85r, 92r–v; vol. 73 (1801-I), f. 146v–147v.

10 ACC, Notaría 1ra., vol. 57 (1791-III), f. 194r–v.

11 ACC, Notaría 1ra., vol. 59 (1793-IV), f. 8r-10r and 104r–112r.

12 Félix José de Restrepo, last will and testament, 1794, ACC, Notaría 1ra., vol. 59 (1794-II), f. 178v–180r; vol. 73 (1808-I), f. 101r–105r, 108v-109v; ACC, sig. 9836 (Col. JII-7cv); "Padrón de la ciudad de Popayán, con once

planes particulares, y uno general que manifiestan el estado de su población hasta 31 de Diciembre de 1807," entry for manzana 27, FHL, International Film, No. 1389116, item 1.

13 ACC, Notaría 1ra., vol. 57 (1790-IV), f. 26v–33r.

14 ACC, Notaría 1ra., vol. 58 (1792-III), f. 12v–20v.

15 ACC, Notaría 1ra., vol. 58 (1792-III), f. 24r–v.

16 ACC, Notaría 1ra., vol 54 (1786-II), f. 36r–37r; vol. 57 (1791-III), f. 260r–261r; vol. 59 (1792-I), f. 246r–247r; AHA, Escribanos de Medellín, Trujillo, 1805, f. 72r–74r and Miguel María Uribe, last will and testament, Trujillo, 1843, f. 79r–82v; Mariano Ospina Rodríguez, *El doctor*, 92–93.

17 Restrepo and his clients were well aware that in the governorate of Popayán, freedom was almost impossible to obtain. Between 1781 and 1830, 4,811 slaves were sold in Popayán, but only 432 slaves obtained their freedom papers. Up to 1810, registered manumissions averaged seven every year, but slave sales averaged 125. While slave sales sharply declined over the following decades, the number of manumissions rose only slightly. ACC, Notaría 1ra., vols. 51 (1781-III) to 82 (1830-I).

18 "Alejandro." On *papel*, see Alejandro de la Fuente, "Slaves and the Creation of Legal Rights in Cuba: Coartación and Papel," *Hispanic American Historical Review* 87.4 (2007): 659–692.

19 "Solicitud de Francisco," f. 5v; *Qvarta Partida* (Salamanca: Andrea de Portonariis, 1555), Tit. XXII, Law VII, f. 57v. On *prescripción*, see Rebecca J. Scott, "Social Facts, Legal Fictions, and the Attribution of Slave Status: The Puzzle of Prescription," *Law & History Review* 35.1 (2017): 9–30.

20 *Qvarta Partida*, Tit. V, preamble, Tit. XXI, Law I, Tit. XXII, preamble, f. 15r, 54v, and 56v.

21 See the notarial records at ACC, and *Tercera Partida* (Salamanca: Andrea de Portonariis, 1555), Tit. XXIX, Laws XXIII–XXV, f. 170v; *Qvarta Partida*, Tit. XXI, Law VI, f. 55v–56r; José Luis Cortés López, "Esclavos en medios eclesiásticos entre los siglos XII–XIV: apuntes para el estudio de la esclavitud en la Edad Media," *Espacio, tiempo y forma* 3.5 (1992): 423–440; Carlos Eduardo Valencia Villa, *Alma en boca y huesos en costal. Una aproximación a los contrastes socio-económicos de la esclavitud: Santafé, Mariquita y Mompox (1610–1660)* (Bogotá: Instituto Colombiano de Antropología e Historia, 2003); Ángel Muñoz García, "La condición del hombre en la Edad Media: ¿siervo, esclavo o qué?," *Revista de Filosofía* 25.57 (2007): 115–142; William D. Phillips, Jr., *Slavery in Medieval and Early Modern Iberia* (Philadelphia: University of Pennsylvania Press, 2014), ch. 2.

22 "Solicitud de Francisco," f. 19r.

23 TLC, 472; DA, vol. 2, book 1, 279; Antonio Manuel Hespanha, *Como os juristas viam o mundo. 1550–1750. Direitos, estados, pessoas, coisas, contratos, ações e crimes* (Lisbon: 2015), 153, 367.

24 Félix José de Restrepo, "Reglamento para las escuelas de la provincia de Antioquia," Medellín, December 6, 1819, Rafael Montoya y Montoya, ed., *Obras completas de José Félix de Restrepo* (Medellín: Bedout, 1961), 186–210.

25 Renán Silva, *Los ilustrados*, 50–56, 62–69; Renán Silva, *La Ilustración en el virreinato de la Nueva Granada. Estudios de historia cultural* (Medellín: La Carreta, 2005), 15–45; Daniel Herrera Restrepo, *El pensamiento filosófico de José Félix de Restrepo* (Bogotá: Universidad Santo Tomás, 2006), 37–47; Edgardo Pérez Morales, "Félix."

26 Félix José de Restrepo, "Oración."

27 Renán Silva, *Los ilustrados*, ch. 2.

28 José Hilario López, *Memorias* 1st ed. 1857 (Bogotá: Biblioteca Popular de Cultura Colombiana, 1942), 15–17; David Fernando Prado Valencia, "Tensiones en la ciudad. Popayán, 1808–1822" (Undergraduate thesis, Universidad del Cauca, Popayán, 2008), 54–56.

29 Samuel Pufendorf, *De Jure Naturae et Gentium. Libri Octo* 1st ed. 1688, ed., trans. C. H. Oldfather and W. A. Oldfather (Oxford and London: Clarendon Press, Humphrey Milford, 1934), vol II, 38, 330–345, 934–946; Cicero, *On Duties* ed., trans. M. T. Griffin and E. M. Atkins (Cambridge: Cambridge University Press, 1991), 18, 41–42. See also Kari Saastamoinen, "Pufendorf on Natural Equality, Human Dignity, and Self-Esteem," *Journal of the History of Ideas* 71.1 (2010): 39–62. On ideas on human dignity more generally, see Herschel Baker, *The Image of Man: A Study of the Idea of Human Dignity in Classical Antiquity, the Middle Ages, and the Renaissance* (New York: Harper & Row, 1961).

30 "Solicitud de Francisco," f. 5v; Gaetano Filangieri, *La scienza della legislazione* 1st ed. 1780–1791 (Venice: Centro di Studi sull'Illuminismo europeo "G. Stiffoni," 2003–2004), 7 vols; See also Vincenzo Ferrone, *The Politics of Enlightenment: Constitutionalism, Republicanism, and the Rights of Man in Gaetano Filangieri* (New York: Anthem Press, 2012) and Alessandro Tuccillo, *Il commercio infame. Antischiavismo e diritti dell'uomo nel Settecento italiano* (Naples: Università degli Studi di Napoli Federico II, 2013).

31 According to Finestrad, the comuneros had criminally stolen this prerogative in the year 1781. Fr. Joaquín de Finestrad, *El vasallo instruído en el estado del Nuevo Reino de Granada y en sus respectivas obligaciones ca. 1789* (Bogotá: Universidad Nacional de Colombia, 2000), 178–181. See also Isidro Vanegas, "Justicia y ley en el Nuevo Reino de Granada, periodo Borbónico," *Historia y Espacio* 16.54 (2020): 55–58.

32 Alexander von Humboldt, Diario VII a and b, 173, *Alexander von Humboldt en Colombia. Extractos de sus diarios* (Bogotá: Flota Mercante Grancolombiana, 1982), 90a. Ibargüen was a common last name among Chocó slaves. Orián Jiménez, *El Chocó: un paraíso del demonio. Nóvita, Citará y el Baudó, siglo XVIII* (Medellín: Universidad de Antioquia, 2004), 34, 79–80.
33 "Pedro Antonio Ibargüen," f. 1r, 16v; "José Ignacio de Castro," f. 21r–23v.
34 "Pedro Antonio Ibargüen," f. 1r–2v.
35 "Pedro Antonio Ibargüen," f. 2r–v.
36 "Pedro Antonio Ibargüen," f. 2v–r.
37 "Pedro Antonio Ibargüen," f. 6r, 8r–v.
38 "Pedro Antonio Ibargüen," f. 11v.
39 "Pedro Antonio Ibargüen," f. 12r.
40 "Pedro Antonio Ibargüen," f. 12r, 17v.
41 "Pedro Antonio Ibargüen," f. 17v–87r; untitled document, ACC, sig. 11383 (Col. JI-17mn), f. 17r–26v.
42 "José Ignacio de Castro," f. 21r–23v.
43 "Pedro Antonio Ibargüen," f. 18r.
44 Untitled document, ACC, sig. 11383 (Col. JI-17mn), f. 17r.
45 Untitled document, ACC, sig. 11383 (Col. JI-17mn), f. 31r–32r.
46 Alonso de Sandoval, *De Instauranda Aethiopum Salute* 1st ed. 1627 (Bogotá: Empresa Nacional de Publicaciones, 1956), 175–187.
47 "José Ignacio de Castro," f. 1v–2r.
48 Doc. 308, "R. Instrucción sobre la educación, trato y ocupación de los esclavos," Aranjuez, May 31, 1789, Richard Konetzke, *Colección de documentos para la historia de la formación social Hispanoamericana. 1493–1810* (Madrid: Consejo Superior de Investigaciones Científicas, 1962), vol. III, book 2 (1780–1807), 643–652; Manuel Lucena Salmoral, *Los códigos negros de la América Española* (Alcalá de Henares: Ediciones Unesco, Universidad de Alcalá, 1996), 115–117.
49 "José Ignacio de Castro," f. 8r–14r.
50 "José Ignacio de Castro," f. 15r–33v.
51 Agustín Gutiérrez Moreno to José Gregorio Gutiérrez Moreno, Maracaibo, July 21, 1808, Isidro Vanegas Useche, ed., *Dos vidas, una revolución. Epistolario de José Gregorio y Agustín Gutiérrez Moreno* (Bogotá: Universidad del Rosario, 2011), 33–34; Acta capitular, Medellín, October 3, 1808, AHM, Libros Capitulares, vol. 73, f. 189v–190v; Acta capitular, Cartagena de Indias, October 27, 1808, AGI, Santa Fe, 1011; Acta capitular, Popayán, October 29, 1808, ACC, Capitulares, vol. 54, 1808, f. 25v.
52 Alfonso Múnera, *El fracaso de la nación: Región, clase y raza en el Caribe colombiano (1717–1821)* (Bogotá: Planeta, 2008); Jaime E. Rodríguez O., "Las primeras juntas autonomistas. 1808–1812," Germán Carrera

Damas, ed., *Historia de América Andina, vol. 4, Crisis del régimen colonial en Independencia* (Quito: Universidad Andina Simón Bolívar, Corporación Editora Nacional, 2003), 129–168; Daniel Gutiérrez Ardila, *Un Nuevo Reino*.

53 Camilo Torres to Ignacio Tenorio, Santa Fe, May 29, 1810, 260, 264–265, 269–270; H. J. König, "Metáforas y símbolos de legitimidad e identidad nacional en Nueva Granada (1810–1830)," Antonio Annino et al. ed., *America Latina: dallo stato coloniale allo stato nazionale* (Milan: Franco Angeli, 1987), vol. 2, 773–788; Daniel Gutiérrez Ardila, *Un Nuevo Reino*, 135–137.

54 Camilo Torres to Ignacio Tenorio, Santa Fe, May 29, 1810, 261, 265–270.

55 HRC, vol. 1, 106–115; Alfonso Múnera, *El fracaso*, 170–171.

56 *Aviso al Público* (Santa Fe), October 13, December 8, 1810; Jaime E. Rodríguez O., *La revolución política durante la época de la independencia. El Reino de Quito, 1808–1822* (Quito: Universidad Andina Simón Bolívar, Corporación Editora Nacional, 2006); Armando Martínez Garnica, *El legado de la "Patria Boba"* (Bucaramanga: Universidad Industrial de Santander, 1998); Armando Martínez Garnica, "Las juntas neogranadinas de 1810," Armando Martínez Garnica and Guillermo Bustos, ed., *La Independencia en los países andinos: Nuevas perspectivas* (Bucaramanga: Universidad Andina Simón Bolívar-Ecuador, Organización de los Estados Iberoamericanos para la Educación, la Ciencia y la Cultura, 2004), 112–134; Daniel Gutiérrez Ardila, *Un Nuevo Reino*, part 1; David Fernando Prado Valencia, "Tensiones," 51–59.

57 Cabildo de Popayán (Manuel José de Borja, Antonio Bueno, José Solís, Felipe Grueso Rodríguez and Joaquín Gutiérrez) to Secretario del despacho universal de Estado, Pasto, May 16, 1811, AGI, Quito, 386; David Fernando Prado Valencia, "Tensiones," 56–58, 61–63.

58 Cabildo de Popayán (Manuel José de Borja, Antonio Bueno, José Solís, Felipe Grueso Rodríguez and Joaquín Gutiérrez) to Secretario del despacho universal de Estado, Pasto, May 16, 1811; Ignacio Torres to Camilo Torres, Popayán, May 7, 1811, *Boletín de Historia y Antigüedades* 26 (1905): 74–79; David Fernando Prado Valencia, "Tensiones," 56–65.

59 "Acta de instalación de la Junta Provisional de gobierno de las seis ciudades confederadas del Valle del Cauca, en Cali, a 10 de Febrero de 1811," Alfonso Zawadsky Colmenares, *Las Ciudades Confederadas del Valle del Cauca en 1811* (Cali: Centro de Estudios Históricos y Sociales Santiago de Cali, Gerencia Cultural de la Gobernación del Valle, 1996), 91–93; HRC, vol. 1, 120–121, 128, 135–137; Zamira Díaz López, "Las transformaciones políticas de los cabildos de la provincia de Popayán durante la Primera República neogranadina," *Anuario de Historia Regional y de las Fronteras* 11 (2006): 301–317.

60 David Fernando Prado Valencia, "Tensiones," 64.

61 Miguel Tacón to Primer secretario del despacho universal de Estado, Tumaco, December 7, 1811, AGI, Quito, 386; HRC, vol. 1, 135; Alfonso Zawadsky Colmenares, *Las Ciudades*; Daniel Gutiérrez Ardila, *Un Nuevo Reino*, 364–365.

62 Peter Blanchard, *Under the Flags of Freedom: Slave Soldiers and the Wars of Independence in Spanish South America* (Pittsburgh, PA: University of Pittsburgh Press, 2008), 26, 29, 34, 66, 70, 74.

63 "Causa contra Juan Manuel Mosquera comenzada a 15 de diciembre. Juez el comandante de Patriotas, escribano, el público y comercio [sic]," ACC, sig. 6384 (Ind. MI-3j), f. 2r; HRC, vol. I, 145–149, 169–179; Peter Blanchard, *Under*, 22–24.

64 Gerónimo Torres to Miguel Tacón, Tambo, January 24, 1811, ACC, sig. 6597 (Ind. CII-2g); Gerónimo Torres to Señor Gobernador, Mina de San Juan, June 20, 1820, ACC, sig. 6596, (Ind. CIII-2g), f. 1r–v.

65 Gerónimo Torres to Señor Gobernador, Mina de San Juan, June 20, 1820, f. 1r–v.

66 José Gregorio Gutiérrez Moreno to Agustín Gutiérrez Moreno, Santa Fe, May 9, 1811, Isidro Vanegas Useche, ed., *Dos vidas*, 208–209; HRC, vol. 1, 135–137; "Causa contra Juan Manuel Mosquera," f. 1r–v.

67 Cabildo de Popayán (Manuel José de Borja, Antonio Bueno, José Solís, Felipe Grueso Rodríguez and Joaquín Gutiérrez) to Secretario del despacho universal de estado, Pasto, May 16, 1811, depositions of Victoriano Sarasti, Cayetano Sarasti, Nicolás Sarasti, Pasto, June 10, 11, 14, 1811, and deposition of Victoriano Sarasti, Pasto, June 10, 1811, AGI, Quito, 386.

68 In August 1810, Tacón had agreed to the formation of a "Junta provisional de salud y seguridad pública." The governor, however, was able to keep full control of the government, making the new arrangement a junta in name only. "Popayán. Acta del cabildo abierto convocado por el gobernador de Popayán y Proclama de la Junta Provisional de Seguridad Pública, 11 y 14 de agosto de 1810," and "Noticia de la instalación de la Junta de Gobierno de la Provincia de Popayán 21 de junio 1811," Ines Quintero Montiel and Armando Martínez Garnica, ed., *Actas de formación de juntas y declaraciones de independencia (1809–1822). Reales Audiencias de Quito, Caracas y Santa Fe* (Bucaramanga: Universidad Industrial de Santander, 2008), vol. 2, 202–208.

69 Cabildo de Barbacoas to Miguel Tacón, Barbacoas, August 28, 1811, AGI, Quito, 386; José Nicolás de Urigüen to Miguel Tacón, Tumaco, September 30, 1811, Miguel Tacón to Joaquín de Molina, Castigo, August 7, 1811 and Tumaco, November 23, 1811, Ignacio Rodríguez to Miguel Tacón, Guapi, November 8, 1811, June 6, 1811, and conditions of transport agreement between Francisco Ramírez, owner and captain of the

Cantabro, and Andrés Quintián y Ponte, bishop of Cuenca, Guayaquil July 14, 1811, AGI, Quito, 386.

70 HRC, vol. 1, 135–136. Dictamen by Manuel José de Borja, Pasto, June 7, 1811, AGI, Quito, 386.

71 Actas capitulares, Popayán, March 10, 20, 25, 1811, AGI, Quito, 386; Santiago Arroyo, *Apuntes históricos sobre la revolución de la independencia de Popayán* (Bogotá: Librería Nueva, 1896), March 24, 1811, 71; Miguel Tacón to Primer secretario del despacho universal de Estado, Tumaco, December 7, 1811, AGI, Quito, 386. Some patricians in Popayán allegedly read copies of the proceedings of the Buenos Aires cabildo, where magistrates discussed offering freedom to the slaves on account of the lack of people in arms to defend the city. See Dictamen by Manuel José de Borja, Pasto, June 7, 1811, AGI, Quito, 386.

72 Acta capitular, Popayán, April 15, 1811, and "cabildo intruso" to Muy Ilustre Cabildo, April 22, 1811, AGI, Quito, 386.

73 "Causa contra Juan Manuel Mosquera," f. 2r–4v.

74 Miguel Tacón to Primer secretario del despacho universal de Estado, Tumaco, December 7, 1811, AGI, Quito, 386.

75 J. D. Monsalve, *Antonio*; Armando Martínez Garnica and Daniel Gutiérrez Ardila, ed., *Quién es quién en 1810. Guía de Forasteros del Virreinato de Santafé* (Bogotá: Universidad del Rosario, 2010), 313; Daniel Gutiérrez Ardila, *Un Nuevo Reino*, 132–135.

76 Antonio de Villavicencio to Miguel de Tacón y Rosique, Santa Fe, May 4, 1810, and June 6, 1811, AGI, Quito, 386; Antonio de Villavicencio, "Delicadísimo."

77 Antonio de Villavicencio to señores Lardizábal and Primer secretario de Estado y del despacho, Cartagena de Indias, May 24, 1810, *Boletín Historial* 1.12 (1916): 448–463; Antonio de Villavicencio to the Regency Council, Cartagena de Indias, May 29, 1810, *Boletín Historial* 2.15–16 (1916): 113–117.

78 Antonio de Villavicencio, "Delicadísimo," f. 3v, 4r–v, 5r.

79 Antonio de Villavicencio, "Delicadísimo," f. 4r–5v.

80 Antonio de Villavicencio, "Delicadísimo," f. 5v.

81 Antonio de Villavicencio, "Delicadísimo," f. 3r.

82 Antonio de Villavicencio, "Delicadísimo." f. 6v.

83 "Memoria histórica de los acontecimientos militares que tuvieron lugar en las provincias del Cauca y Popayán desde el principio de la Revolución de la Nueva Granada en 1809. Por un Alférez de las tropas republicanas," 1840, ACC, Sala Mosquera, folder 48, doc. 11602; HRC, vol. 1, 192; M. Leonidas Scarpetta and Saturnino Vergara, *Diccionario biográfico de los campeones de la libertad de Nueva Granada, Venezuela, Ecuador y Perú. Que comprende sus servicios, hazañas y virtudes* (Bogotá: Imprenta de

Zalamea, por M. Díaz, 1879), 504, 701; Mariano Ospina Rodríguez, *El doctor*, 92–93; María Eugenia Chaves Maldonado, "El oxímoron de la libertad. La esclavitud de los vientres libres y la crítica a la esclavización africana en tres discursos revolucionarios," *Fronteras de la Historia* 19.1 (2014): 174–200.

84 Antonio de Villavicencio, "Delicadísimo," f. 6r.

85 Simón Sáenz de Vergara and Felipe Grueso Rodríguez to Miguel Tacón, Tumaco, December 7, 1811, AGI, Quito, 386. On popular royalism in the governorate of Popayán, see Marcela Echeverri, *Indian and Slave Royalists in the Age of Revolution: Reform, Revolution, and Royalism in the Northern Andes, 1780–1825* (New York: Cambridge University Press, 2016).

86 Santiago Arroyo, *Apuntes*, April, 1812, 86; Jose Hilario López, *Memorias*, 19–20; HRC, vol. 1, 170–172; M. Leonidas Scarpetta and Saturnino Vergara, *Diccionario*, 504–505; Mariano Ospina Rodríguez, *El doctor*, 60–61, 65–66, 82–83.

87 "Libro primero de la Contaduría, para compras de metales de oro, y plata para los años de 1811 y 1812," ACC, sig. 6195 (Ind. CI-11f), f. 45v.

88 "Libro primero," f. 95r, 97r, 98v, 102r, 108r, 112r, 119v, 120r.

4 Cartagena: Equality and Natural Law

1 Exposition by Melchor Sáenz de Ortíz, Mompox, December 6, 1804, "Don Melchor Sáenz de Ortíz contra don Francisco de la Barcena Posada sobre la libertad de una esclava," AGN, C, NEB, vol. 9, doc. 3, f. 265v.

2 On natural law and rights-claiming by slaves in Spanish America, see Bianca Premo, *The Enlightenment on Trial: Ordinary Litigants and Colonialism in the Spanish Empire* (New York: Oxford University Press, 2017), 207–212. On the place of slavery in the development of natural law theories, see Alessandro Tuccillo, *Il commercio infame. Antischiavismo e diritti dell'uomo nel Settecento italiano* (Naples: Università degli Studi di Napoli Federico II, 2013), 129–139, 268–282.

3 On natural law and the intellectual formation of the viceroyalty's jurists, see Renán Silva, *Universidad y sociedad en el Nuevo Reino de Granada. Contribución a un análisis histórico de la formación intelectual de la sociedad colombiana* (Bogotá: Banco de la República, 1992); Renán Silva, *Los ilustrados de Nueva Granada, 1760–1808. Genealogía de una comunidad de interpretación* (Medellín: Banco de la República, Universidad EAFIT, 2002); Daniel Gutiérrez Ardila, *Un Nuevo Reino. Geografía política, pactismo y diplomacia durante el interregno en Nueva Granada (1808–1816)* (Bogotá: Universidad Externado de Colombia, 2010), ch. 2.

4 José Antonio Maldonado to Real Audiencia, Santa Fe, *ca.* August 8, 1777, "Don José Antonio Ambrosi [sic] de Arango sobre la venta que se le quiere precisar de un negro esclavo," AGN, C, NEA, vol. 1, doc. 23, f. 716r–v.

5 José Ignacio de San Miguel, Mompox, February 28, 1777, "Don José Antonio Ambrosi," f. 703r–v.

6 Daniel Gutiérrez Ardila, "Las querellas de Mompox: Subordinación estratégica, erección de junta provincial e invención historiográfica de la independencia absoluta, 1805–1811," *Historia y Sociedad* 23 (2012): 111–146.

7 Gabriel Gutiérrez de Piñeres to Pantaleón Germán Ribón, Cartagena de Indias, October 12, 1812, Concejo Municipal, *Documentos para la historia de Cartagena, 1810–1812* (Cartagena: Tipografía Hernández, 1963), 242–245; Armando Martínez Garnica and Daniel Gutiérrez Ardila, ed., *Quién es quién en 1810. Guía de Forasteros del Virreinato de Santafé* (Bogotá: Universidad del Rosario, 2010), 62, 115; Alfonso Múnera, *El fracaso de la nación. Región, clase y raza en el Caribe colombiano (1717–1821)* 1st ed. 1998 (Bogotá: Planeta, 2008), 188–191; Aline Helg, *Liberty and Equality in Caribbean Colombia, 1770–1835* (Chapel Hill: The University of North Carolina Press, 2004), 90; Renán Silva, *Los ilustrados*, 83–90, 459–460.

8 Henry Louis Ducoudray Holstein, *Memoirs of Simón Bolívar and of His Principal Generals* 1st ed. 1828 (Middletown: Terra Firma, 2010), 132.

9 The 1822 statement by Juan Guillermo Ros is quoted in Adelaida Sourdis, *Cartagena de Indias durante la primera República, 1810–1815* (Bogotá: Banco de la República, 1988), 35.

10 Anthony McFarlane, *Colombia before Independence: Economy, Society, and Politics under Bourbon Rule* (New York: Cambridge University Press, 1993), 44–45; Vladimir Daza Villar, ed., *Los Libros de contabilidad del marqués de Santa Coa, Mompox, provincia de Cartagena, siglo XVIII* (Bogotá: Banco de la República, 2016); Hermes Tovar Pinzón, *Hacienda colonial y formación social* (Barcelona: Sendai Ediciones, n.d.), 93–119; Aline Helg, *Liberty*, 49–53.

11 "Testimonio de Real Provisión a favor de los naturales del pueblo de Talaigua de las tierras frontero a su pueblo," AGN, C, Resguardos de Bolívar y Magdalena, vol. 1, doc. 18; AGN, C, Milicias y Marina, vol. 86, f. 560–563, vol. 43, doc. 6, f. 246–250, 256r and Juan Manuel de la Carrera to the Arzobispo Virrey, Mompox, August 21, 1786, with accusation, in f. 262r–263r; Antonio Joseph García de la Guardia, *Kalendario manual y guía de forasteros en Santa Fé de Bogotá capital del Nuevo Reyno de Granada, para el año de 1805* (Santa Fe: Imprenta Real, n.d.), 235; *Alexander von Humboldt en Colombia. Extractos de sus diarios* (Bogotá: Flota Mercante Grancolombiana, 1982), Diario VII a and b, 16a.

12 Hermes Tovar Pinzón, Camilo Tovar M. and Jorge Tovar M, *Convocatoria al poder del número. Censos y estadísticas de la Nueva Granada (1750–1830)* (Bogotá: Archivo General de la Nación, 1994), 498–499, 515; Aline Helg, *Liberty*, 84.

13 *Alexander*, Diario VII a and b, 16a, 39–40.

14 Across the 1820s, Mompox continued to be a nodal transit point for import merchandise en route to the Andean highlands and export gold bound for Kingston, London, and New York. A Swedish traveler reported that the most prosperous merchants from the United States, Jamaica, England, and France residing in Cartagena had agents in Mompox. See Carl August Gosselman, *Viaje por Colombia. 1825 y 1826* 1st ed. 1830 (Bogotá: Banco de la República, 1981), 83–85, 117.

15 Juan Manuel de la Carrera to Arzobispo Virrey, Mompox, August 21, 1786, AGN, C, Milicias y Marina, vol 43, doc. 6, f. 262r–263r.

16 Juan Antonio Gutiérrez de Piñeres to Manuel Antonio Flores, Mompox, March 1, 1779, AGN, C, Miscelánea, vol. 18, doc. 39; Pedro Diago to Capitán a Guerra de Barranca, Honda, May 21, 1788, and May 24, 1788, AGN, C, Quinas, vol. 1, doc. 8, f. 160r, 161r; Ramón del Corral y Castro and Juan Antonio Gutiérrez de Piñerez to the viceroy, *ca.* August, 1788, AGN, C, Quinas, vol. 1, doc. 8, f. 170r–171r.

17 Camilo Torres owned a copy of the proceedings of the Sociedad Económica de Madrid in two volumes. José Camilo Torres y Tenorio and Francisca Prieto y Ricaurte, marriage contract, Santa Fe, December 11, 1802, AGN, ACH, Camilo Torres, box 1, folder 2, f. 126r.

18 *Extracto de las primeras juntas, celebradas por la Sociedad Económica de los Amigos del País en la villa de Mompox, provincia de Cartagena de Yndias, desde 12 de septiembre, hasta 19 de diciembre de 1784* (Santa Fe de Bogotá: Antonio Espinosa de los Monteros, Ympresor Real, *ca.* 1785); François-Xavier Guerra, *Modernidad e independencias. Ensayos sobre las revoluciones hispánicas* (Madrid: MAPFRE, 1992), 92–104.

19 José Celestino Mutis to Gonzálo José de Hoyos, Mariquita, January 18, 1785, Guillermo Hernández de Alba, ed., *Archivo epistolar del sabio naturalista don José Celestino Mutis* (Bogotá: Instituto Colombiano de Cultura Hispánica, 1968), vol. 1, 217–218.

20 *Extracto*, 6–7, 35–36; Pedro Rodríguez de Campomanes, *Discurso sobre el fomento de la industria popular* (Madrid: D. Antonio de Sancha, 1774), 152–154. See also François-Xavier Guerra, *Modernidad*, ch. 3 and 8; Elisa Martín-Valdepeñas Yagüe, "Del amigo del país al ciudadano útil: uno aproximación al discurso patriótico en la Real Sociedad Económica Matritense de Amigos del País en el Antiguo Régimen," *Cuadernos de Historia Moderna* 11 (2012): 35–39; Robert Jones Shafer, *The Economic*

Societies in the Spanish World (1763–1821) (Syracuse, NY: Syracuse University Press, 1958).

21 Armando Martínez Garnica and Daniel Gutiérrez Ardila, ed., *Quién es Quién*, 55, 89; Roberto Luis Jaramillo, "Notas al Carnero," José Antonio Benítez "El Cojo," *Carnero, y miscelánea de varias noticias, antiguas, y modernas, de esta villa de Medellín* (Medellín: Autores Antioqueños, 1988), 407.

22 "Testimonio que comprende la escritura de fundación de 81.300 pesos hecha por don Pedro Martínez de Pinillos, y su prima consorte doña Manuela de Nájera, a favor de la casa hospicio, y hospital que se va a erigir en esta villa, y otras obras pías en beneficio de la humanidad," 1801, AGI, Santa Fe, 1020; power of attorney, Pedro Martínez de Pinillos to Eloy Valenzuela, Mompox, July 9, 1806, AGN, C, Colegios, vol. 6, f. 504–505; *Relación de los méritos y servicios de Don Pedro Martínez de Pinillos: Regidor, Alcalde mayor Provincial jubilado, y vecino de la Villa de Santa Cruz de Mompox, Provincia de Cartagena de Indias* (Madrid: 1806); Diana Soto Arango, "La primera universidad del Caribe Colombiano: un modelo ilustrado para América colonial," *Destiempos* 3.14 (2008): 512–530.

23 "Constituciones para el Colegio de San Pedro Apóstol, redactadas por el presbítero Eloy Valenzuela," Mompox, April 13, 1806, and "Plan de estudios de filosofía que ha de servir en el Colegio de San Pedro," *ca.* September 2, 1806, Guillermo Hernández de Alba, ed., *Documentos para la historia de la educación en Colombia* (Bogotá: Kelly, 1986), vol. 7 (1804–1809), docs. 286 and 289, 27–71 and 80–96.

24 *Relación*; intervention by Fernando Martínez in "Testimonio," AGI, Santa Fe, 1020.

25 "Constituciones," tit. 3, No. 11 and 13.

26 *Relación de los ejercicios literarios, grados y méritos del doctor D. Juan Fernández de Sotomayor, cura rector de la Iglesia Parroquial de la Villa de Mompox* (Madrid: 1805). Available in AGI, Santa Fe, 1172.

27 "Constituciones," tit. 10, No. 10.

28 *Qvarta Partida* (Salamanca: Andrea de Portonariis, 1555), Tit. V (preamble), Tit. XXI, Law I, Tit. XXII (preamble), Tit. XXIII, Law II, f. 15r, 54v, 56v, and 59r. TLC, 824; DA, vol. 2, book 2, 650–651. See also Raymond Williams, *Keywords: A Vocabulary of Culture and Society* (New York: Oxford University Press, 1983), 219–224.

29 *Tercera Partida* (Salamanca: Andrea de Portonariis, 1555), Tit. XXIX, Laws XXIII–XXV, f. 170v; *Qvarta Partida*, Tit. V (preamble), Tit. XXI, Laws I and VI, Tit. XXII (preamble), Tit. XXIII, Law II, f. 15r, 54v, 55v, and 56v; Bianca Premo, *The Enlightenment*, 198.

30 Bianca Premo, *The Enlightenment*, 37, 131–37. On justice administration via oral and other non-judicial transactions, see also Antonio Manuel Hespanha, *La gracia del derecho. Economía de la cultura en la edad moderna* (Madrid: Centro de Estudios Constitucionales, 1993), 21; Tomás A. Mantecón Movellán, "Justicia y fronteras del derecho en la España del antiguo Régimen" and María Eugenia Albornoz Vásquez, "Cortar la causa, no admitir más escrito, obligar al perdón. Sentencias judiciales para administrar la paz quebrada por las injurias (Chile, 1790–1873)," Elisa Caselli, ed., *Justicias, agentes y jurisdicciones. De la Monarquía Hispánica a los Estados Nacionales (España y América, siglos XVI-XIX)* (Madrid and Mexico City: Fondo de Cultura Económica, 2016), 25–58 and 125–157.

31 A case in point is Francisco Javier de Mier, a slave who worked in the "exercise of the quill" for one of the richest men in Mompox, the first marquis of Santa Coa. See Francisco Javier de Mier to José Solis Folch de Cardona, Mompox, December 24, 1760, AGN, C, NEB, vol. 9, doc. 16.

32 TLC, 851; DA, vol. 3, book 5, 114; Kathryn Burns, *Into the Archive: Writing and Power in Colonial Peru* (Durham, NC: Duke University Press, 2010), 132–135. Another slave of the Santa Coa estate, José Antonio Molla, African of the Chalá nation, secured the services of a writer who drafted and signed for him a petition of emancipation. See "Pretensión del esclavo José Antonio Moya sobre su libertad, perteneciente que dijo ser a la causa mortuoria del difunto señor marqués de Santa Coa don Julián Trespalacios Mier," AGN, C, NEB, vol. 2, doc. 18. See also "Autos sobre la libertad de Fermín, y su hija Norberta esclavos de la testamentaría del señor marqués de Santa Coa don Julián de Trespalacios Mier," AGN, C, NEA, vol. 6, doc. 10.

33 Bianca Premo, *The Enlightenment*; Bianca Premo, "Before the Law: Women's Petitions in the Eighteenth-Century Spanish Empire," *Comparative Studies in Society and History* 53.2 (2011): 272–276, 288; Edgardo Pérez Morales, "Manumission on the Land: Slaves, Masters, and Magistrates in Eighteenth-Century Mompox (Colombia)," *Law & History Review* 35.2 (2017): 511–543. See also Judy Kalman, *Writing on the Plaza: Mediated Literacy Practice among Scribes and Clients in Mexico City* (Cresskill: Hampton Press, 1999); José Ramón Jouve Martín, *Esclavos de la ciudad letrada. Esclavitud, escritura y colonialismo en Lima (1650–1700)* (Lima: Instituto de Estudios Peruanos, 2005); Kathryn Burns, *Into the Archive*; Sandra Lauderdale Graham, "Writing from the Margins: Brazilian Slaves and Written Culture," *Comparative Studies in Society and History* 49.3 (2007): 611–636.

34 José Ignacio de San Miguel, Mompox, February 28, 1777, "Don José Antonio Ambrosi," f. 703r-v; Victor M. Uribe-Urán, *Honorable Lives.*

Lawyers, Family, and Politics in Colombia, 1780–1850 (Pittsburgh: University of Pittsburgh Press, 2000), 42.

35 "Don José Antonio Ambrosi," f. 701v, 703v, 704r, 705v, 706r, 711r–712r.

36 On Pedro Bravo de Lagunas y Castilla, see Bianca Premo, *The Enlightenment*, 77–84, 198–200.

37 Pablo Sarmiento to Real Audiencia, Santa Fe, *ca.* July 1777, "Don José Antonio Ambrosi," f. 713v–714r. Sarmiento used a handwritten copy of the 1746 disquisition to craft his argument. The copy in question might be the incomplete document at AGN, AAI, Esclavos, vol. 3, f. 656r–667v. For the entire disquisition, see Pedro Bravo de Lagunas y Castilla, "Carta en que se trata: si por el favor de la libertad pueda obligarse al Señor, a que reciba el precio de su siervo; y del derecho que éste tiene para ser preferido en caso de enajenarse," in his *Colección legal de cartas, dictámenes, y otros papeles en derecho* (Lima: Oficina de los Huérfanos, 1761), 194–239.

38 On varying interpretations and the social use of custom, see Bianca Premo, *The Enlightenment*, 178–184.

39 Gregorio José Cevallos to Ignacio de San Miguel, Mompox, February 17, 1777, "Don José Antonio Ambrosi," f. 701v.

40 José Antonio Maldonado to Real Audiencia, Santa Fe, *ca.* August 8, 1777, f. 716r–717r. On Francisco González Manrique, see Armando Martínez Garnica and Daniel Gutiérrez Ardila, ed., *Quién es quién*, 31.

41 Alessandro Tuccillo, *Il commercio*, 130–140.

42 Samuel Pufendorf, *De Jure Naturae et Gentium. Libri Octo* 1st ed. 1688, ed., trans. C. H. Oldfather and W. A. Oldfather (Oxford and London: Clarendon Press, Humphrey Milford, 1934), vol 2, 154–230; Antoine-Gaspard Boucher d'Argis, "Droit de la Nature, ou Droit Naturel," *Encyclopédie ou dictionnaire raisonné des sciences, des arts et des métiers* (Paris: Chez Briasson, David, Le Breton, Durand, 1755), vol. 5, 131–134; Montesquieu, *De l'esprit des lois* (London: 1768), vol. 1, 6–9; Renán Silva, *Los ilustrados*; Daniel Gutiérrez Ardila, *Un Nuevo Reino*, 81–110. Se also Leo Strauss, *Natural Right and History* (Chicago: The University of Chicago Press, 1953).

43 "Discurso inaugural de estudios que como Catedrático de Filosofía leyó el doctor José María Gutiérrez de Caviedes," Mompox, *ca.* 1809, Guillermo Hernández de Alba, ed., *Documentos*, doc. 298, 179–180; Gaetano Filangieri, *La scienza della legislazione* 1st ed. 1780–1791 (Venice: Centro di Studi sull'Illuminismo europeo "G. Stiffoni," 2003–2004), vol. 5, 189.

44 Montesquieu, *De l'esprit*, vol 2, 61–95; Gaetano Filangieri, *La scienza*, vol. 1, 61–72; Alessandro Tuccillo, *Il commercio*, ch. 2 and 4.

45 Exposition by Melchor Sáenz de Ortíz, Mompox, December 6, 1804, f. 265v.

46 Exposition by Melchor Sáenz de Ortíz, Mompox, December 10, 1804, "Don Melchor," f. 265v–266r; *Febrero reformado y anotado, o librería de escribanos que compuso don Joseph Febrero Escribano Real y del Colegio de la corte, y ha reformado en su lenguaje, método, estilo y muchas de sus doctrinas, ilustrándola y enriqueciéndola con varias notas y adiciones para que se han tenido presentes las Reales Órdenes modernas, el Lic. D. Joseph Márcos Gutierrez: Obra no solo necesaria á los escribanos sino tambien utilísima á todos los jueces, abogados, procuradores, agentes de negocios y á toda clase de personas. Parte II. De inventarios, tasaciones y particiones de bienes, y de los juicios ordinario, ejecutivo y de concurso de acreedores, como tambien del criminal que faltaba y se añade á esta obra* (Madrid: Imprenta de Villalpando, 1802, 2nd ed.), vol. 3, 211.

47 Antonio de Villavicencio, "Delicadísimo punto y plan sobre el comercio de esclavos y la absoluta abolición de la esclavitud en ambas Américas, propuesto por un propietario," Seville, November 16, 1809, BNC, Fondo Antiguo, RM 223, pza 1.

48 As we know from abundant notarial documents, in Antioquia and Popayán the grip of the masters over their slaves was almost unshakable. The evidence is less abundant for the province of Cartagena, but surviving documentary shards suggest slave sales outnumbered manumissions in 1814, 1815, 1824, 1825, and 1832, with a total of ten people granted freedom against 144 slaves exchanged. It was very difficult to obtain emancipation. AHCI, catalogues for Protocolos Notariales, 1814, 1815, 1824, 1825, and 1832. The information from these catalogues was checked against the original ledgers as far as it was possible in May 2017. While most ledgers are practically unreadable because of deterioration, a photostatic copy for the 1815 ledger made it easier to corroborate information on the catalogue for this particular year.

49 Edgardo Pérez Morales, "Manumission," 538–541.

50 Most dramatically, the cabildo had quickly overturned the practical effects of a 1774 royal decree and a 1777 governor's act that erected Mompox as seat of a new *corregimiento* (a jurisdiction carved out of Antioquia and Cartagena), placing it under the authority of a *corregidor* directly appointed by the viceroy. See AHA, vol. 375, doc. 7003; Daniel Gutiérrez Ardila, "Las querellas," 112–115; "Reseña histórica," *Estadística de Mompós (Entrega primera)* (Mompox: Imprenta de La Palestra, 1880), 17.

51 Cabildo de Mompox to the viceroy, Mompox, October 13, 1809, "El Excelentísimo señor Don Antonio Narváez. Acompaña el oficio, y documento que le dirigió el cabildo de Mompox, solicitando su mediación en la desavenencia, y recurso que se ha suscitado con el teniente coronel de ingenieros Don Vicente Talledo, con motivo de la posesión del empleo de subdelegado de rentas, que el cabildo ha suspendido darle por las causas

que expresa," AGN, C, Miscelánea, vol. 40, doc 27, f. 973r; Daniel Gutiérrez Ardila, "Las querellas," 119–127.

52 Vicente Talledo to the viceroy, Mompox, November 13, 1809, March 23, 1810, and May 3, 1810, DHPC, docs. 8, 21 and 22, 20–21, 49–55.

53 "Reseña," 27; Daniel Gutiérrez Ardila, "Las querellas," 133–135.

54 "Oficios cambiados entre los señores Gobernador de Cartagena y Alcaldes ordinarios, sobre los temores de una subversión del orden," Cartagena de Indias, May 15, 1810, "Acta de la sesión del Cabildo de Cartagena tenida el 14 de junio de 1810, en que, por los graves motivos que se expresan, dicha Corporación tuvo por conveniente separar, y separó, al Gobernador Don Francisco de Montes del ejercicio de su empleo," and José María García de Toledo to Antonio Amar y Borbón, Cartagena de Indias, July 10, 1810, DHPC, docs. 26, 37, and 52, 65–66, 81–90, 116–118; *A todos los estantes y habitantes de esta plaza y su provincia* (Cartagena de Indias: November 9, 1810); Alfonso Múnera, *El fracaso*, 164–172; Daniel Gutiérrez Ardila, *Un Nuevo Reino*, 194–198; Adolfo Meisel Roca, "La crisis fiscal de Cartagena en la era de la independencia, 1808–1821," Haroldo Calvo Stevenson and AdolfoMeisel Roca, ed., *Cartagena de Indias en la Independencia* (Cartagena: Banco de la República, 2011), 371–403.

55 "Edicto por el cual el Cabildo de Cartagena excita a los habitantes de las ciudad a procurar la unión, a que respeten y obedezcan a las Autoridades, y ordena la formación de dos batallones," Cartagena de Indias, June 19, 1810, and Manuel Marcelino Núñez, "Exposición de los acontecimientos memorables relacionados con mi vida política, que tuvieron lugar en este país desde 1810 en adelante," Cartagena de Indias, February 22, 1864, DHPC, doc. 40 and doc. 114, 94, 411; Alfonso Múnera, *El fracaso*, 186–189, 208. On Pedro Romero, see Alfonso Múnera, "Pedro Romero: el rostro impreciso de los mulatos libres," Alfonso Múnera, *Fronteras imaginadas. La construcción de las razas y de la geografía en el siglo XIX colombiano* (Bogotá: Planeta, 2005), 153–174 and Sergio Paolo Solano D., "Pedro Romero, el artesano: trabajo, raza y diferenciación social en Cartagena de Indias a finales del dominio colonial," *Historia Crítica* 61 (2016): 151–170.

56 HRC, vol. 1, 168.

57 Armando Martínez Garnica and Daniel Gutiérrez Ardila, ed., *Quién es quién*, 115.

58 Alfonso Múnera, *El fracaso*; Armando Martínez Garnica, "Prejuicio moral e instrucción: dos obstáculos para la incorporación de los pardos a la Nación," *Revista Colombiana de Educación* 59 (2010): 14–32; Sergio Solano de las Aguas and Roicer Flórez, "Los 'Artilleros pardos y morenos artistas': Artesanos, raza, milicias y reconocimiento social en el Nuevo Reino de Granada, 1770–1812," *Historia Crítica* 48 (2012): 11–37;

Sergio Solano de las Aguas, "Artesanos, bellas artes, raza y política en Cartagena de Indias a finales del siglo XVIII," Alcides Beretta Curi, ed., *Inmigración europea, artesanado y orígenes de la industria en América Latina* (Montevideo: Universidad de la República, 2016), 113–142; Sergio Solano D., "Pedro Romero."

59 José María Gutiérrez de Caviedes to the cabildo, Mompox, *ca.* August 14, 1810, "El mes de agosto de 1810 en la Villa de Mompox," DHPC, doc. 73, 191–195.

60 "Lista de los sujetos que se citan en el adjunto oficia de esta fecha," Mompox, January 31, 1811, AGN, AAI, Embargos, vol. 1, f. 443r; José María García de toledo and José María Benito Revollo, "Exposición de la Junta de Cartagena de Indias, sobre los sucesos de Mompox, encaminados a formar una Provincia independiente," Cartagena de Indias, December 4, 1810, and "Combates habidos entre las fuerzas de Cartagena de Indias y las de Mompox, en Enero de 1811," DHPC, docs. 74 and 77, 201–217, 234–235; Armando Martínez Garnica and Daniel Gutiérrez Ardila, ed., *La contrarevolución de los pueblos de las Sabanas de Tolú y el Sinú (1812)* (Bucaramanga: Universidad Industrial de Santander, 2010), 14–17.

61 Alfonso Múnera, *El fracaso*, 200–203; Armando Martínez Garnica, "Prejuicio;" Adelaida Sourdis, *Cartagena*, 44–47; María Teresa Ripoll, "El Argos Americano: crónica de una desilusión," Haroldo Calvo Stevenson and Adolfo Meisel Roca, ed., *Cartagena*, 529–560.

62 Manuel Marcelino Núñez, "Exposición," 410–412; "Acta de independencia," DHPC, doc. 108, 351–356; HRC, vol. 1, 157–168; Alfonso Múnera, *El fracaso*, 204–208.

63 DHPC, 545–546. For a direct reference to Filangieri by the revolutionary government, see *Gazeta de Cartagena de Indias*, June 18, 1812. On the US federal and state constitutions in the New Kingdom, see Isidro Vanegas, *El constitucionalismo fundacional* (Bogotá: Ediciones Plural, 2014); Isidro Vanegas, "La revolution angloamericana como herramienta. Nueva Granada, 1808–1816," *Co-herenia* 25.13 (2016): 89–118; Edgardo Pérez Morales, *No Limits to Their Sway: Cartagena's Privateers and the Masterless Caribbean in the Age of Revolutions* (Nashville, TN: Vanderbilt University Press, 2018), ch. 3 and 4.

64 "Constitución política del Estado de Cartagena de Indias," Cartagena de Indias, June 14, 1812, DHPC, 485–546.

65 *Gazeta de Cartagena de Indias*, June 11, 1812 (in circulation June 12).

66 Armando Martínez Garnica, "Prejuicio."

67 Armando Martínez Garnica and Daniel Gutiérrez Ardila, *La contrarevolución.*

68 *Gazeta de Cartagena de Indias*, April 8, 1813. For critical accounts of this emerging ideology of equality and the subsequent struggles for inclusion,

see Aline Helg, *Liberty*; Marixa Lasso, *Myths of Harmony: Race and Republicanism during the Age of Revolution, Colombia 1795–1831* (Pittsburgh, PA: University of Pittsburgh Press, 2007); Jason McGraw, *The Work of Recognition: Caribbean Colombia and the Postemancipation Struggle for Citizenship* (Chapel Hill: The University of North Carolina Press, 2014).

69 Edgardo Pérez Morales, *No Limits*.

70 "Constitución," Tit. 13, art. 1, 540; Adelaida Sourdis, *Cartagena*, 56.

71 *Gazeta de Cartagena de Indias*, May 27, 1813 and January 6, 1814. See the notarial transaction for slave sales at AHCI, Notaría, 1814, f. 60; January 21, 1815, f.18v–20v; March 16, 1815, f. 50–51; August 22, 1815, f. 26–28.

5 Antioquia: Free Womb, Captive Slaves

1 José Manuel Restrepo, "Ensayo sobre la geografía, producciones, industria y población de la Provincia de Antioquia en el Nuevo Reino de Granada," 1809, *Semanario del Nuevo Reino de Granada* (Bogotá: Biblioteca Popular de Cultura Colombiana, 1942, vol. 1, 243–286; Vicente Restrepo, *Estudio sobre las minas de oro y plata en Colombia* (Bogotá: Imprenta de Silvestre y Compañía, 1888); Ann Twinam, *Miners, Merchants, and Farmers in Colonial Colombia* (Austin: University of Texas Press, 1982); Anthony McFarlane, *Colombia Before Independence: Economy, Society, and Politics under Bourbon Rule* (New York: Cambridge University Press, 1993), ch. 3; Jorge Orlando Melo, ed., *Historia de Antioquia* (Medellín: Suramericana de Seguros, 1988); Jorge Orlando Melo, ed., *Historia de Medellín (Bogotá: Suramericana de Seguros, 1998); Beatriz Patiño Millán, Riqueza, pobreza y diferenciación social en la provincia de Antioquia durante el siglo XVIII* (Medellín: Universidad de Antioquia, 2011).

2 Out of thousands of slaves in the province, only around 400 achieved manumission over the fifty years between 1780 and 1830. AHA, Escribanos de Medellín, 1781–1810; Convenio Alcaldía de Santa Fé de Antioquia-Fundación Rodrigo Escobar Restrepo, *Índice analítico del Protocolo de Escribanos de 1821–1840* (Santa Fe de Antioquia, n.d.); Karen Mejía Velázquez and Luis Miguel Córdoba Ochoa, "La manumisión de esclavos por compra y gracia en la Provincia de Antioquia, 1780-1830," *Historelo* 9.17 (2017): 252–291.

3 "Testimonio del expediente formado sobre las inquietudes de los naturales de Guarne, y La Mosca, en la jurisdicción de Río Negro y el pueblo de Sopetrán de la de esta ciudad; de las providencias tomadas sobre dichas inquietudes, y sobre las noticias que a este gobierno se han dado, de intentarse invadir esta provincia," 1781, BNC, Comuneros, rm 372; "Don Alonso Elías Jaramillo Capitán a Guerra del valle de Río Negro

dando cuenta con testimonio de lo actuado en asunto del levantamiento que proclamando libertad, tenían proyectado los negros, y demás esclavos de aquel valle coligados con los de las Ciudad de Antioquia, y Villa de Medellín," 1781–1782, BNC, Comuneros, rm 376; "Testimonio de un expediente relativo al levantamiento o insurrección de esclavos en la provincia de Antioquia," 1781, *Documentos para la historia de la insurrección Comunera en la provincia de Antioquia. 1765–1785* (Medellín: Universidad de Antioquia, 1982), 441–588; "Expediente seguido en la villa de Medellín, sobre las voces, que se esparcieron en ella de que los negros esclavos, se hallaban impresionados en que habían venido providencias para su libertad, y que intentaban solicitarla, cuyos rumores promovieron la averiguación del origen de ellas," 1798, AGN, AAI, Esclavos, vol. 2; "Expediente de la Candanga. Criminal contra los esclavos de esta jurisdicción porque se les presumía alzamiento," 1806, AHJM, box 171, doc. 3532.

4 On the State of Antioquia, see Daniel Gutiérrez Ardila, "Introducción. Un estado al borde del precipicio: el caso de la provincia de Antioquia (1810–1812)," Daniel Gutiérrez Ardila, ed., *Las asambleas constituyentes de la Independencia. Actas de Cundinamarca y Antioquia (1811–1812)* (Bogotá: Corte Constitucional de Colombia, Universidad Externado de Colombia, 2010), 169–186; Daniel Gutiérrez Ardila, *La Restauración en la Nueva Granada (1815–1819)* (Bogotá: Universidad Externado de Colombia, 2016), ch. 2; Edgardo Pérez Morales, "José Manuel Restrepo: un mediador cultural en la Independencia de Antioquia. 1808–1813," Rodrigo Campuzano Cuartas, ed., *Política, guerra y cultura en la Independencia de Antioquia* (Medellín: Academia Antioqueña de Historia, 2013), 351–391.

5 *Constitución del Estado de Antioquia sancionada por los representantes de toda la provincia. Y aceptada por el pueblo en tres de mayo del año de 1812* (Santa Fe de Bogotá: Imprenta de D. Bruno Espinosa, Por D. Nicomedes Lora, 1812), tit. 1, sections 1 and 2, 4–5.

6 We ten thousand and seven hundred slaves to the Supreme Tribunal of Justice, Medellín, August 25, 1812, "Contra varios de los Etíopes, por haber intentado su liberated con violencia," ACCR, Gobierno, vol. 93, f. 3r–v, 7r. See also Eduardo Zuleta, "Movimiento antiesclavista en Antioquia," *Boletín de Historia y Antigüedades* 109 (1915): 32–37; María Eugenia Chaves, "Nos, los esclavos de Medellín." La polisemia de la libertad y las voces subalternas en la primera república antioqueña," *Nómadas* 33 (2010): 43–55; Daniel Gutiérrez Ardila, "La politique aboli-tionniste dans le'État d'Antioquia, Colombie (1812-1816)," *Le Mouvement social* 252 (2015): 55–70.

7 Daniel Gutiérrez Ardila, *Un Nuevo Reino. Geografía política, pactismo y diplomacia durante el interregno en Nueva Granada (1808-1816)* (Bogotá: Universidad Externado de Colombia, 2010), 130, 133, 138, 245, 351.

8 "Ley sobre la manumisión de la posteridad de los esclavos africanos y sobre los medios de redimir sucesivamente a sus padres, extendida y propuesta para su sanción a la Cámara de Representantes del Pueblo, por el Excelentísimo Dictador Ciudadano Juan B. del Corral," *Gazeta Ministerial de la República de Antioquia* (Medellín), October 2, 1814.

9 "Mortuoria de don Bacilio Jaramillo sus inventarios, y valuos [sic]," AHA, Mortuorias, vol. 238, doc. 5376.

10 "Mortuoria," f. 512r–514r, 517r, 546r–547r.

11 Salvadora Jaramillo to Señor Alcalde Ordinario, February 25, 1807, "Mortuoria," f. 544r.

12 Salvadora Jaramillo to Señor Alcalde Ordinario, February 25, 1807.

13 Salvadora Jaramillo to Señor Alcalde Ordinario, February 25, 1807.

14 "Mortuoria," f. 544r.

15 "Mortuoria," f. 596r.

16 Salvadora Jaramillo to Señor Alcalde Ordinario, February 25, 1807.

17 "Mortuoria," f. 553r, 554r, and Salvadora Jaramillo to Pedro Campero, October 20, 1807, "Mortuoria," f. 555r.

18 "Mortuoria," f. 563r–v; Armando Martínez Garnica and Daniel Gutiérrez Ardila, ed., *Quién es quién en 1810. Guía de Forasteros del Virreinato de Santafé* (Bogotá: Universidad del Rosario, 2010), 59.

19 "Auto sobre la ninguna asistencia de los regidores al cabildo de Medellín y al folio VII se hallan las diligencias sobre empleo de alguacil mayor rematado en el doctor don Faustino Martínez," AHA, Empleos, vol. 100, doc. 2664, f. 29r–v.

20 "Don Juan Esteban Martínez mayordomo de nuestro Amo y Señor Sacramentado hace presente que don Pablo de Vargas consignó cien castellanos que reconocía a favor de su cofradía los que se pasaron a la caja de consolidación y hasta ahora se hallan sin asegurar," AHA, Eclesiásticos, vol. 83, doc. 2322, f. 32r; "Don Juan Esteban Martínez hace presente que por final del presbítero don Ignacio Tabares cura de Sopetrán resultaron algunas cantidades a favor de las cofradías que eran a su cargo y promete entregarlas al mayor que se nombre," AHA, Eclesiásticos, vol. 83, doc. 2325; cabildo de Antioquia to the viceroy, Antioquia, August 3, 1795, AGN, C, Miscelánea, vol. 122, doc. 94, f. 771r–v and 774r.

21 HRC, vol. 1, ch. 3–4; Daniel Gutiérrez Ardila, "Introducción."

22 José Miguel de la Calle and José María Montoya, September 2, 1810, AGN, Archivo José Manuel Restrepo, reel 4, ff, 12r–13r. A transcription of this document is available in Martín Alonso Medina Restrepo, *Historia*

de la Independencia del departamento de Antioquia. Período comprendido entre 1810-1816 (Medellín: Universo, 1984), 18–20.

23 Armando Martínez Garnica, "Las juntas neogranadinas de 1810," Armando Martínez Garnica and Guillermo Bustos, ed., *La Independencia en los países andinos: Nuevas perspectivas. Memorias del Primer Módulo Itinerante de la Cátedra de Historia de Iberoamerica. Quito, diciembre 9 al 12 de 2003* (Bucaramanga: Universidad Andina Simón Bolívar-Ecuador, Organización de los Estados Iberoamericanos para la Educación, la Ciencia y la Cultura, 2004), 127–128; Daniel Gutiérrez Ardila, "Introducción;" Daniel Gutiérrez Ardila, *Un Nuevo Reino*, ch. 1 and 5.

24 AHM, Libros Capitulares, vol. 76, f. 42v, 170v–175r; AHA, Documentos, vol. 818, doc. 12858; Armando Martínez Garnica, "Las juntas neogranadinas," 130; Daniel Gutiérrez Ardila, "Introducción."

25 Roberto Luis Jaramillo, "Notas al Carnero," José Antonio Benítez "El Cojo," *Carnero, y miscelánea de varias noticias, antiguas, y modernas, de esta villa de Medellín* (Medellín: Autores Antioqueños, 1988), 407. Juan del Corral's baptismal record of June 30, 1778 is transcribed in *Repertorio Histórico* 16.148 (1941): 117–118.

26 "Actas del Colegio Electoral y Constituyente de Antioquia," 1811–1812, Daniel Gutiérrez Ardila, ed., *Las asambleas*; *Constitución del Estado*; José Manuel Restrepo, *Autobiografía. Apuntamientos sobre la emigración de 1816, e índices del "Diario Político"* (Bogotá: Biblioteca de la Presidencia de Colombia, 1957), 13.

27 *Constitución del Estado*, tit. 1, section 1, art. 2, section 2, arts. 1–8 and 28, 4–6, 9–10; Daniel Gutiérrez Ardila, *Un Nuevo Reino*, 239–243; Isidro Vanegas, *El constitucionalismo fundacional* (Bogotá: Ediciones Plural, 2014), 95–130, *passim*.

28 Juan del Corral, "Reglamento de Milicias de Infantería, Caballería, Artillería, y Zapadores para la Provincia de Antioquia," Antioquia, July 27, 1812, AHA, Reglamento militar, vol. 656, f. 4r–v.

29 "Reglamento definitivo para las elecciones," Antioquia, September 28, 1811, tit. 2, art. 1, Daniel Gutiérrez Ardila, ed., *Las asambleas*, 232; *Constitución del Estado*, tit. 1, section 2, arts. 1, 7, 13, 15, tit. 2, art. 3, pages 5, 6, 7, 13; José Manuel Restrepo to cabildo de Medellín, Antioquia, August 18, 1811, "Oficios," 218.

30 AHM, Libros Capitulares, vol. 76, f. 168v; José Manuel Restrepo to cabildo de Medellín, Antioquia, August 18, 1811, "Oficios del Dr. José Manuel Restrepo al cabildo de Medellín," Daniel Gutiérrez Ardila, ed., *Las asambleas*, 218; Daniel Gutiérrez Ardila, "Introducción," 171.

31 *Constitución del Estado*, tit. 1, art. 2, 4.

32 *Constitución del Estado*, tit. 1, section 2, art. 29, tit. 5, section 1, arts. 1–17, 10, 50–53. Along with the establishment of the new tribunal, the

Constitution also stipulated that the "people," and every "citizen" individually, had the right to file *representaciones* to "legally, and peacefully request" redress from the authorities. The slave petitioners might have also relied on this explicit mechanism, understanding themselves as constituents of the Antioquia people.

33 We ten thousand and seven hundred slaves to the Supreme Tribunal of Justice, Medellín, August 25, 1812, f. 3r–v, 7r. See also Eduardo Zuleta, "Movimiento;" María Eugenia Chaves, "'Nos, los esclavos;" Daniel Gutiérrez Ardila, "La politique."

34 Isidro Vanegas, *El constitucionalismo*, 19

35 We ten thousand and seven hundred slaves to the Supreme Tribunal of Justice, Medellín, August 25, 1812, f. 7v–9r; *Constitución del Estado*, tit. 1, section 1, preamble.

36 HRC, vol. I, 239–246; José Manuel Restrepo, *Autobiografía*, 15.

37 "Relación que hace a los Representantes de la República de Antioquia el C. Dictador Juan del Corral, acerca de las medidas que ha tomado para sus progresos en el discurso de los últimos cuatro meses de su administración, y del estado en que deja sus intereses al concluirse el término de su Gobierno Dictarorio," Rionegro, February 20, 1814, BNC, JMR, fondo 1, vol. 7, f. 404v; José María Martínez to Señor teniente asesor, Antioquia, *ca.* September 6, 1822, "José María Martínez hace recuento de su libertad, méritos y servicios durante la época de la Independencia," AHA, Esclavos, vol. 38, doc. 1283, f. 410r; HRC, vol. 1, 239–246; José Manuel Restrepo, *Autobiografía*, 15.

38 "Relación que hace," f. 414v; *Gazeta Ministerial de la República de Antioquia* (Medellín), December 25, 1814; HRC, vol. 1, 192–193; Mariano Ospina Rodríguez, *El doctor José Félix de Restrepo y su época* 1st ed. 1888 (Bogotá: Biblioteca Aldeana de Colombia, 1936), 85; Daniel Gutiérrez Ardila, "Juan del Corral: dictadura, leyes de excepción y revolución sin terror (1812–1813)," paper delivered at the conference *Guerra y revolución en Antioquia*, Medellín, Banco de la República, September 18, 2012.

39 Acto de Independencia de Antioquia, Antioquia, August 11, 1813, AHA, Documentos Generales, vol. 827, doc. 13054, f. 1r–2v; Daniel Gutiérrez Ardila, *La Restauración*, 251–253.

40 Daniel Gutiérrez Ardila, "Juan del Corral," 5.

41 Juan del Corral to Presidente de la Unión, Antioquia, December 12, 1813, *Memorias del General O'Leary* (Caracas: Imprenta de la Gaceta Oficial, 1881), vol. 13, 493–494; "Relación que hace," f. 383v–384r.

42 Juan del Corral to Presidente de la Unión, Antioquia, December 12, 1813; "Relación que hace," f. 384v–385r; Antonio de Villavicencio, "Delicadísimo punto y plan sobre el comercio de esclavos y la absoluta

abolición de la esclavitud en ambas Américas, propuesto por un propietario," Seville, November 16, 1809, BNC, Fondo Antiguo, RM 223, pza 1.

43 "Ley," arts. 1, 2, 4, 6, 9 and 11; "Relación que hace," f. 385v.

44 "Observaciones sobre la manumisión de los esclavos, extractadas del *Espíritu de las leyes* de Montesquieu, para servir de comentario a la ley de libertad de vientres, publicada en el número 2 de la Gazeta Ministerial," *Gazeta Ministerial de la República de Antioquia* (Medellín), November 13, 20, 27, 1814; Gaetano Filangieri, *La scienza della legislazione* 1st ed. 1780–1791 (Venice: Centro di studi sull'Illuminismo Europeo "G. Stiffoni," 2003), vol. 1, book 1.

45 Gaetano Filangieri, *La scienza*, 68–72.

46 "Relación que hace," f. 386r.

47 "Ley," arts. 7 and 11.

48 "Ley," arts. 3, 5, 12 and 15; "Relación que hace," f. 385r.

49 *Febrero reformado y anotado, o librería de escribanos que compuso don Joseph Febrero Escribano Real y del Colegio de la corte, y ha reformado en su lenguaje, método, estilo y muchas de sus doctrinas, ilustrándola y enriqueciéndola con varias notas y adiciones para que se han tenido presentes las Reales Órdenes modernas, el Lic. D. Joseph Márcos Gutierrez* (Madrid: Imprenta de Villalpando, 1802, 2nd. ed.), vol. 4, 218.

50 "Ley," arts. 7, 9 and 10.

51 "Decreto para ejecutar en todas sus partes a Ley sobre la manumisión de esclavos publicada en el numero 2 de esta Gazeta," Rionegro, September 19, 1814, *Gazeta Ministerial de la República de Antioquia* (Medellín), November 6, 1814.

52 Harold A. Bierck, Jr., "The Struggle for Abolition in Gran Colombia," *Hispanic American Historical Review* 33.3 (1953): 365–386; Pablo Rodríguez J., "La manumisión en Popayán, 1800–1851," *Revista de Extensión Cultural* 9–10 (1980): 77–85; Jorge Castellanos, "The Failure of the Manumission Juntas in the Colombian Province of Popayán, 1821–1851," *Michigan Academician* 14.4 (1982): 427–443; Russell Lohse, "Reconciling Freedom with the Rights of Property: Slave Emancipation in Colombia, 1821–1852, With Special Reference to La Plata," *The Journal of Negro History* 86.3 (2001): 203–227; Jorge Andrés Tovar Mora and Hermes Tovar Pinzón, *El oscuro camino de la libertad. Los esclavos en Colombia, 1821–1851* (Bogotá: Universidad de los Andes, 2009), 90; Rocío Rueda Novoa, "Desesclavización, manumisión jurídica y defensa del territorio en el norte de Esmeraldas (siglos XVIII–XIX)," *Procesos. Revista Ecuatoriana de Historia* 43 (2016): 9–35; Marcela Echeverri, "Esclavitud y tráfico de esclavos en el Pacífico suramericano durante la era de la abolición," *Historia Mexicana* 69.2 (2019): 627–691.

53 *Gazeta Ministerial de la República de Antioquia* (Medellín), January 29, 1815; Daniel Gutiérrez Ardila, "La politique," 63–65.

54 Daniel Gutiérrez Ardila, "La politique," 60–61.

55 Antonio de Villavicencio, "Delicadísimo."

56 Daniel Gutiérrez Ardila, "La politique," 70.

57 *Gazeta Ministerial de la República de Antioquia* (Medellín), September 25, 1814; Daniel Gutiérrez Ardila, *La Restauración*, 17–68.

58 HRC, vol. 1, 399–424.

59 *Número Extraordinario (Estrella de Occidente)* (Medellín), March 22, 1816.

60 "Solicitudes de varios individuos sobre diversas materias," AHA, Documentos, vol. 898, f. 625r–639r; José Manuel Restrepo, "Apuntes sobre la emigración que hice en 1816 de la provincia de Antioquia a la de Popayán," José Manuel Restrepo, *Autobiografía*, 63–77; Daniel Gutiérrez Ardila, *La Restauración*, ch. 2, 4, and 5.

61 "José María Martínez," f. 410r.

62 "José María Martínez," f. 410r.

63 "José María Martínez," f. 411r.

64 AGN, AAI, Guerra y Marina, vol. 135, doc. 19, N 119-A.

65 HRC, vol. 1, 427, 443.

66 "José María Martínez," f. 410r.

67 HRC, vol. 1, 391–466; Juan Friede, *La otra verdad. La independencia americana vista por los españoles* (Bogotá: Carlos Valencia, 1979); Daniel Gutiérrez Ardila, *La Restauración*, part 2.

68 HRC, vol. 1, 989–998, 1012–1024; Barreyro to Sámano, July 19, 1819, and "Diario histórico de la división," Juan Friede, *La batalla de Boyacá -7 de agosto de 1819- a través de los archivos españoles* (Bogotá: Banco de la República, 1969), docs. 39 and 54, 83–87, 115–122; Clément Thibaud, *Repúblicas en armas. Los ejércitos bolivarianos en la guerra de independencia en Colombia y Venezuela* (Bogotá: Planeta, 2003), ch. 6–8. On the concept of *libertadores* and its political and historiographical implications, see Daniel Gutiérrez Ardila, *La Restauración*, ch. 7, and Sergio Mejía, *La revolución en letras. La Historia de la Revolución de Colombia de José Manuel Restrepo (1781–1863)* (Bogotá: Universidad de los Andes, 2007).

69 HRC, vol. 1, 1042–1045.

70 HRC, vol. 1, 1026.

71 José María Córdova to Carlos Soublette, Medellín, August 30, 1819, José María Córdova to Simón Bolívar, Medellín, September 1, 1819, José María Córdova to Carlos Soublette, Rionegro, September 3, 1819, José María Córdova to Félix de Restrepo, Rionegro, October 22, 1819, Pilar

Moreno de Ángel, *Correspondencia y documentos del General José María Córdova* (Bogotá: Editorial Kelly, 1974), vol. 1, 14–15, 16–17, 19–20, 63.

72 "Lista de los Patriotas que deben contribuir según sus facultades, y en calidad de empréstito para la defensa del Estado," AHA, Documentos, vol. 875, doc. 13721, f. 239r, 240r; "José María Martínez," f. 410r.

73 Peter Blanchard, *Under the Flags of Freedom: Slave Soldiers and the Wars of Independence in Spanish South America* (Pittsburgh, PA: University of Pittsburgh Press, 2008), 74.

74 "José María Martínez," f. 410r.

75 Capitán Buenaventura Correa, military service record, AGN, República, Hojas de Servicios, vol. 9, f. 241v, 250r–253r; "Relación de los militares que hicieron la campaña del 'Bajo Magdalena,' que comprende los años de 1820 y 1821," DHPC, vol. 2, doc. 384, 487; Peter Blanchard, *Under the Flags*, 72–73.

76 José Manuel Restrepo, *Diario político y militar. Memorias sobre los sucesos importantes de la época para servir a la Historia de la Revolución de Colombia y de la Nueva Granada, desde 1819 para adelante* (Bogotá: Imprenta Nacional, 1954), vol. 1, 23, 26–27.

77 Buenaventura Correa to José María Córdova, Marinilla, August 27, 1819, Yolombó, August 31, 1819 and October 6, 1819, Zaragoza, October 7, 1819 and October 12, 1819, Carlos Robledo to José María Córdova, Sabanalarga, September 3, 1819, "Contiene partes militares de varios jefes remitidos al gobernador comandante general José María Córdova," AHA, Documentos, vol. 879, doc. 13734; José de Villa to José María Córdova?, "Contiene comunicaciones de varios empleados para el gobernador con 126 fojas. 1820," AHA, Documentos, vol. 904, doc. 13944; Capitán Buenaventura Correa, military service record, f. 241v, 250r–253r; José María Córdova to Francisco de Paula Santander, Rionegro, October 16, 1819, Pilar Moreno de Ángel, *Correspondencia y documentos*, vol. 2, 58–60.

78 "José María Martínez," f. 410r.

79 Peter Blanchard, *Under the Flags*, 82.

80 José María Martínez, copy of recruitment record, "Plaza de Medellín. Año 1824. Compañía de Guarnición. Causa criminal contra José María Martínez soldado de la misma compañía, por haber caído alevosamente al ciudadano José Moreno de que le resultó la muerte en la tarde del 31 de diciembre. Juez fiscal el señor capitán José María Botero," AHA, Documentos, vol. 962, doc. 14388, f. 9v; José María Córdova to General José Mires, Popayán, December 28, 1823, José María Córdova to José Manuel Restrepo, Guayaquil, February 20, 1824, José María Córdova to Antonio José de Sucre, Otuzco, April 14, 1824, Pilar

Moreno de Ángel, *Correspondencia y documentos*, vol. 2, 100, 120, 121; Peter Blanchard, *Under the Flags*, 64–112.

81 "Plaza de Medellín," f. 2v, 9r–v, 10v.
82 "Plaza de Medellín," f. 2r–v, 3r. At the time of the fight, José María was working as an assistant to Manuela Girardot, the new governor's wife. Girardot turned José María over to the authorities after realizing he had wounded a man and fled the scene. In his deposition, José María declared he had drunk some *aguardiente* before the fight. Enrique Zabala, a witness in the criminal proceedings, assured magistrates that another soldier had unsheathed José María's sword. But José María stated that the sword had come out of its sheath unintentionally, after he fell on the ground. Whatever the circumstances, a sword was run through Moreno, probably when he charged against José María as the latter felt on to the ground. In his deposition, José María implied that Moreno had thrown himself against his sword. (The governor, Francisco Urdaneta Rivadavia was a cousin of General Rafael Urdaneta, while Girardot was the sister of Atanasio Girardot Díaz, an officer killed in 1813). See Sergio Elías Ortíz, *Franceses en la independencia de Colombia* (Bogotá: Academia Colombiana de Historia, Editorial ABC, 1971), 77–83; "Plaza de Medellín," f. 6v–7v, 11r–v.
83 "Plaza de Medellín," f. 43r–44r.
84 Alta Corte Marcial, AGN, Colecciones, Enrique Ortega Ricaurte, box 85, folder 35. On the High Court, see David Bushnell, *The Santander Regime in Gran Colombia* (Westport: Greenwood Press, 1970), 45–50.
85 Capitán Buenaventura Correa, military service record, f. 242r, 258r.
86 "Relación que hace," f. 380r, 382r.
87 The person in question was Pedro José de Ibarra, who filled the vacant post in 1812. See Daniel Gutiérrez Ardila, "Pedro José de Ibarra: A Mulatto Senator in Colombia's Antioquia," Josep M. Fradera, José María Portillo, and Teresa Segura-García, ed., *Unexpected Voices in Imperial Parliaments* (London: Bloomsbury Academic, 2021), 75–96.

6 An Exegesis of Liberty

1 *Constitución del Estado de Antioquia sancionada por los representantes de toda la provincia. Y aceptada por el pueblo en tres de mayo del año de 1812* (Santa Fe de Bogotá: Imprenta de D. Bruno Espinosa, Por D. Nicomedes Lora, 1812), tit. 1, sections 1 and 2, 4–5.
2 This formulation owes to Manisha Sinha, *The Slave's Cause: A History of Abolition* (New Haven, CT: Yale University Press, 2016).
3 "Criminal contra Cornelio Sarrazola esclavo de Manuel Herrón por pretender su libertad a fuerza," AHA, Criminal, B-84, 1820–1840, doc. 14.

4 On the Republic of Colombia, see David Bushnell, *The Santander Regime in Gran Colombia* (Westport: Greenwood Press, 1970); Daniel Gutiérrez Ardila, *El reconocimiento de Colombia: Diplomacia y propaganda en la coyuntura de las Restauraciones (1819–1821)* (Bogotá: Universidad Externado de Colombia, 2012); Armando Martínez Garnica, *Historia de la Primera República de Colombia, 1819–1831: "Decid Colombia sea, y Colombia será"* (Bogotá: Universidad del Rosario, 2018).

5 "Constitución de la República de Colombia," tit. I, arts. 1, 2, 3, tit. VIII, art. 181, *Cuerpo de leyes de la República de Colombia. Tomo 1°. Contiene la Constitución y leyes sancionadas por el primer congreso general en las sesiones que celebró desde el 6 de mayo hasta el 14 de octubre de 1821* (Bogotá: Por Bruno Espinosa impresor del Gobierno General, 1822), 7, 8, 41.

6 José Félix de Restrepo [sic], "Discurso sobre la manumisión de esclavos, pronunciado en el soberano Congreso de Colombia reunido en la villa del Rosario de Cúcuta en el año de 1821," Rosario de Cúcuta, June 28 and July 5, 1821, *Obras completas de José Félix de Restrepo* (Medellín: Bedout, 1961), 296–342; Law of July 21, 1821, *Gazeta de Colombia* (Rosario de Cúcuta), September 9, 1821.

7 José María Martínez to Señor teniente asesor, Antioquia, *ca.* September 6, 1822, "José María Martínez hace recuento de su libertad, méritos y servicios durante la época de la Independencia," AHA, Esclavos, vol. 38, doc. 1283, f. 410r.

8 David Bushnell, *The Santander*, 169; Gerónimo Torres, *Observaciones de G.T. sobre la ley de manumisión del soberano congreso de Colombia* (Bogotá: En la Patriótica de la Capital de Bogotá, por José Manuel Galagarza, 1822); *Respuesta documentada a la imputación hecha a la Asamblea Electoral de Popayán con motivo de la petición que dio sobre la ley de manumisión* (Popayán: Imprenta del Gobierno, por Rafael Viteri, 1823); José Rafael Mosquera, *Proyecto de ley sobre manumisión de esclavos, e indemnización a los amos* (Bogotá: Imprenta de Espinoza, por V. E. Molano, 1824); Joaquín Mosquera, *Memoria sobre la necesidad de reformar la ley del congreso constituyente de Colombia, de 21 de julio, de 1821, que sancionó la libertad de los partos, manumisión, y abolición del tráfico de esclavos: y bases que podrían adoptarse para la reforma. Por el Senador Joaquín Mosquera* (Bogotá: Impreso por F. M. Stokes, 1825).

9 Gerónimo Torres, *Observaciones*, 35, 37–38.

10 "Posesorio promovido por Pedro Antonio Ibargüen contra Guillermo Segura por despojo de un territorio en «Pique»," ACC, sig. 5624 (Ind. CII-24mn), f. 105v–106r.

11 "Posesorio promovido," f. 105r.

12 "Pedro Antonio Ibargüen contra Manuel José Grueso por despojo de una mina de Iscundé," ACC, sig. 11367, (Col. JI-17mn), f. 18r.

13 Tamar Herzog, *Defining Nations: Immigrants and Citizens in Early Modern Spain and Spanish America* (New Haven: Yale University Press, 2003); François-Xavier Guerra, "De la política antigua a la política moderna. La revolución de la soberanía," François-Xavier Guerra et al. ed., *Los espacios públicos en Iberoamérica* (Mexico City: Fondo de Cultura Económica, 2008), 109–139.

14 *Constitución*, tit. 1, section 3, art. 4, tit. 2, art. 3, tit. 3, section 2, arts. 2, 3, 7, pages 12–13, 26–28.

15 We ten thousand and seven hundred slaves to the Supreme Tribunal of Justice, Medellín, August 25, 1812, "Contra varios de los Etíopes, por haber intentado su liberated con violencia," ACCR, Gobierno, vol. 93, f. 3r.

16 We ten thousand and seven hundred slaves to the Supreme Tribunal of Justice, Medellín, August 25, 1812, deposition of Pedro Antonio, Rionegro, September 17, 1812, "Contra varios de los Etíopes," f. 3r, 27v.

17 We ten thousand and seven hundred slaves to the Supreme Tribunal of Justice, Medellín, August 25, 1812, deposition of José Antonio, Rionegro, September 13, 1812, deposition of Pedro Antonio, Rionegro, September 17, 1812, sentence by Manuel José Bernal, Bernardino Álvarez and José Manuel Restrepo, Medellín, October 16, 1812, "Contra varios de los Etíopes," f. 3r, 7r, 4r, 22r–v, 27r–28v, 32v–33r.

18 Ángel Martínez to cabildo de Rionegro, Antioquia, September 1, 1812, José Manuel Restrepo to mayor of Rionegro, Medellín, September 10, 1812, "Contra varios de los Etíopes," f. 2r, 13r. Magistrates at the Supreme Tribunal recognized the radical implications of the slaves' petition, even considering that the logic behind the petitioners' propositions might apply to other sovereign provinces like Cartagena. See Resolution by the Supreme Tribunal of Justice, Medellín, September 7, 1812, and sentence by Manuel José Bernal, Bernardino Álvarez and José Manuel Restrepo, Medellín, October 8, 1812, "Contra varios de los Etíopes," f. 4r–5r, 9r–v.

19 Deposition of José María Vallejo, Rionegro, October 15, 1812, "Contra varios de los Etíopes," f. 24v.

20 Deposition of Narciso Marín, Antioquia, September 24, 1814, "Criminal contra Cornelio," f. 3v.

21 Auto, Antioquia, September 22, 1814, "Criminal contra Cornelio," f. 2r.

22 *Constitución*, title 1, section 2, art. 3, 5.

23 Deposition of Vitorino Garro, Antioquia, September 26, 1814, "Criminal contra Cornelio," f. 4r.

24 Deposition of Cornelio, Antioquia, September 26, 1814, "Criminal contra Cornelio," f. 5r–v.

25 Pedro José de Garro to José Pantaleón González de Mendoza, Antioquia, September 28, 1814, "Criminal contra Cornelio," f. 7r.

26 Cayetano Buelta Lorenzana to José Pantaleón González de Mendoza, Antioquia, October 11, 1814, "Criminal contra Cornelio," f. 8r–9r.

27 José Manuel Restrepo to Presidente de la República, Rionegro, November 17, 1814, Pedro José de Garro to José Pantaleón González de Mendoza, Antioquia, September 28, 1814, "Criminal contra Cornelio," f. 14v.

28 Daniel Gutiérrez Ardila, "La politique abolitionniste dans le'État d'Antioquia, Colombie (1812–1816)," *Le Mouvement social* 252 (2015): 70.

29 José María Martínez to Señor teniente asesor, Antioquia, *ca.* September 6, 1822, f. 410r.

30 José María Martínez to Señor teniente asesor, Antioquia, *ca.* September 6, 1822, f. 410v; "Relación de los militares que hicieron la campaña del 'Bajo Magdalena,' que comprende los años de 1820 y 1821, y la cual dio por resultado la recuperación de las Provincias antiguas de Cartagena, Riohacha y Santa Marta por las autoridades y fuerzas colombianas," DHPC, vol. 2, doc. 384, 487.

31 Peter Blanchard, *Under the Flags of Freedom: Slave Soldiers and the Wars of Independence in Spanish South America* (Pittsburgh, PA: University of Pittsburgh Press, 2008), 82.

32 José María Martínez to Señor teniente asesor, Antioquia, *ca.* September 6, 1822, f. 409r, 410r; John V. Lombardi, *The Decline and Abolition of Negro Slavery in Venezuela* (Westport: Greenwood Press, 1971).

33 José María Martínez to Señor teniente asesor, Antioquia, *ca.* September 6, 1822, f. 410r.

34 *Quarta Partida* (Salamanca: Andrea de Portonariis, 1555), Tit. XXII, Law I, f. 56v.

35 José María Martínez to Señor teniente asesor, Antioquia, *ca.* September 6, 1822, f. 410v, 411r.

36 José María Martínez to Señor teniente asesor, Antioquia, *ca.* September 6, 1822, f. 410r.

37 This unorthodox proposition had a clear (though maybe only coincidental) affinity with the principle of compensation for the masters stipulated first by Antioquia's manumission law, and now by its successor, Colombia's manumission law of 1821. These gradual slave emancipation laws ordered that all masters whose female slaves birthed free children had an obligation to care for those children and a right to be compensated for this care. The masters, however, would not receive a cash compensation but rather be paid by with "works and services" provided to them by the children in question. Law of July 21, 1821, art. 2.

38 José María Martínez to Señor teniente asesor, Antioquia, *ca.* September 6, 1822, f. 410r.

39 José María Martínez to Señor teniente asesor, Antioquia, *ca.* September 6, 1822, f. 410r.

40 "Contra Manuel Herrera por heridas que dio a un esclavo del doctor Faustino Martínez," AHA, Criminal, B-78, 1800–1820, doc. 10; *Quarta Partida* (Salamanca: Andrea de Portonariis, 1555), Tit. XXII, Laws I and III, f. 56v and 57r.

41 José María Martínez to Señor teniente asesor, Antioquia, *ca.* September 6, 1822, f. 410r; deposition of Rita Pimienta, Antioquia, October 23, 1822, "José María Martínez," f. 411v–412r.

42 *Qvarta Partida*, Tit. XXII, Law VII, f. 57v. On *prescripción*, see Rebecca J. Scott, "Social Facts, Legal Fictions, and the Attribution of Slave Status: The Puzzle of Prescription," *Law & History Review* 35.1 (2017): 10–11.

43 José María Martínez to Señor teniente asesor, Antioquia, *ca.* September 6, 1822, f. 410v.

44 José María Martínez to Señor teniente asesor, Antioquia, *ca.* September 6, 1822, f. 410r.

45 *Diccionario de la lengua Castellana compuesto por la Real Academia Española, reducido a un tomo para sumás fácil uso. Tercera edición, en la cual se han colocado en los lugares correspondientes todas las voces de los suplementos, que se pusieron al fin de las ediciones de los años de 1780 y 1783, y se han intercalado en las letras D. E. y F. nuevos artículos, de los cuales se dará un suplemento separado* (Madrid: Viuda de Joaquín Ibarra, 1791), 384; DA, vol. 3, book 1, 539–540; Bianca Premo, *The Enlightenment on Trial: Ordinary Litigants and Colonialism in the Spanish Empire* (New York: Oxford University Press, 2017), 82, 119–120, 199; Bianca Premo, "An Equity against the Law: Slave Rights and Creole Jurisprudence in Spanish America," *Slavery & Abolition* 32.4 (2011): 507, 510.

46 Pedro Antonio Ibargüen to the governor, Popayán, February 16, 1793, "Pedro Antonio Ibargüen," f. 18r.

47 "Constitución de la República de Colombia," Rosario de Cúcuta, August 30, 1821, Manuel Antonio Pombo and José Joaquín Guerra, ed., *Constituciones de Colombia* (Bogotá: Imprenta de Echeverri Hermanos, 1892), preamble, Tit. 1, section 1, art. 3, 119.

48 "Constitución de la República de Colombia," preamble, Tit. 1, section 2, art. 4, Tit. 3, section 1, article 21, 119 and 122. Unlike Cartagena's Constitution (1812), Colombia's Constitution (1821) mentions "equality" but not "equality before the law." The Constitution of Cartagena defined equality before the law in contrast to unequal corporate and inherited privileges. Even before declaring independence, revolutionary Cartagena granted voting rights to heads of households who made a living from their work, regardless of the income they drew from their workshops or

occupations. The guidelines for the first popular elections in Cartagena specifically invited "blancos, indios, mestizos, mulatos, zambos y negros" to participate as voters. See "Instrucciones que deberán observarse en las elecciones parroquiales, en las de partido y en las capitulares, para el nombramiento de diputados en la Suprema Junta de la provincia de Cartagena," Cartagena de Indias, December 11, 1810, Manuel Ezequiel Corrales, ed., *Efemérides y anales del Estado de Bolívar* (Bogotá: Casa Editorial de J. J. Pérez, 1889), vol. 2, 48; "Constitución política del Estado de Cartagena de Indias," Cartagena de Indias, June 14, 1812, Tit. 1 art. 8, DHPC, vol. 1, 487; Marixa Lasso, "Race War and Nation in Caribbean Gran Colombia, Cartagena, 1810–1832," *American Historical Review* 111.2 (2006): 345–346; Roger Pita Pico, *La manumisión de esclavos en el proceso de independencia de Colombia: realidades, promesas y desilusiones* (Bogotá: Editorial Kimpres, 2014), 193–201; Muriel Laurent, *Contrabando, poder y color en los albores de la república. Nueva Granada, 1822–1824* (Bogotá: Universidad de los Andes, 2014).

49 José Ignacio de Pombo, *Comercio y contrabando en Cartagena de Indias* (Bogotá: Nueva Biblioteca Colombiana de Cultura, 1986), 88–90.

50 Pedro Gual to Manual José Hurtado, Bogotá, July 19, 1824, AGN, Ministerio de Relaciones Exteriores, Delegaciones, Transferencia 2, vol. 300, f. 90v.

51 HRC, vol. 2, 17; Daniel Gutiérrez Ardila, "La politique," 70.

52 Daniel Gutiérrez Ardila, "El coronel Concha en el Cauca o la gestación de un vórtice político, 1821-1824," *Historia Crítica* 78 (2020): 65–86.

53 José Félix de Restrepo, "Discurso," 334.

54 "Posesorio promovido," f. 1r–3v. See also ACC, sig. 11383 (Col. JI-17mn), f. 1r–7v. War and revolution slowed down judicial business in Popayán, leaving us with a gap in the evidence of Ibargüen's difficulties with his "arrogant" opponents. In 1818, however, Ibargüen, who had once promised to go on a legal pilgrimage to Madrid and plead his case before the king, traveled to Santa Fe, where he requested protection from the restored (but soon to be ousted again) Spanish authorities. Ibargüen complained against Manuel Silvestre Balverde, lieutenant governor of Guapi, who now emerged as his antagonist in the Pacific district of Micay. Balverde allowed people to enter Ibargüen's mines and pan for gold. In 1814, Balverde allegedly took away Juana Tenorio, a woman held in slavery by Ibargüen. The lieutenant governor also seems to have been in cahoots with a priest who refused to celebrate Ibargüen's marriage to Feliciana Alvarado. The would-be spouses had met in Quito during one of Ibargüen's legal quests. See the complaints by Pedro Antonio Ibargüen, Santafé, November 24, 1818, "Pedro Antonio Ibargüen vecino del pueblo de Guapi en Micay, provincia del Chocó se queja de los procedimientos del

teniente de dicho pueblo por haberle quitado de propia autoridad una negra, pide providencia para su devolución," AGN, C, NEC, vol. 3, doc. 9, f. 820r–821r.

55 José Ignacio de San Miguel, Mompox, February 28, 1777, "Don José Antonio Ambrosi [sic] de Arango sobre la venta que se le quiere precisar de un negro esclavo," AGN, C, NEA, vol. 1, doc. 23, f. 703r–v; José Ignacio San Miguel, *Para perpetua memoria. Se manifiesta la necesidad, la obligación, la razón, y la justicia con que la valerosa República de Colombia sostiene su libertad e independencia* (Bogotá: Espinoza impresor del gobierno, 1821), 61–68.

56 "Posesorio promovido," f. 7r–50r.

57 "Posesorio promovido," f. 57v–98v.

58 "Pedro Antonio Ibargüen," f. 12r. 17v, 18r.

59 A popular inexpensive newspaper, written in plain language and circulated among republican soldiers, for example, drew sharp but forced distinctions between Spaniards and Colombians. See *El patriota* (Bogotá), 42 issues, 1823. Legal theorists publicized their arguments on the illegitimacy of Spain's legal claims over Colombian lands and citizens. See San Miguel, *Para perpetua*.

60 "Posesorio promovido," f. 95v.

61 "Posesorio promovido," f. 105r.

62 "Posesorio promovido," f. 105v–106r.

63 "Posesorio promovido," f. 105v–106r–v.

64 "Posesorio promovido," f. 106v–107r.

65 "Posesorio promovido," f. 110v–112r.

66 "Posesorio promovido," f. 113r–137v. "Guillermo Antonio Segura y Pedro Antonio Ibargüen, sobre posesión y propiedad de los derechos de minas del río «Pique»," and "Entre Pedro Antonio Ibargüen y Guillermo Segura sobre despojo de tierras, y minas," both in ACC, sig. 5625 (Ind. CII-24mn).

67 "Posesorio promovido," f. 113r–137v. "Guillermo Antonio" and "Entre Pedro Antonio."

68 ACC, Notaría 1ra., 1829-I, f. 48r–49v, 49v–50r; 1866-I, f. 161v.

69 ACC, Notaría 1ra., 1829-I, f. 48r–49v, 49v–50r; 1850-II, f. 113r–115v.

70 For leads on these attitudes, see the 1820s correspondence between Manuel José Mosquera and Tomás Cipriano de Mosquera, BLAA, Libros Raros y Manuscritos, Ms. 588, Archivo Familiar Mosquera. See also Daniel Gutiérrez Ardila, "El coronel" and Marcela Echeverri, "Esclavitud y tráfico de esclavos en el Pacífico suramericano durante la era de la abolición," *Historia Mexicana* 69.2 (2019): 627–691.

71 José Manuel Restrepo, *Memoria sobre Amonedación de Oro i Plata en la Nueva Granada. Desde 12 de julio de 1753 hasta 31 de agosto de 1859* (Bogota: Imprenta de la Nación, 1860), 28.

72 Pablo Rodríguez J., "La manumisión en Popayán, 1800-1851," *Revista de Extensión Cultural* 9–10 (1980): 77–85; Jorge Castellanos, "The Failure of the Manumission Juntas in the Colombian Province of Popayán, 1821–1851," *Michigan Academician* 14.4 (1982): 427–443; Roger Pita Pico, *La manumisión de los esclavos en el proceso de independencia de Colombia: Realidades, promesas y desilusiones* (Bogotá: Kimpres, 2014), ch. 12 and 13; Daniel Gutiérrez Ardila, "El coronel."

73 "Concurso de acreedores de los bienes de José Tenorio," ACC, sig. 11273 (Col. J III-9su), f. 46v; Juan Camilo Torres to Señor Teniente Gobernador, Guapi, August 26, 1816, ACC, sig. 6598 (Ind. CIII-2g), f. 1r–v; Manuel Alonso de Velasco to Señor Gobernador, Popayán, February 14, 1818, ACC, sig. 6598 (Ind. CIII-2g), f. 6r-8r; Gerónimo Torres to Señor Gobernador, San Juan mine, June 20, 1820, ACC, sig. 6596, (Ind. CIII-2g); Marcela Echeverri, *Indian and Slave Royalists in the Age of Revolution: Reform, Revolution, and Royalism in the Northern Andes, 1780-1825* (New York: Cambridge University Press, 2016), 175–183.

74 Gerónimo Torres to Señor Gobernador, San Juan mine, June 20 1820, f. 1r.

75 Gerónimo Torres to Señor Gobernador, San Juan mine, June 20 1820, f. 1r-v.

76 "Expediente seguido contra don Casimiro Cortés, sobre la averiguación de la muerte de dos Negros en la mina de don Marcos Cortés por maltratos y azotes," ANE, Popayán, box No. 284, exp. 7; "Expediente contra don Casimiro Cortés por querella de sus esclavos, probando sevicia autuada por los tres señores jueces año de 1798," AGN, C, NEC, vol. 2, doc. 13; ACC, Notaría 1ra., vol 54 1786-IV, f. 21r–23r; AHC, Notaría 1ra., vol. 73A, 1807, f. 198r–199v; AGS, Secretaría de Guerra, 7087, exp. 24; Marcela Echeverri, "'Enraged to the Limit of Despair': Infanticide and Slave Judicial Strategies in Barbacoas, 1789–1798," *Slavery & Abolition* 30.3 (2009): 403–426.

77 Gerónimo Torres to Señor Gobernador, San Juan mine, June 20, 1820, f. 2r-v.

78 "Libro copiador intendencia," May 23, 1846, ACC, Archivo Muerto, bundle 40, leg. 65.

79 Victor M. Uribe-Uran, *Honorable Lives. Lawyers, Family, and Politics in Colombia, 1780–1850* (Pittsburgh, PA: University of Pittsburgh Press, 2000), 170.

80 Gerónimo Torres, *Observaciones*; *El Fósforo* (Popayán), February 27 and June 5, 1823.

81 Gerónimo Torres, *Observaciones*, 17–18, 23–24, 26 29, 33, 36–37; Jorge Andrés Tovar Mora and Hermes Tovar Pinzón, *El oscuro camino de la libertad. Los esclavos en Colombia, 1821–1851* (Bogotá: Universidad de los Andes, 2009), 74.

82 Gerónimo Torres, *Observaciones*, 33–34.
83 Gerónimo Torres, *Observaciones*, 33–34.
84 Gerónimo Torres, *Observaciones*, 35, 37–38. On "race war," see Marixa Lasso, "Race War."
85 Joaquín Mosquera, *Memoria*, 4. See also *Respuesta*; José Rafael Mosquera, *Proyecto*.
86 José Félix de Restrepo, "Discurso," 329–330, 337.
87 Restrepo bought at least one slave as late as 1819 and owned other slaves at the time. See slave purchase, Félix de Restrepo from Pedro Muñoz, Medellín, July 15, 1819, AHA, Escribanos, 1819, José Vicente de la Calle, f. 288r-299v.
88 José María Mosquera to Gerónimo Torres, Popayán, August 13, 1827, AGN, ACH, Camilo Torres, box 3, folder 6, f. 56r.
89 Fredy Enrique Martínez Pérez, "Manumisión en Colombia: Cauca y Antioquia 1821–1830" (MA Thesis, Universidad Nacional de Colombia, Bogotá, 2014), 162–166; Karen Mejía Velázquez and Luis Miguel Córdoba Ochoa, "La manumisión de esclavos por compra y gracia en la Provincia de Antioquia, 1780–1830," *Historelo* 9.17 (2017): 281–283; Armando Martínez Garnica, *Historia*, 300.
90 José Félix de Restrepo, "Discurso," 337.

Epilogue: The Slaves Before the Law

1 Rebecca J. Scott, "Slavery and the Law in Atlantic Perspective: Jurisdiction, Jurisprudence, and Justice," *Law & History Review* 29.4 (2011): 922–923.
2 The vocabulary can be found in many sources, most importantly in notarial records formalizing the sale, purchase, and emacipation of slaves. See, for example, the notarial records at ACC. On the differences, overlaps, and implications of these labels, see José Luis Cortés López, "Esclavos en medios eclesiásticos entre los siglos XII–XIV: apuntes para el estudio de la esclavitud en la Edad Media," *Espacio, tiempo y forma* 3.5 (1992): 423–440; Carlos Eduardo Valencia Villa, *Alma en boca y huesos en costal. Una aproximación a los contrastes socio-económicos de la esclavitud: Santafé, Mariquita y Mompox (1610–1660)* (Bogotá: Instituto Colombiano de Antropología e Historia, 2003); Ángel Muñoz García, "La condición del hombre en la Edad Media: ¿siervo, esclavo o qué?," *Revista de Filosofía* 25.57 (2007): 115–142; William D. Phillips, Jr., *Slavery in Medieval and Early Modern Iberia* (Philadelphia: University of Pennsylvania Press, 2014), 39–40.
3 Elizabeth Heyrick, *Immediate, Not Gradual Abolition; Or, An Inquiry Into the Shortest, Safest, and Most Effectual Means of Getting Rid of West Indian Slavery* (London: 1824), 11.

4 Juan del Corral to Presidente de la Unión, Antioquia, December 12, 1813, *Memorias del General O'Leary* (Caracas: Imprenta de la Gaceta Oficial, 1881), vol. 13, 494; Montesquieu, *De l'esprit des lois* (London: 1768), vol. 2, ch. 3, vol. 4, ch. 10–11; Antoine-Gaspard Boucher d'Argis, "Esclave," *Encyclopédie ou dictionnaire raisonné des sciences, des arts et des métiers* (Paris: chez Briasson, David, Le Breton, Durand, 1755), vol. 5, 939; Antoine-Gaspard Boucher d'Argis, "Serf," *Encyclopédie ou dictionnaire raisonné des sciences, des arts et des métiers* (Neuchâtel: chez Samuel Faulche, 1765), vol. 15, 82; Marc Bloch, "Serf de la glébe. Histoire d'une expression toute faite," *Revue Historique* 136.2 (1921): 220–242.

5 "Ley sobre la manumisión de la posteridad de los esclavos africanos y sobre los medios de redimir sucesivamente a sus padres, extendida y propuesta para su sanción a la Cámara de Representantes del Pueblo, por el Excelentísimo Dictador Ciudadano Juan B. del Corral," Antioquia, April 20, 1814, *Gazeta Ministerial de la República de Antioquia* (Medellín), October 2, 1814; "Decreto para ejecutar en todas sus partes a Ley sobre la manumisión de esclavos publicada en el numero 2 de esta Gazeta," Rionegro, September 19, 1814, *Gazeta Ministerial de la República de Antioquia* (Medellín), November 6, 1814.

6 Law of July 21, 1821, art. 8, *Gazeta de Colombia* (Rosario de Cúcuta), September 9, 1821.

7 Bartolomé and Lucille Bennassar, *Los cristianos de Alá. La fascinante aventura de los renegados* (Madrid: Nerea, 1989); Robert C. Davis, *Christian Slaves, Muslim Masters: White Slavery in the Mediterranean, The Barbary Coast, and Italy, 1500–1800* (New York: Palgrave Macmillan, 2003).

8 We ten thousand and seven hundred slaves to the Supreme Tribunal of Justice, Medellín, August 25, 1812, "Contra varios de los Etíopes, por haber intentado su libertad con violencia," ACCR, Gobierno, vol. 93, f. 3r, 7r–9r.

9 "Ley."

10 Simón Sáenz de Vergara and Felipe Grueso Rodríguez to Miguel Tacón, Tumaco, December 7, 1811, AGI, Quito, 386; We ten thousand and seven hundred slaves to the Supreme Tribunal of Justice, Medellín, August 25, 1812; "Criminal contra Cornelio Sarrazola esclavo de Manuel Herrón por pretender su libertad a fuerza," AHA, Criminal, B-84, 1820–1840, doc. 14; Acta 63, July 4, 1821, Acta 80, July 16, 1821, and Protesta No. 29 by Juan Bautista Estévez, *Congreso de Cúcuta 1821. Libro de Actas* (Bogotá: Banco de la República, 1971), 195, 254, 706–707; José María Martínez to Señor teniente asesor, Antioquia, *ca.* September 6, 1822, "José María Martínez hace recuento de su libertad, méritos y servicios durante la época de la Independencia," AHA, Esclavos, vol. 38, doc. 1283; Pedro Antonio Ibargüen to Corte del Cauca, Popayán, July 7,

1827, "Posesorio promovido por Pedro Antonio Ibargüen contra Guillermo Segura por despojo de un terreno en 'Pique,'" ACC, sig. 5624 (Ind. C II-24mn), f. 105v–106r.

11 Martha S. Jones, *Birthright Citizens: A History of Race and Rights in Antebellum America* (New York: Cambridge University Press, 2018).

Index

Printed by Printforce, United Kingdom